S0-BEG-326

The New Family Office

Innovative Strategies for Consulting to the Affluent

The New Family Office

Innovative Strategies for Consulting to the Affluent

Institutional
Investor Books

Published by

Euromoney Institutional Investor Plc

Nestor House, Playhouse Yard

London EC4V 5EX

United Kingdom

Tel: +44 (0) 20 7779 8999 or USA +1 800 437 9997

Fax: +44 (0) 20 7779 8300

www.euromoneybooks.com

E-mail:hotline@euromoneyplc.com

Copyright © 2004 Euromoney Institutional Investor plc

ISBN 1 84374 064 8

This publication is not included in the CLA Licence and must not be copied without the permission of the publisher.

All rights reserved. No part of this publication may be reproduced or used in any form (graphic, electronic or mechanical, including photocopying, recording, taping or information storage and retrieval systems) without permission by the publisher.

The views and opinions expressed in the book are solely those of the authors and need not necessarily reflect those of the institutions which have acted as co-publishers to the book. Although Euromoney has made every effort to ensure the complete accuracy of the text, neither it nor the authors nor any co-publisher can accept any legal responsibility whatsoever for consequences that may arise from errors or omissions or any opinions or advice given. Nothing in this book is, or is intended to constitute the provision of, taxation or investment advice. Readers are strongly advised to take professional independent advice on these matters.

Printed by Cromwell Press Ltd

To Adrianne and Tripp

The meaning of your support and belief in me cannot be measured

Contents

Author biography

Lisa Gray is a 15-year veteran of the investment industry. She began her career at Union Planters Investment Bankers Group in 1998 working with individual investors in the fixed-income markets. She continued her career at Morgan Keegan and Company, Inc. During her tenure with the firm, she became a student of technical analysis of equities and the financial markets. Ms Gray continued that study at PaineWebber, Inc. (now UBS), where she completed Level 1 of the requirement for earning the Chartered Market Technician (CMT) designation. She began a career in financial journalism in 2001.

Ms Gray offers in-the-trenches experience and expertise in a variety of areas including creating and developing business initiatives, strategic marketing, business and investment planning, alternative investments, the financial markets, fostering ultra high net worth client relationships, and family wealth optimization. She holds the Certified Investment Management Consultant (CIMC) designation and is a member of the Investment Management Consultants Association (IMCA). She is also a Level 1 CFA candidate and is a member of the Association for Investment Management and Research (AIMR) and the Memphis Society for Financial Analysts. She has recently been selected as a member of the editorial board for AIMR's *Financial Journalist e-Newsletter*, a global newsletter 'providing educational insight for journalists on the intricacies of the financial world'. Ms Gray has an extensive industry-training background, and is actively involved in promoting internet-based training and education throughout the industry. In 2002, she founded graymatter STRATEGIES LLC a financial marketing consulting firm that leverages educational and relationship marketing through the written word.

Foreword

Frank L. Campanale
Former president and CEO, Salomon Smith Barney Consulting Group

Today's high-level advisors and investment management consultants are saying to themselves: 'I want to attract wealthier families. I'm a good relationship manager; I get along well with wealthy people; I understand their needs, their desires, and their eccentricities, but I'm having problems. There are gaps between the way my practice is set up and the services I want to offer my clients, and I don't know how to fill in the blanks.'

In this book, the author fills in those blanks. She does it in an easy-to-understand format by using case studies and examples to which advisors and consultants can readily relate. In essence, this book is a business plan for transforming the businesses of advisors and consultants to meet the challenges of the future, and to thrive in doing so.

All revolutions cause disruption. When my colleagues and I began the consulting group at E.F. Hutton in the late 1970s, we knew that what we were doing would revolutionize the financial services industry. We knew that doing the right thing for the client would translate into a better way of doing business. But we also knew that the industry would be slow to adopt such a process because people are naturally slow to accept and adapt to change, especially when it involves changing an established culture and way of doing business. By 1987, when Hutton came out with its pioneering Hutton Select Managers product, the revolution started by our group at Hutton began to take hold. Today, it has spread throughout the industry and is spurring even greater revolution through new products designed to offer better integration of services to clients.

Today's clients, however, are looking for more than just a better mousetrap. As the former president and CEO of Salomon's Consulting Group, which grew out of the original Hutton Consulting Group, I had the privilege of educating advisors and consultants in giving their clients more than just new product offerings that used the elements of the consulting process as a superficial side offering. Today, through my work and that of my colleagues, Salomon Smith Barney has the most advanced level of consulting support for advisors and consultants in the financial services industry, but that level is still not developed enough to fully address today's market-place demands. Long before I left the firm in August of 2003, I realized that a new phase of the revolution my colleagues and I started at Hutton was beginning to spread throughout the industry – that of providing a fuller, more personalized level of service based on the family office service model not only to ultra-wealthy clients, but to clients with assets as small as US$5 million, US$20 million, and US$50 million on up.

This new phase is having the same effect as the initial stage – a burst of firms trying to get in on the action and the subsequent fall-off as the realities of adapting to provocative and irreversible change begin to set in. Now, advisors and consultants (and their firms) are struggling to develop the right business models that will serve the demands of the market-place, while allowing them to still make a profit. In this book, the author lays the groundwork for high-level advisors and investment management consultants to do just that. She nails the issues at the heart of both industries today, and outlines the cultural changes that will have to take place for advisors and consultants to remain competitive.

She pulls together top professionals from both the family office and financial services industries to assist individual consultants, financial planners, or independent broker/dealers thinking about entering the high net worth servicing/family office business in addressing those issues. The author gives advisors and consultants a complete view of the market-place opportunities available in both industries to those willing to take advantage of them. She proposes a new answer to the demands of today's more sophisticated and exacting market-place – wealth optimization consulting – and she deftly posits this answer through clear examples and historical comparisons. She effectively pulls together all the moving parts of the industry and translates them into English so people can understand what is happening and how they can benefit.

The author does a wonderful job of taking the reader from the genesis of both the family office and financial services industries to where the industries are converging today and where they are probably going to be five to 10 years from now.

The histories of both industries are easily explained so that advisors and consultants can fully understand the background of the services that today's market-place demands. She shows how elements from both industries are converging, adding confusion for investors and opportunity for advisors and consultants.

The book also brings together all the possibilities in terms of servicing mechanisms available to advisors and consultants. In successfully bringing together all of these elements, the author has created an invaluable resource. The reader can go through each chapter, outline or highlight the piece that sounds most interesting, and be able to find the resources that will provide the services needed to transform his or her practice into a wealth optimization consulting business.

In short, the author of this book has accomplished what no one else in the industry has had time to accomplish: she has taken the disparate parts of both industries and shown advisors and consultants how they can fill in the blanks by using those disparate parts to create optimal business models for themselves and optimal service models for their clients.

Acknowledgements

Undertaking a work in the hope that it will be a profoundly positive influence on people's business and personal lives is a monumental task; undertaking such a work in the hope that it will be a positive influence on an entire industry is even more daunting. Neither can be accomplished on one's own. The graciousness of industry experts, leaders, and pioneers such as Charlotte Beyer, Sara Hamilton, Frank Campanale, and Richard Joyner make such a task even more humbling to the author undertaking it. It is with deep thanks to these exceptional people that I present this work for your contemplation, consideration, and (hopefully) enjoyment.

The research required to properly present such a work is also invaluable. In that regard, I would like to thank the many experts who wrote the materials referenced throughout. They are important contributors to an industry I love and have enjoyed being a part of for 15 years.

Of course, this book would never have become a reality without the vision and insight of Euromoney/Institutional Investor's Dr Elizabeth Gray. Liz's unceasing patience and invaluable contributions to the book's quality are immensely appreciated. Many thanks also to her staff and to all of the people both abroad and here in the United States, whose names I do not know, who were instrumental in bringing this work to publication and are contributing to its success.

I would never have had the opportunity to write this work without the early and continuing mentoring and career encouragement from my dear friend and colleague Sydney LeBlanc. Sydney continually gives of herself to help others succeed, and I feel most fortunate to be one of her beneficiaries. Thanks to her for reviewing the work and contributing her usual wonderful words of wisdom.

To those influential industry experts who took the time to contribute personally to this effort, I give heartfelt thanks. To Dr Lee Hausner, Stan Pantowich, Tom Livergood, Pat Soldano, Susan Snyder, Amy Braden, Andrew Keyt, Eric Bennett, and John Tolleson on the practitioner and advisory side, and to Mike Cagney, Ward McGraw, Jon Carroll, Steve DeAngelis, and Scott Welch on the technology side – the ability to tap into your exceptional abilities and experience added the highest quality to this work. Thanks particularly to those whose contribution to this work was just as invaluable, but who preferred not to be named. Your courage in making such contributions offers this book's readers extremely important insights that they would not otherwise be able to access.

Finally, I'd like to offer a special thanks to my friend Frank Campanale. In addition to being the incredible person that he is, Frank is an influential pioneer who does not compromise his beliefs and principles. He continually offers those who will listen wise counsel for achieving the best success in an industry charged with the welfare of many individuals and their families. Thank you, Frank, for your continued encouragement, support, and words of wisdom in my quest to make this book everything it should be.

It is with humility and great pleasure that I present this work to you. If it can influence one industry practitioner to reinvent herself to better fulfill her charge, my strongest hopes of success for this work will have been realized.

Lisa Gray, CIMC

Introduction

This book is a guide to building and maintaining exceptional businesses that will generate exceptional revenues for astute practitioners in the midst of ongoing challenges in the market-place. The book is not a simple, how-to manual, nor does it attempt to provide a turnkey solution to financial services advisors' ailing practices. Rather, it is designed as an educational tool that will prove its value through the successful implementation of its guidelines.

The challenges financial advisors and investment management consultants face in the financial services industry today are significant and unprecedented. Top-level investment management consultants are coping with them more effectively than the bulk of the financial services advisory. What makes these consultants better able to make the challenges work in their favor? *By basing everything they do on each client's unique vision for successful wealth management rather than their own, they command higher fees and enjoy exposure to high-quality business opportunities.* These consultants have also realized that there is a price for attaining and maintaining this level of success: they must operate with the paradoxical mind-set that monetary reward is a natural by-product of doing the right thing for the client. In other words, by switching their focus from increasing revenues to providing clients with the service they demand, not only do they attract the profits the entire industry craves, but they also achieve more personal satisfaction in the process.

Problems for the financial services industry

Despite its efforts to convince the investing public otherwise, the financial services industry is still primarily profit-driven, often at the expense of investors. Its profit-driven culture is deeply embedded in its history. It has attempted to shift to a family office style service focus in a furious effort to replace the cash cow of commission-generating business that carried it through the early 1990s only to quickly abandon that focus because it did not generate the immediate profit panacea demanded by shareholders. That cash cow is on the way out, but it still dominates the financial services industry.

The vast majority of advisors at large financial services firms continue to receive their compensation from transaction-based business. They are milking the cash cow for everything it is worth, which is diametrically opposed to the way solid, long-lasting profits are generated in today's world. Granted, the firms employing today's advisors are verbally encouraging them to make the switch to fee-based compensation, but the firms' actions to date in supporting that encouragement have been less than spectacular. This lack of deep-seated support may be rooted in the industry's general failure to fully appreciate or understand how people feel about their money, suggests Charlotte B. Beyer, founder and CEO of the Institute for Private Investors (IPI),[1] as well as industry firms' overall feeling that they cannot make money by providing open architecture, individually customized, client-focused service. As a result, the proportion of revenues generated at financial services firms today from family wealth is under 15%, according to Family Office Exchange (FOX) founder and CEO Sara Hamilton.[2]

These factors cause firms to focus on the goals of increasing margins and satisfying shareholder demands and, paradoxically, to miss the mark for sustained achievement of those goals. This sets up a difficult hurdle for financial services firms and the advisors and consultants who work for them. By definition, the interests of shareholders and clients conflict. Shareholders tend not to be patient and this adds significant pressure on financial institutions to 'perform'.

Although some firms have done a much better job of accomplishing the shift in focus than their less committed counterparts, the overriding pull of shareholder demands and expectations still dominates. The answer to these problems lies in educating shareholders that a long-term, high-quality approach to profit generation is actually more lucrative than the current short-term approach. The responsibility for providing this education lies with the financial services firms themselves, who, so far, have made little attempt to come to grips with the issue. As a result, at most financial services firms, attempts to boost margins continue to address the symptoms rather than the root causes of the problem. Thus, astute investment consultants are placed in the frustrating position of having a clear understanding of what they need in order to move their businesses forward while not having the appropriate tools to accomplish that goal.

Problems for the family office industry

The family office industry has had the right focus, but feasible business models and retention of the level of professional talent required to implement that focus in recent decades have been elusive. The family office traditionally has been viewed as an entity designed to provide the ultimate level of service to the family rather than as a business designed to make a profit. But as families and their wealth grow in size and complexity, the costs of managing the family and the wealth also grow. This increase in costs eats into investment returns from all sources of capital – financial, human, intellectual, and social. Families have attempted to achieve more cost-effective and profitable ways of managing their portfolio of assets by adopting the multi-family office structure and/or specializing in niche offerings such as hedge funds or private equity funds. However, these efforts can only be rewarding if the family views the office as a separate, formal business entity, not simply as a way to get the service they demand with the bonus of a little profit thrown in.

So an overlap in the focuses of the two industries is occurring: the financial services industry is attempting to emulate the family office industry's level of service in order to boost profits, whereas the family office industry is attempting to add greater cost-effectiveness and even profitability to its unsurpassed service mix. This overlap is limited and it is the author's view that, unless fundamental changes occur in the financial services industry, it will remain so. However, the family office industry's inclusion of profits within its focus offers it much greater reciprocal benefit than the financial industry's frustrated attempts to lay claim to the profits from the larger assets indigenous to the family office industry.

The financial services industry's view that capturing the larger assets of families would automatically generate larger profits has proven to be erroneous. The industry miscalculated the costs required to offer the broad range of services required by wealthy families; therefore, they are now trying to reinvent the wheel. In times past the financial services industry created the service models offered to clients; now, client demand is dictating the service models that the industry adopts.

The family office industry has the optimal service model. Its challenge is to contain costs and increase profits without unduly compromising the quality of that service model. The financial services industry had the optimal profit model, but that entire model is being undermined by market forces stemming from the desire of a more sophisticated investing public to have stable, more responsible, and more knowledgeable management of its assets. The growing momentum of these forces has been accelerated by corporate scandal in the midst of one of the worst bear markets in capital market history.

The solution

The solution for both the financial services and family office industries and their advisors and consultants lies in optimizing all sources of client wealth and consultant wealth. Today's leading investment management consultants are already well on the road to such optimization, but even the top consultants must constantly re-examine their business models to ensure continued success. They must transform their identities from investment management consultants into wealth optimization consultants[SM], realizing that the wealth optimization consulting model[SM] provides the basis for long-term competitive superiority.[3]

The need for investment management consultants to be skilled in wealth management is already apparent to the Investment Management Consultants Association (IMCA), the industry organization that licenses the Certified Investment Management Analyst (CIMA) designation. IMCA has acknowledged this need by creating a wealth management certification course among its other certification courses designed to help consultants remain competitive.

But educating investment management consultants in such wealth management disciplines as compensation plans, retirement plans, alternative investment strategies, fiduciary tax planning, asset protection, estate and gift tax codes, and charitable planning – with little mention of the effects that family dynamics and other aspects indigenous to the wealthy have on the employment of these skills – leaves high-level advisors and investment management consultants only partially equipped to work effectively with owners of significant wealth. In fact, only one organization – the IPI – has structured a formalized program designed to educate its high-level advisory and investment management consultant members in these so-called 'softer' service areas of wealth management.[4] Yet, these are the areas that hold the greatest influence over wealth management results, and they are also the areas most sought after by today's increasingly sophisticated investors.

The author expects that several such programs will be in place by 2005 due to demand from high-level advisors and investment management consultants and an increasingly challenging market-place. An integrated, comprehensive application of traditional wealth management skills and softer service skills optimizes all forms of a family's wealth – financial, human, intellectual, and social. Thus, a practitioner sufficiently educated and experienced in both skill sets becomes a consultant not just for wealth management, but for wealth optimization, and wealth optimization is the key to competitive excellence through any type of challenge or industry climate.

The future of the financial services industry

Unless the industry makes an 'about face' commitment to addressing the needs of the wealthy, it will succumb to the commoditization forces at work in all tactical areas of service, including setting up separately managed accounts (SMAs) and unified managed accounts (UMAs) and the front and back office services so critical to those investment products. Chapters 4 and 6 explore both aspects of this industry metamorphosis.

Without such a commitment, the author sees the market for financial services lying predominantly with investors having net worth of between US$500,000 and US$5 million.[5] The ultra-wealthy will always be the smallest market segment (and the most eagerly sought after), but the ultra-wealthy will continue to demand single family office (SFO) level services regardless of whether they exist in the traditional format. However, there is a middle market that is being virtually ignored. This market is divided into two segments – US$5 million to US$24 million and US$25 million to US$100 million.[6]

Wealth optimization will enjoy the luxury of being able to address this middle market range of needs, signified at the extremes by the US$5 million investor and the ultra-wealthy, plus everything in between. This is not to encourage consultants to be all things to all wealthy people; however, the wealth optimization model is flexible enough to accommodate various market level focuses of individual wealth optimization consultants and wealth optimization consulting teams. There are three basic levels or tiers of service in the new model: services targeting the US$5 million to US$24 million market, the US$25 million to US$100 million market, and the ultra-wealthy. Whichever service level a consultant chooses, the wealth optimization model can be adapted accordingly.

The purpose and structure of this book

This book is designed to offer a new, objective view of the state of the financial services and family office industries from a knowledgeable, experienced third party. The author's objective is to enlighten financial industry advisors and consultants to competitive solutions that will allow them to create thriving businesses.

The transformation to wealth optimization begins in this book with a thorough examination of the histories of both the family office and financial services industries, followed by a full exploration of the factors that make family office models so attractive, the essential ingredients of the new wealth optimization model, and what high-level advisors and consultants must do in order to realize their business objectives despite the contradictory backdrop of the financial services industry.

Part I encompasses the history of both industries from the 19th century onwards. The two histories are laid side by side so that their concurrent development may be examined and the ways in which they are beginning to overlap may be clearly seen. Layered on top is an overview of current family office service models and the elements that will be retained and/or tweaked in creating successful models for the future. Part I closes with a reality check covering the current state of both industries and defining choices and opportunities presented to today's high-level advisors and investment management consultants.

Part II contains an exploration of the new wealth optimization model and the formats through which it can be implemented. It explains the collaborative relationships that must be created between family advisors and the comprehensive integration of services that attract wealthy families. It examines the technology requirement, plus the costs and education needed by the wealth optimization consultant, and also explores traditional wealth management skills in a new light. From this point, the book predicts the development and characteristics of wealth optimization consulting into the future.

Part III of the book encapsulates the considerations necessary for transforming a practice to the wealth optimization model. A fresh look at traditional wealth management skills is followed by the marketing and client education guidelines that will position the advisor/consultant and build his or her identity as a wealth optimization consultant.

---

[1] Personal interview with Charlotte B. Beyer, founder and CEO, IPI, November 2003.
[2] Personal interview with Sara Hamilton, founder and CEO, Family Office Exchange (FOX), September 2003.
[3] The terms 'wealth optimization consultant' and 'wealth optimization consulting model' are the marked property of graymatter STRATEGIES LLC.
[4] IPI offers one-day seminars designed to give both private investor attendees and their advisors hands-on opportunities to find solutions to common challenges through its Investor–Advisor Dialogue sessions. FOX offers educational conferences for its family client members and their advisors. However, there are no programs available focused on the education of advisors or consultants wishing to attract wealthy family clients.
[5] IBM Business Consulting Services (in *Technology is Not the Trump Card in Mass Affluent Wealth Management Game*, 2003) places the ideal financial services market at between US$100,000 and US$1 million in investable assets beyond the traditional ultra high net worth and high net worth focuses of the industry.
[6] The founder and CEO of FOX, Sara Hamilton, states that most experienced professionals identify that the complexities of managing wealth start to change dramatically at the US$25 million level. Hence, the author's service tier division at that level. (Personal interview with Sara Hamilton, September 2003.)

Part I

The historical basis for the family office's appeal

Introduction to Part I

Since the formation of the first family office in the 19th century, it has been considered the ultimate model of customized service. Family offices arose from the need of the ultra-wealthy to have a continuous thread connecting the many disparate parts of the professional advisory, including attorneys, certified public accountants (CPAs), investment managers, stockbrokers, insurance agents, and bank and independent trust entities.[1] Having a separate set of professional advisors, housed in one office and focusing strictly on one family's needs, has provided this connecting thread.

The family office has been the caretaker of the family fortune, has provided on-demand availability, and has offered understanding, care, and support for family members whenever needed. Financial services institutions of all kinds are attempting to replicate the superior service for which the family office is famous in an effort to attract larger assets and build deeper relationships, and, in so doing, to slow or halt the erosion of profits caused by fee compression and narrowing margins.

The history and development of the financial services industry are related to the history and development of the family office: both were spurred by courageous entrepreneurs and the new money-making opportunities generated from their success; both have been shaped by the powerful and influential; and both are going through a significant metamorphosis.

What is the appeal of the family office model and why is it being emulated and copied by every segment of the financial advisory? The events of 11 September 2001, the 2000–03 bear market, and the ensuing corporate scandals have brought a hefty dose of reality to investors as well as to both industries. Investors of all wealth levels – including those classified as 'less wealthy' – are clamoring for good advice. They are looking for trustworthy relationships with credentialed, experienced advisors who are interested enough in their personal situations to provide services, or access to services, outside investors' normal scope of involvement.

The migration of services formerly reserved for the ultra-wealthy to their less wealthy counterparts began with the offering of separately managed accounts (SMAs) to individuals. The important companion to this offering was the process of consulting with clients about their investments and their long-term objectives rather than simply peddling the investment product of the day. Formalizing the consulting process at the retail client level was the beginning of the transformation now occurring. However, it was not the only catalyst for change. The advent of the personal computer in the late 1980s carried the development of SMAs to the major firms, who really did not pay much attention to the new model until the mid-1990s when the internet began stealing high-margin commission business from the big firms, much like Dr. Seuss's Grinch stole Christmas.

Part I of this book offers a detailed history of these events from the perspective of both the family office and financial services industries. It then outlines current family office models and their appeal to the owners of significant wealth, followed by an examination of the forces behind the sea change occurring in both industries and what this monumental change may ultimately mean for investment management consultants and their clients.

---

[1] Beyer, C.B., and Brown, T.P. (2003), 'Does a Multi-Family Office Make Sense for You?', *Families in Business,* January 2003.

Chapter 1

Evolution of the family office model

Introduction

This chapter discusses the nature of the family office model, how it developed, and its role in managing family wealth. Only by examining the history of the family office can the value of its service model to the wealthy be fully appreciated. As its history unfolds throughout the chapter, its appeal to the wealthy and to those who would advise them also will become apparent. Such a comprehensive review of family office history will serve as the basis for designing effective service models to the three markets listed in the Introduction to this book – the US$5–24 million market, the US$25–100 million market, and the ultra-wealthy.

The 'business of the family' has been the inspiration of wealth management models for over two centuries. It is simultaneously a uniquely U.S. phenomenon and an Old World legacy. The success of family businesses created the need for management of the 'other' family business – the family's hard-earned assets. Those assets have, and continue to carry, great influence over family members and, collectively, over the investment industry as a whole. (For the purposes of this book, the term 'the industry' will be used to refer to both the family office and the financial industry, while the 'financial industry' will be used to refer to both the institutional and retail sides of the securities/investment industry.) The financial industry is undergoing a major revolution and the family office concept is inspiring its direction. The resolution to this metamorphosis is far from certain, but one thing is sure: financial industry firms and practitioners who survive the metamorphosis will have fundamentally reversed their business focuses.

Regarding the family office, the structure, size, and shape of the family office model is experiencing substantial redefinition. The exact models of the future remain to be seen, but it is the author's view that there will be several viable structures to choose from based on a number of factors. Until now, one family office structure or another has predominated through long developmental periods of the family office's history. In the future, dominant models will arise from the service satisfaction (both hard and soft areas), cost-effectiveness, efficiency, and profit considerations for both the family and the advisors who serve them.

Generally, from the 19th century to the 1980s, the single family office (SFO) concept reigned. An SFO is a staff of administrative, legal, accounting, investment, and other professionals hired to work in a single office location exclusively for the benefit of the hiring family. Services delivered range from managing the assets of the family's operating business and personal investment portfolios to scheduling corporate and family events, to arranging business trips and family vacations, to hiring nannies for the grandchildren. During the 1980s and 1990s, multi-family offices (MFOs) took off. An MFO strives to provide the same intensely customized, high-quality services as an SFO for more than one family, allowing the costs of providing those services to be spread over a larger asset base. MFOs are usually formed by an initial family's SFO opening its doors to other families who may share certain interests or dynamics or who have fewer assets than the original family. The difficulty is in preventing too significant a trade-off between the cost savings and the privacy and exclusive service provisions that may be sacrificed in order to achieve those savings.

The intriguing and exciting phenomenon now occurring is the evolution of financial industry consulting toward a family office level of service. This evolution, combined with new technologies and demands by the investing public, is inspiring new levels of family office service. The interest in family office services currently has the flavor of the interest in internet stocks during the late 1990s – models to emulate the service level have been thrown together in a variety of forms in order to use the 'family office services' label. This has caused confusion for families and investors who seek family office level services because the name 'family office' is being used by many who may provide disappointing experiences.

As a result, talented advisors and consultants to the wealthy who have a sincere desire to succeed have an unparalleled opportunity to do so. Examining the histories of both the family office and financial industries will give a more complete perspective and will open thought processes regarding the pragmatic and realistic opportunities that currently exist within this burgeoning market-place.

Origins of the family office

According to a report by Cerulli Associates, the original U.S. family offices were created by wealthy merchants early in the 19th century who hired trusted comrades or advisors to oversee their wealth and provide for their families while they were traveling. European history dates family office services in the form of private banks back 300 years, when the wealthy merchants began setting up banks that became the foundations for some of the top modern-day wealth managers. The threads of these early European private banks have woven themselves into modern times, as some Swiss banks are still owned by descendants of the original merchants and, in some cases, continue to invest on the same side with their clients.[1] These were the first fiduciary relationships. They represented the foundation for the relationships provided by bank trust officers, which blossomed during the Industrial Revolution.

The private banks founded in Europe were an offshoot from goldsmith banks, which held gold deposits in order to extend credit to successful monarchs and merchants entering into new business ventures worldwide.[2] European private banks at that time were unregulated and unlicensed, enabling wealthy businessmen to conduct their affairs in a private manner and with little or no governmental regulation. European private bankers of the 17th century through to the first quarter of the 19th century included the Rothschilds and all the English banks (apart from the Bank of England).[3]

The tradition of unregulated, unlicensed private banking was unsurprisingly carried to the New World, led by figures such as Alexander Hamilton (Bank of New York, 1784), John Pierpont Morgan (J.P. Morgan, 1800s), and Stephen Girard (Bank of Stephen Girard in Philadelphia, 1812, which became part of Mellon Financial Corporation in 1983[4]). Politically based state chartering set the stage for the development of private banks in the United States, since political deal-making influenced which banks received lucrative state charters. The charters granted economically favorable privileges to the banks, making it difficult for banks without charters to compete. This competitive landscape, along with the high demand for banking services, spawned the adoption of the unregulated European private banking model.

However, the intertwined financial interests of state governments and state chartered banks were to number the days of these unregulated 'encroachers'. The private banks, as well as the early federal banks, were considered trespassers on the lucrative deals set up between the states and their chartered banks and were forced to become regulated in consideration of the 'public interest'.[5] Nonetheless, private banks continued to provide specialized, personal services to the wealthy, and later teamed with trust companies to offer a more complete selection of services catering to high net worth individuals.

Early securities investment and the construct of family assets

In 19th century America, most wealth was in the form of local business ventures or real estate and was easily managed by its owners. There was little available in the form of cash instruments. Following on from the signing of the Buttonwood Agreement in 1792, the New York Stock and Exchange Board (later to be renamed the New York Stock Exchange) was founded in 1817 (see Exhibit 1.1). Few financial instruments traded at the time, and those that did primarily consisted of U.S. government bonds[6] and a few bank, insurance company, and canal company stocks.[7]

The early entrepreneurs comprised railroad barons, merchants, shipbuilders, and industrialists, and in 1853 the first trust company, U.S. Trust, was formed by a group of forward-thinking industrialists including Peter Cooper, Erastus Corning, Marshall Field, John Phelps, and Jacob Westervelt. The purpose of this early financial institution was to help other entrepreneurs execute financial transactions and manage their wealth. Prior to the formation of U.S. Trust, the only trustees had been individuals; creating a financial institution to handle trust and banking functions for the early business barons was an innovative, prescient idea.

Exhibit 1.1

Timeline of U.S. securities investment and wealth development

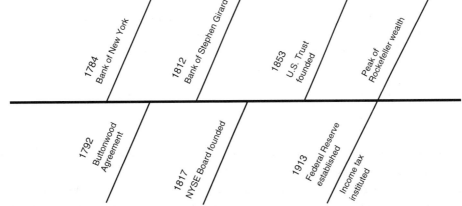

Source: Author's own.

The establishment of the Federal Reserve in 1913 gave stability to the growing financial markets, which contributed greatly to restoring prosperity in the United States during this great industrial period. By the beginning of the 20th century, the securitization of more and more large companies initiated a shift in the creation of wealth. Publicly traded securities grew to include railroad companies, banks, insurance companies, and mining companies. Some entrepreneurs became executives of the new large corporations that were springing up, while others continued to grow their businesses or start new ones. Both types of entrepreneurs had built up enough capital to invest in other companies, which diversified their holdings and contributed to the growth of liquidity in the market-place.

Industrial icons create a need for larger family offices

It was during this period that the first great American entrepreneurs arose – the Rockefellers, Carnegies, Fords, Vanderbilts, Roosevelts, Morgans, and a long list of other famous names – whose businesses influence the U.S. economy to this day. Many of these entrepreneurs (the Rockefellers will be used for ease of example) built companies into trusts (for example, Standard Oil) with very centralized structures that virtually eliminated competition of any consequence by simply purchasing it.[8] The Rockefeller wealth peaked in 1913 at US$900 million with the court-ordered break-up of Standard Oil. Half of the Rockefeller wealth was lost during the Great Depression; however, there was plenty left to ensure the family fortune. In 1931, construction of 14 buildings that would be called Rockefeller Center began.[9] Multiply the Rockefeller's reinvestment and ability to thrive during this devastating period by the number of 'legacy' families, and the foundation for the tremendous wealth of the 1950s and 1960s becomes readily apparent.

As early as the mid-19th century, the pioneering entrepreneurs found themselves immersed not only in the day-to-day operations of the larger-than-life businesses they had built, but also inadvertently in the business of managing the by-product of those businesses – their enormous wealth.[10] The businesses they founded grew to require more and more of their time. Wealth management was becoming an increasingly involved process and the entrepreneurs had neither the time to give nor the expertise required for successful management.

Exhibit 1.2

Early family office structure

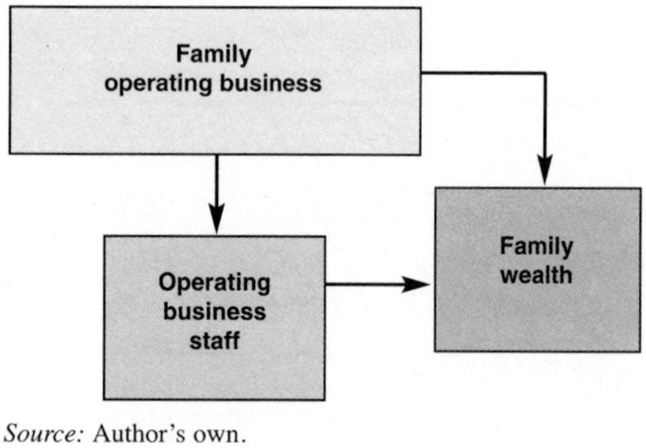

Source: Author's own.

The management of the family wealth was initially the responsibility of internal corporate staff members, who in some cases were also family members (see Exhibit 1.2). In addition to their normal duties, these staff members began handling such broad family matters as paying the bills for both the business and the family, hiring household help, planning business and social events, overseeing bank accounts, helping children finance their first homes, seeing to personal and corporate tax matters, and monitoring investment management. As the business and the family grew, the business and family needs also grew and demanded more of the staff's time, which began diverting resources from the primary focus of managing the operating business. Increased knowledge of personal family matters by the company staff, even if those staff were family members themselves, often tended to create an uncomfortable situation.

So the founders and their families began to hire outside advisors, primarily at trust companies and banks, to handle the business of managing their wealth so that they and their staffs could continue to effectively manage their corporate businesses and keep private family information and financial activities private. At this point, there was little definition or guidance regarding the involvement and influence of other family members in the business. The involvement of the company staff in both businesses was originally viewed as providing a connection between the two. But this connection would only breed confusion regarding family members' roles, greatly increase overhead for the operating business, and foster confidentiality concerns.[11]

Businessmen and wealthy investors came to depend on financial professionals to advise them on increasingly demanding wealth management issues. After the income tax and the Federal Reserve were established in 1913, new complications were added to the management of these entrepreneurs' portfolios.[12] Having to manage their operating businesses, which by now had grown quite large, plus their investment portfolios, trusts, and other business of the family began to develop into quite a daunting task. The next generation was coming of age, adding more variables to the mix as the original founders of these now enormous business concerns began to pass on.

The first significant transfer of wealth in the United States began to occur as the next generation (in our example, signified by John D. Rockefeller, Jr.) inherited the businesses and investments of their fathers, and the duties of the trustees expanded accordingly. Rather than working for one 'master' in the form of the patriarchal founder, the trustees now answered to two or more siblings or even a group of cousins. The industrialization of the United States, giving rise to large corporations with different forms of ownership and producing new sources of wealth, had begun.

As needs outside of trust concerns continued to develop, the founding families of the businesses realized the management of their two businesses – the operating business and the family's personal and financial affairs – needed to be split. The result was the formation of the first separate family offices.

'Waves of wealth' and multiple generations complicate family wealth

Entrepreneurial activity in the aftermath of World War II brought the United States out of the Great Depression, giving birth in its wake to a second, much larger wave of family office creation.[13] Coming on the heels of the Depression and World War II, these entrepreneurs appreciated the value of what they had created and wanted to preserve it for their progeny. The family attorney, the family accountant, or other family advisors began to be hired to work exclusively for these entrepreneurs, and their combined role was to work toward preservation of the wealth for future generations.

It is critical to realize the meaning of this wealth creation from the personal view of the business owner and his family and from the standpoint of the economic future of the United States. Because of their unprecedented wealth, these entrepreneurs had, unlike the vast

Exhibit 1.3

Waves of wealth and market-place changes

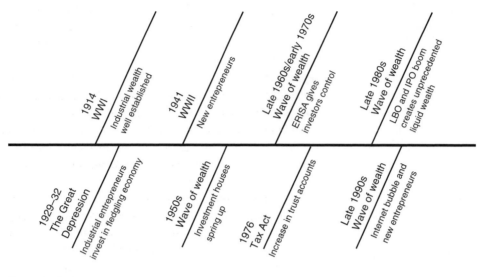

Source: Author's own.

majority of the population, survived an unimaginable time of poverty and economic devastation and were even able to bolster their wealth by taking advantage of the best bargains and investment opportunities. Although the manner in which their wealth was created and maintained may have produced enemies for these entrepreneurs and their families, their ability to survive the Depression and reinvest in their businesses and in the economy provided much needed jobs and economic support in the 1929–32 period. In fact, many such entrepreneurs purposely became philanthropically focused in order to repair the ill will fostered by their great success.[14]

The waves of wealth began to restructure the economy and the investment market-place (see Exhibit 1.3). As we have seen, during the 1920s the first advisors outside the family were hired and later began to be brought in-house. By the 1940s and 1950s, investment houses had sprung up to manage the investments of institutions such as foundations, endowments, and large pension funds. Since such institutional accounts were not concerned with tax consequences, the portfolio managers at the investment houses did not take the taxable assets of individuals. The bigger money was in the tax-exempt institutions, so firms were not willing to deal with the complications that taxable accounts presented. As a result, many of the families now known as the 'legacy' families, such as the Duponts, Fords, Pitcairns, Phipps, Vanderbilts, Rockefellers, and Morgans, had portfolio managers in-house to manage the financial assets of the family plus maintain the privacy that was so precious to them.

According to Sara Hamilton, CEO of the Family Office Exchange (FOX), a resource for families of exceptional wealth, changes occur in the financial markets whenever large amounts of wealth are transferred; hence her term, 'waves of wealth'. In the private wealth arena, Hamilton says such waves occurred during the late 1800s, the 1950s, the late 1960s and early 1970s, the late 1980s (as a result of unprecedented

16

Exhibit 1.4

The family office becomes a separate entity

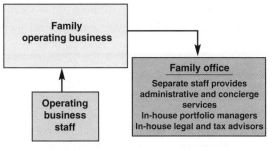

Source: Author's own.

merger and acquisition activity), and, most recently, the 1990s.

Some of the wealth created in the mid-19th century by the industrial powerhouse entrepreneurs was pooled in small networks of sophisticated owners to create companies such as U.S. Trust and J.P. Morgan, which still exist in some form today. Many other companies created during this period have now consolidated. Recent examples include the Chase Manhattan merger with J.P. Morgan and the merger of U.S. Trust with Charles Schwab Corporation. The firms that have survived, at least in name, of course look quite different from what their founders could possibly have envisioned.

There were other services such as trust, accounting, and concierge operations and families who had enough assets to merit a full staff to perform these services hired them (see Exhibit 1.4). These families also benefited from the synergies created by having all their advisors under one roof; the accountant, attorney, and portfolio manager worked as a team to benefit the family wealth in a more coordinated and comprehensive manner. During this period, families either set up their family offices as private trust companies or hired an independent trust company to serve as trustee.

The post-World War II entrepreneurs' businesses that began in the late 1940s and early 1950s ran as autonomous entities until the 1980s when many families took advantage of unprecedented leveraged buyout activity and sold their businesses. This created an entirely new slate of wealth management needs for the families. The founders had established these businesses, had loved their work, and had never envisioned selling the businesses. But offers of double what the owners felt the businesses were worth were just too tempting. So another great wave of wealth changing hands completely altered the face of the investment management business.

A further conduit for sudden, large cash flows came from taking these companies public. The initial public offering (IPO) markets of the late 1980s were quite favorable and remained so throughout a major portion of the 1990s. Business owners were accustomed to having great wealth, but had never before experienced the level of liquidity generated from the IPOs or by the outright sales of their businesses. For the first time in history, first generation, intelligent business people were faced with the challenges of managing their wealth like they had managed their businesses – only it was a different type of management that the entrepreneurs knew little about, and if they had sold the business, they no longer had the corporate staff at their disposal.[15]

The stark reality of no longer having an operating business to run and a staff to assist in day-to-day activities hit home quickly. Many of the entrepreneurs were so confused they became paralyzed, placing their money in low-yielding Treasury bills while they tried to figure out how, as soon as possible, to become adept wealth managers. Through the buyouts or successful public offerings, their wealth had become large enough to last not only through their lifetimes, but also through the lifetimes of their children.[16]

Other emerging wealth concerns

New estate and gift tax rules enacted by the Tax Reform Act of 1976[17] brought insurers into the mix who convinced business owners to transfer ownership of most of the wealth to their children through trusts. These children were suddenly quite wealthy and their entrepreneurial parents became concerned that the work ethic they held so dear would not be passed on. They were also concerned about the children's ability to manage the wealth appropriately.

The financial industry of the 1980s was vertically integrated; services were segmented, compartmentalized, and very technical. For example, estate planners never consulted with tax planners; tax planners never consulted with art collectors; art collectors never consulted with people who sold airplanes.[18] Business owners were receiving advice that was as segmented as the professionals who advised them, and with whom they had often developed long-term relationships. As owners of more wealth than they had probably ever imagined, they were faced with trying to decide who would manage it for them. Would it be John, the attorney who had set up the business structure and had handled the family affairs for decades; Mark, the CPA who had protected the wealth from taxes year after year; or Joe, the investment broker who had managed the family's investments since the children had been born?

In the early 1980s, these questions had been easily answered for some families – the family wealth management business was dominated by trust companies (that were also the estate planners of the time) who managed the wealth and private bankers who were lenders. Some trust companies also owned private banks and, in those cases, the two services became integrated. As the decade developed and large financial institutions opened their money management services to wealthy families, private bankers became money managers and asset gatherers in order to compete.[19]

The wealth owners were also faced with a plethora of new opportunities and needs. There were new investment vehicles such as hedge funds and derivatives, new retirement plan structures and reporting requirements enacted under the Employee Retirement Income Security Act (ERISA), philanthropic considerations, new tax laws, new legal structures, and different insurance needs.[20] Concierge services offering everything from personal shoppers to scheduling the family plane were also desired. Meanwhile, the impending transfer of this wealth to succeeding generations also presented new challenges. Concerns about the friction great wealth can cause among family members and, with the significant growth in the divorce rate beginning in the 1960s and 1970s, the possible threat of family wealth falling into the hands of ex-spouses and away from the original family heirs made the lives of entrepreneurs and their families even more complicated.

Against this background, the need for trusted family advisors to manage the wealth in a more collaborative fashion was mounting. Wealth management as another 'business' of the family became more pronounced and came to include more services from more advisors. But the only place where all of these services were available under one roof was the family office.[21] Meanwhile, this expansion in the need for services also increased the costs of the business of managing the family wealth, so the family office was a tool for pooling assets to increase buying and negotiating power in order to cut overall costs and still be able to hire the best advisors.

Expansion of the family office

This need of wealthy families to run their wealth like a business and the pooling of assets to create a larger block began to attract the attention of institutional money managers. The pooled asset levels of these families were as large as some of the managers' institutional accounts, so the managers saw the opportunity to expand their businesses by offering their services to wealthy families. Families were already experiencing institutional level service with their corporate and foundation accounts; they wanted the same service for their personal wealth.[22] This added to the sense that managing the family wealth was indeed a business. The process should be the same as the institutional process and should involve the creation of written investment plans, asset allocation services, access to the best managers to accomplish the families' financial objectives and goals, ongoing monitoring of performance, and institutional level performance reporting and attribution. This new level of management for personal wealth also gave families access to investment vehicles not available to the general investing public, such as hedge funds, private equity funds, and commodity pools.

The migration from a couple of trusted advisors (the trust officer and the private banker) managing one entrepreneur's cache to the business of managing the collective pool of assets from the entrepreneur's children, siblings, and cousins also tended to keep primary control of those assets in the hands of the entrepreneurs. Although the assets were legally owned by the heirs through trusts, the agreement among family members regarding the management of the pooled assets usually followed along the lines of the founder's (the family patriarch's) wishes. It allowed the original objectives of the entrepreneur to be achieved and safeguarded the assets from early and indiscriminant dissipation (see Exhibit 1.5).

The concerns of the entrepreneurs regarding their heirs' ability to manage their new holdings would eventually prove to be well founded. The heirs of these great entrepreneurs had no inkling about the complications of managing immense wealth. The longest bull market in history would begin in 1982, checked only briefly by the crash of 1987. As the trusts began to be dispersed, the markets of the 1990s would lull these heirs into thinking that managing wealth was easy, but the severe bear market of 2000–03 would bring the complications into stark focus.

Exhibit 1.5

Patriarchal control maintained via the trustee system

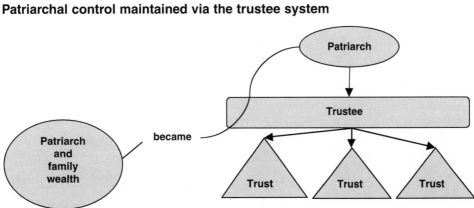

Source: Author's own.

Since the management of the pooled assets also brought new dynamics to the relationships between family members, organization of the family office into a separate legal entity allowed those relationships and sometimes disparate views to be governed and managed by the structure of the business. In some instances, the family office became an official business organization in the form of a partnership, limited partnership, corporation, Subchapter 'S' corporation, or a limited liability company (LLC).

By this point, the primary purposes of the family office were to provide personal care for the family and to optimize the management of the family's wealth. Setting up the family office as a formal business entity enabled it to have just enough of a degree of separation to provide the objective guidance that can be so beneficial to families, yet maintain the all-important level of support and customized service family offices were designed to provide. The creation of the family office proved to be a major task in itself, so wealthy entrepreneurs hired consultants to facilitate their set-up and to preside over the families' financial needs during the process.[23]

Services and structure of the family office

The responsibility of the family office is to serve the family's needs, both financially and personally. Wealthy families traditionally have realized the power of pooling their assets to obtain the best in service in just about any area they desire. Since managing the family wealth is a significant component of that service, it is important to realize the connection of the wealth with other aspects of the family's assets. A family's wealth obviously includes the money accumulated from the business and financial investments, but it also may include hard assets such as art collections, jewelry, gold, real estate, and the family plane. A family's wealth also comprises human, intellectual, and social capital. These components are often overlooked by outside observers, but are some of the most important of the family's assets.

It was the founder's intelligence and human capital that created the wealth in the first place. Having the business acumen, drive, intuition, and foresight to take timely advantage of the opportunities that allowed the wealth to be created are attributes not only to be admired, but also nourished in the other family members. There are countless stories about the family member who is only involved in the family business because he or she is a member of the family. These stories often are unfavorable – to either the family member or the business – but there are just as many stories about talented family members who make a significant contribution to the business's continuing success story.

The complication for a family office staff is in supporting both types of family members. Although it may not be desirable for a family member to be involved in the business, whether he or she actually is, the family office may be called upon to help that family member discover his or her true talents, or at least feel no less an important part of the family. The entrepreneurs who founded the business may also have a difficult time with these family members, especially in the case of a son or daughter. These are examples of the difficult questions to which family offices are called upon to provide answers, and that task may involve outsourcing a psychologist or similar counselor.

Business of the family office

The family office ideally should be run as a separate business – in reality, not just conceptually. It should have a formal business structure with a board of directors that is actively involved and meets regularly. The board can consist of certain family members as well as outside advisors, and it should report to the family on normal business matters such as cash flow, investment performance, the activities of the staff, and other operating information.

The primary services of the first family offices have involved managing the family's financial affairs and a limited list of personal activities including bill-paying, planning social events, income tax planning, and trust services, which oversaw transfer of the wealth to the next generation. During the 1980s and 1990s, the list of family office services expanded greatly. The basic services offered by today's family offices vary widely, but they commonly include:[24]

- income tax, retirement, financial, succession, and estate planning;
- integration of services related to all aspects of the family's financial matters;
- cash flow management;
- financial reporting, on family office functions as well as investment management;
- implementing philanthropic strategies;
- mentoring;
- investment management services;
- holding family meetings;
- managing debt and leverage;
- multi-generational education;
- mediation of internal family conflicts;
- bill-paying;
- payroll tax administration for household help;
- coordination with bankers, attorneys, and insurance brokers;
- oversight of real estate investments;
- wealth transfer strategies;
- trust services; and
- family governance.

In addition to these basic services, family offices may also offer:[25]

- a total wealth audit designed to help the family understand its holdings on a more comprehensive basis;
- monitoring all risk coverage, from property and casualty to substantial life insurance programs;
- offshore solutions where appropriate;
- overseeing and monitoring of outside trustees;
- creating educational programs for the next generation, giving them skills needed to make independent evaluations regarding the family wealth and preparing them to serve as valuable board members for other organizations; and
- facilitating family meetings, either at the family foundation or with the family council.

Listing the services that family offices provide can easily mislead the reader into thinking that all family offices offer at least the basic slate of services. In reality, no two family offices are the same. Family offices were developed to serve the individual needs of their families; therefore, the services offered and the systems designed for offering those services are as varied as the individual families who own them.

Key objectives of the family office

Originally, the family office represented a method by which family members could create more value for the family as a whole. Then, the combined assets increased purchasing power, provided the luxury of having a dedicated staff available on demand, offered a source of understanding and caring for each family member, coordinated outsourced services for the maximum benefit to the family, and created a legacy for the founding member.[26]

In the 1960s and 1970s, these luxuries sometimes gave rise to unproductive, irresponsible adults who abused privileges and squandered their share of the assets. 'Family offices can very often contribute to the total financial ineptitude of wealthy families,' offers Lee Hausner, Ph.D. and partner at DoudHausnerVistar Strategic Family Business Advisors. She explains: 'When someone else is doing everything – writing the checks, planning the budget – you don't get financially competent. There's a much greater awareness now on the part of family office personnel and staff on empowering family members. It's much easier to serve an empowered family member than an incompetent.'

Today, there is also more interest on the part of entrepreneurs in educating heirs about their responsibilities and giving back some of their good fortune to the community (see Exhibit 1.6). According to Stanley H. Pantowich, partner and CEO at TAG Associates, a leading multi-client family office and portfolio management services company:

> The biggest evolution that I've seen is that people who have made great wealth are thinking twice about leaving that great wealth to their children. They're saying, 'I'm worth US$500 million and I've got three kids. Am I doing them a favor by leaving them each US$100 million (after taxes)? Or am I hurting them?' And many are concluding that they'd like their kids to have the benefit of the money, but that US$10 million is enough. If they want to own a jet, they're going to have to earn enough to buy it themselves. This trend is very powerful and that wasn't the case when I started this business in 1983. People said, 'I made it; I'm giving it to my kids.' Now people are recognizing that too much money is not the right thing.

Exhibit 1.6

The change in family philanthropic objectives

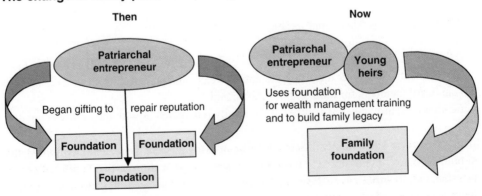

Source: Author's own.

The sufficiency or otherwise of specific sums of money may be debatable, but the new focus on responsibility regarding wealth is, indeed, a genuine one.

So what are the key objectives of today's family office? The primary purposes have changed very little since the family offices created during the Industrial Revolution, or even since the wealthy merchants of old. 'Its entire mission is to manage the wealth of the family for the benefit of the family,' offers Amy Braden, managing director and head of the Family Wealth Center at J.P. Morgan Chase. The family office as a business is 'really a resource to leverage the family wealth and to use that wealth for the benefit of the objectives of the family'.

Another important purpose is to provide cohesiveness to the family by realizing the legacy of the original founder. The family office serves to coordinate all of the functions of the family, which may include everything from making a hair appointment for 14-year-old Sally and addressing the family greeting cards around holidays to attracting the best money managers and developing a customized transition plan to heirs. But the predominant goals have to do with the overall good of the family and the goals the family has for managing its wealth. 'The goals of the family determine the functions of the office,' says FOX's Sara Hamilton. And the complexity of those functions is determined by the complexity of the ownership structure:

> Family trusts and individual assets owned by different owners and different cousins in a family all use that pooling fund as a way to manage the assets collectively. That creates some very complex and interesting issues around, if it's a partnership, who is going to be the general partner and who is going to control it; and if it's an investment partnership how that is going to be structured; if it's an LLC who is going to be the managing partner of that entity? But (the family office) is still the tool that holds families together.

Large institutions have increasingly attempted to offer effective family office services over the past five to six years. The projections for wealth transfer over the next 50 years are approaching the US$41 trillion mark,[27] triple what was projected just a couple of years ago – figures that continue to spur the development of less traditional family office models. This enormous transfer will create yet another wave of wealth changing hands, but Hamilton projects this wave will be different to those of the past:

> I don't think it's going to be the same kind of wave. I think it's going to be a gradual growth in the number of people with liquid wealth. We want to educate owners. We talk to hundreds of owners a year who are in some kind of financial transition and are wrestling with questions such as, 'What kind of provider do I need? What are my real challenges? How do I educate my kids about wealth management? What do I want to do philanthropically?'

The beneficiaries of this transfer will be the baby boomers, who think differently to their parents about the meaning of wealth, what it means to their future, and how they want it to be used. Successful family offices will initiate steps to address the specific needs and thought processes of this powerful generation; as it has changed every other facet of life it has touched, it is already bringing about unprecedented changes in the functions and structure of the family office.

The family office of today

Today's family office is experiencing greater demands from families. The complexity of the tax laws, the frequency of tax law change, greater interest in alternative investment vehicles such as hedge funds and private equity, and more complex family make-up created by extended families are bringing greater challenges to family offices than ever before.

As family offices grow in size and in the number of services they provide, the costs of running them are growing beyond the boundaries of some single families' financial feasibility. The struggle to find the best and most efficient method of management is not new. In 1974, Bessemer Trust became the first family office to offer management and other services to wealthy families outside the family of origin who needed a family office but whose assets were not large enough to afford one of their own.[28] But as costs have risen, the popularity of multiple family offices has increased – particularly in light of the 2000–03 bear market. Many families realize that managing their wealth is not as easy as it once appeared to be and wish to avail themselves of professional management. Since many of these families cannot afford to open a family office strictly dedicated to their autonomous needs, they have found that the multiple family office can provide the bulk of the same services in an affordable manner and in a customized fashion.

Nevertheless, the MFO experience has been a disappointing one for many families. According to Charlotte B. Beyer, founder and CEO of the Institute for Private Investors (IPI), family offices are notoriously unprofitable because most families do not run them as a business:

> They tell themselves, 'This is what makes us happy. This is what we're doing to keep our wealth.' So they open up to other families because they think, 'Wait a minute! Here's how we can become profitable.' A couple of years later, they decide that was a bad decision and close up again.

MFOs with larger asset bases that offer family office executives ownership in the business are the most successful, says Beyer. Some MFOs serve as many as 150 families, making these offices equal in size to small financial institutions. Such growth has attracted the attention of the financial industry over the past few years, creating competition for family offices' financial management business. The influence of these institutions on family office creation and operation has definitely been felt.

The competition for asset management has added confusion for families seeking family office services. Large financial institutions such as banks, brokerage firms, and insurance companies have created new marketing divisions focused on attracting large-scale family assets. The marketing boasts that these institutions are family offices as a result of some special services they have added to their investment management mix. However, traditional family offices say it is difficult for large financial firms to know families well enough to provide the cohesion and integration of services offered by the traditional family office model.

To combat this problem, some firms hired new groups of advisors dedicated to fostering such cohesion and overseeing better integration of services only to discover the added costs of the increased staff more than offset the benefits of capturing the extra assets. The culture at large financial institutions represents another deterrent. Large financial firms traditionally are product focused; wealthy families demand open architecture and objective advice, and they expect to have access to the best money managers and other advisors as a result. Open architecture brings in lower fees, which has already caused many firms to either abandon their family office models or to try to create a more profitable structure.

Families have begun researching alternatives themselves and, due to technology development, better flow of information, and increased investor education, they are discovering new models and even combinations of models that they can customize to suit their individual needs. This new curiosity and in-depth research on the part of wealthy families, combined with the effort by large financial institutions to get a piece of the wealth transfer that is already beginning, is setting up some interesting dynamics in the industry as a whole.[29] Whether these institutions will be successful in the endeavor to adequately provide family office services remains to be seen. The obvious facts are that the huge, although gradual, transfer of wealth to the baby boomer generation, increased technological capabilities that will boost efficiencies, and the increased focus on philanthropy by today's families are developments that have attracted both new players and new family wealth to the family office industry.

Conclusions

With so many new choices available to wealthy families, industry firms, and professionals alike, the purpose of this book is to explore the validity and feasibility of these new choices. Many firms have rushed into offering family office style services only to hit obstacles, causing them to re-evaluate their approach and redesign their models.

The development of the family office with its comprehensive range of services has been, and continues to be, the response to the needs of wealth creators and their families. Its level of service will remain the vanguard for the stewardship of that wealth by succeeding generations as well as for the new wealth creators and their families. Family office operations were spawned from wealth management service offerings available in Europe at the time of the establishment of the New World. U.S. entrepreneurs put their own stamp on the European models, eventually leading to the family office models of today and the opportunities within those structures for advisors/consultants seeking to develop them further.

At such an interesting time for both the family office and general financial services industries, it is impossible to say which models will succeed and how the family office of the future will ultimately look. Opportunities abound for both industry practitioners and families with wealth. Families with new wealth face a paradox spurred by three factors:

- confusion arising from the number of choices;
- lack of definition regarding those options; and
- the advantages of having access to the new innovations of the family office model.

With that in mind, an attempt to fully explore the possibilities for families as well as industry practitioners unfolds in the chapters to come.

[1] Fleck, Fiona (2002), 'Saving Generations of Wealth: The Rich Move Beyond Private Bankers to "Family Offices" Managing Fortunes With One-Stop Financial Planning', available at www.loedstar.com/press/wsje-december_2002.htm

[2] Barclays (2003), 'Barclays History', available at http://www.personal.barclays.co.uk/BRC1/jsp/brc control?task=articleabout&value=2946&site=pfs

[3] Sylla, Richard, and Kaufman, Henry (1995), 'The Forgotten Private Banker', originally published in *The Freeman,* a publication of the Foundation for Economic Education, Inc, Vol. 34, No. 4 (April).

[4] Mellon Financial Corporation (2003), 'History of Mellon Financial Corporation', available at http://www.mellon.com/aboutmellon/history.html

[5] Sylla, Richard, and Kaufman, Henry (1995), 'The Forgotten Private Banker', originally published in *The Freeman,* a publication of the Foundation for Economic Education, Inc, Vol. 34, No. 4 (April), available at http://www.libertyhaven.com/theoreticalorphilosophicalissues/economichistory/forgotten.html

[6] Investment Research Institute (2002), 'The Beginning', available at http://www.stockmarkettrivia.com/

[7] Smith, B. Mark (2001), 'Toward Irrational Exuberance: The Evolution of the Modern Stock Market', available at http://www.booksense.com/readup/excerpts/rationalexuberance.jsp

[8] PBS. org (2003), 'The Rockefellers: Rockefeller Timeline', available at www.pbs.org/wgbh/amex/rockefellers/timeline/index.html

[9] Ibid., 1930–85.

[10] Ibid., 1839–98.

[11] Hauser, Barbara R. (2001), 'The Family Office: Insights into Their Development in the U.S., a Proposed Prototype, and Advice for Adaptation in Other Countries', *The Journal of Wealth Management* (Fall), p. 16.

[12] U.S. Trust (2002), 'Annual Review' and 'U.S. Trust: A History of Growth with a Commitment to Personal Service'.

[13] Cerulli Associates (2001), *Family Offices.*

[14] PBS (2003), 'The Rockefellers: Rockefeller Timeline, 1839–1898', available at www.pbs.org/wgbh/amex/rockefellers/timeline/index.html

[15] Author's interview with Sara Hamilton, CEO, FOX, September 2003.

[16] Hauser, Barbara R. (2001), 'The Family Office: Insights into Their Development in the U.S., a Proposed Prototype, and Advice for Adaptation in Other Countries', *The Journal of Wealth Management* (Fall), p. 16.

[17] Silberstein, Debra Rahmin (2003), 'A History of the Estate Tax: A Source of Revenue or Vehicle for Wealth Redistribution?', *Brandeis Graduate Journal*, Vol. 1, No. 1, available at http://www.brandeis.edu/gsa/gradjournal/2003/pdf/silberstein.pdf

[18] Author's interview with Sara Hamilton, CEO, FOX, September 2003.

[19] Ibid.

[20] LeBlanc, Sydney (2002), *Legacy: The History of Separately Managed Accounts*, Washington, DC, Money Management Institute, p. 5.

[21] Author's interview with Sara Hamilton, CEO, FOX, September 2003.

[22] Author's interview with Frank L. Campanale, former president and CEO, Salomon Smith Barney Consulting Group, September 2003.

[23] Hauser, Barbara R. (2001), 'The Family Office: Insights into Their Development in the U.S., a Proposed Prototype, and Advice for Adaptation in Other Countries', *The Journal of Wealth Management* (Fall), p. 16.

[24] Ibid., pp. 17–18; and Cymric Family Office Services (2002), 'Functions of a Family Office', available at http://www.cymricfamilyoffice.com/html/ functions.html

[25] Hauser, Barbara R. (2001), 'The Family Office: Insights into Their Development in the U.S., a Proposed Prototype, and Advice for Adaptation in Other Countries', *The Journal of Wealth Management* (Fall), pp. 17–18.

[26] Ibid., p. 19.

[27] Boston College (2003), 'Why the US$41 Trillion Wealth Transfer is Still Valid: A Review of Challenges and Questions', The National Committee on Planned Giving's *The Journal of Gift Planning,* Vol. 7, No. 1, First Quarter 2003, pp. 11–15 and 47–50, available at http://www.bc.edu/research/swri/features/wealth

[28] Bessemer Trust (2003), 'Our Heritage', available at https://www.bessemer.com/WebSite/PageLoad.asp?PageKey=OurHeritage

[29] Beyer, Charlotte B. (1999), 'Family Offices in America: Why the Bloom is Off the Rose', *The Journal of Private Portfolio Management,* Vol. 2, No. 2, pp. 26–29.

Chapter 2

Separately managed accounts: the 'Holy Grail' of the financial services industry

Introduction

This chapter focuses on the history of the modern-day separately managed account (SMA) industry and its relationship to family office style services.

To fully appreciate the family office's standing in today's investment industry, a view of the 'other side' of customized wealth management must be explored – that of SMAs,[1] sometimes referred to as 'managed money'. SMAs as investment vehicles are unique and fill the distinct, historic role of initiating the migration of services formerly reserved for institutions and the ultra-wealthy to the broader investing public. Reviewing the history of SMAs will lead to a better understanding of the convergence of the financial services and family office industries, and of the unprecedented opportunities arising from their development.

SMAs began as a new way of investing for small businesses and super-wealthy individuals during the late 1970s when the previously unquestioned investment dominance of bank trust departments and insurance companies began to break down. They developed in the midst of other revolutionary changes that were occurring in society, business, and government, and, to an extent, were conceived as the natural offspring of the environment.

Indeed, the whole financial services industry has developed as a product of its environment. Its vehicles have arisen from economic conditions, the needs of the investing public, and the desire of capitalist societies to prosper. However, along the way, the financial services industry began shifting its focus to the profits it could achieve by selling investment products to the beneficiaries of that prosperity rather than truly serving them. Therefore, the greatest beneficiaries either hired their own investment counsel to work exclusively on their behalf or sought the guidance of a private trust company. They continue to demand the privilege of having 'the best' in investment management and financial services.

Financial industry firms that have capitalized the most on this product-driven culture have been extremely resistant to change – even as they now face the demise of their product-driven businesses. So they cut costs and add more controls over the processes they are trying to protect and the people who implement those processes. Those who have been forced to realize they must adapt to the new environment have had to be dragged into it; once there, they have begun the process of trying to control the lifetime and profitability of the new environment just as they did the old.

Legislative changes foster the development of SMAs

The changes that began in the 1970s would also plant the seeds of accessibility by the mass affluent to the levels of investment counsel traditionally accessed only by the privileged. Investors with assets worth less than the US$10 million minimum then required by most

Exhibit 2.1

Retirement plan disclosure rules enacted by the U.S. government

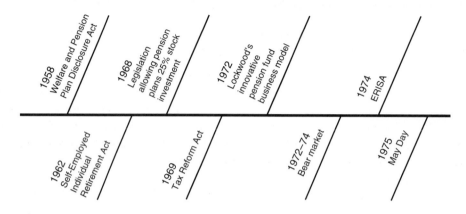

Source: Author's own.

money managers would gain access to the same managers through the SMA platform. The precursor to this accessibility was the issuance of new rules of accountability by the U.S. government through several pieces of legislation affecting retirement plan disclosure (see Exhibit 2.1).

The Welfare and Pension Plan Disclosure Act of 1958 and the amendments that were enacted in 1962, the Self-Employed Individual Retirement Act of 1962, and the Tax Reform Act of 1969 began to force disclosure of money managers' activities in these accounts and provided for a closer look at returns. The Self-Employed Individual Retirement Act of 1962 provided incentives for the self-employed to establish retirement plans in the form of Keogh plans or individual retirement accounts (IRAs). In 1974, the Employee Retirement Income Security Act (ERISA) was introduced to protect the retirement benefits of participants in private pension plans set up by their large company employers.

Prior to ERISA, most of the retirement and general investment assets of the wealthy, including their estates, corporate funds and public funds, and foundation and endowment assets, were controlled by banks and insurance companies, which were blindly trusted by investors who lacked information about the (often mediocre) level of returns they were receiving. There was no method of accurately measuring investment performance or comparing performance results to benchmarks or other similar investments. Most significant investment assets of the time were held in defined benefit plans that were invested primarily in fixed-income instruments. Business people (the wealthy founders discussed in Chapter 1) had no real reason to question the advisors at the banks and insurance companies; these were people who had taken care of their interests for years. So the trust departments had a largely free hand to invest the assets as they saw fit, with little conscious thought of the client's best interests.

The regulatory actions from the late 1950s onwards changed all of that. As with any period of cataclysmic change, new opportunities developed for the investment industry as well as its clients. ERISA required that assets be invested 'prudently', that investment decisions be documented, and that performance be reported on a comparative basis.

Unable or unwilling to assume this new accountability themselves, the insurance companies and bank trustees began hiring professional investment managers. This spawned the investment consultant and set the stage for the development of a new and ground-breaking business model.

Lockwood's pension fund business model

James Lockwood, an innovative, forward-thinking pension fund consultant, initiated a very important legislative change governing pension fund investments in 1968. His brother happened to be a state senator and Lockwood convinced his brother to sponsor a bill that would allow city, county, and state pension funds to invest up to 25% of their assets in equities. Because these funds had previously been allowed to invest only in fixed-income instruments, this new legislation opened up greater diversification and higher return opportunities.

In 1972, Lockwood and a team of like-minded peers designed a new business model to offer pension fund trustees a way to organize and document their investment processes and account for the performance of the funds according to the new disclosure legislation criteria. Lockwood's timing was impeccable. The 1972–74 recession would devastate investors' portfolios, resulting in a clamor for investment advice. The new business model represented the birth of the investment management consulting process and consisted at that time of three basic components:

- the formation of written investment guidelines;
- the selection of asset management companies that would invest the funds according to those guidelines; and
- performance measurement and monitoring.

The creation of the investment consulting model was significant. Although investors were accustomed to receiving general activity and performance information on their assets, they had never before been offered a method of assessing the quality of that performance.

The investment consultants who began advising these sponsors revolutionized the institutional investment industry. The consultants began working directly with the money managers to provide performance reporting. Lockwood and his team realized that smaller companies represented an untapped pool of assets, and those smaller companies also provided access to the vast personal assets accumulated by the entrepreneurs who had founded them. By partnering with the money managers to provide performance reporting and other consulting services to smaller institutions, both the consultants and the money managers could gain access to a brand new asset market.

So the money managers left the bank and insurance companies they were working for to establish their own investment management companies (see Exhibit 2.2). They teamed with the consultants, who handled the relationship management and administrative aspects and who had found support for their new business model at E.F. Hutton, to work together for the benefit of their new clients – the US$50 million to US$150 million small to mid-sized companies that had previously been ignored. The money managers liked the new business model because it gave them access to a broad, new pool of assets without the responsibility of handling hundreds of smaller client relationships and the associated burden of small

Exhibit 2.2

Money managers break away to form asset management companies

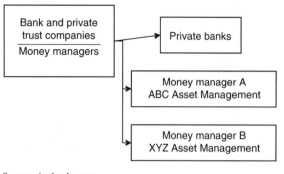

Source: Author's own.

account administrative work. It also allowed them to concentrate on managing money, not administering accounts and creating performance reports. This separation of responsibilities was offered as a trade-off for the money managers' lowering their account minimums and fees in order to attract a larger overall asset base.

In addition to the new relationships gained by working with the broker/consultants, the money managers solicited business from their former employers, the bank trust departments and insurance companies, suggesting they should handle trust and pension fund investment portfolios. The business model shift allowed the money managers access to the funds they had been managing for years, plus extra assets from the smaller companies. Seeing this new willingness of the professional money managers to take on smaller accounts, wealthy families seized the opportunity to secure the same level of investment management for their personal assets.

The introduction of separate accounts for individuals

The ability of wealthy families to meet the new minimums with several different managers gave birth to a new term in investment management, the SMA. Unlike mutual funds, SMAs were managed individually by money managers and the securities were directly owned by the individual clients, not pooled together to form investor units. At this time, commissions were fixed and mutual fund sales loads could be as high as 8%. In May 1975, fixed commission rates became a thing of the past, allowing competitive forces to bring down rates significantly and putting pressure on mutual fund companies to decrease the sales loads on their funds. This also laid the groundwork for another innovative concept, which would, again, be brought to the industry by the new consultants – fee-based compensation. By charging an all-inclusive fee (with no trading commissions) that included administrative costs and fees for the money managers, clients were paying significantly less for the overall services they received than they had been under the fixed commission model. In general, they also received more services.

The fee structure enabled consultants and money managers to work together with no conflict of interest for the benefit of the client. The success of this innovative compensation structure exceeded its originators' expectations. Small businesses were able to receive more personalized treatment on assets of less than US$10 million (the former minimum account size for institutional level management), while wealthy individuals with smaller assets were able to enjoy the same high-quality service for their personal portfolios.

SMAs were nothing new. 'They had been around for hundreds of years,' says Frank L. Campanale, one of the early members of the Hutton consulting team and former president of

Exhibit 2.3

A changed relationship

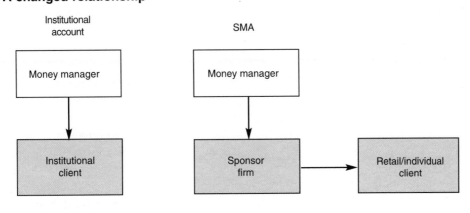

Source: Author's own.

the Consulting Group at Salomon Smith Barney.[2] 'It was the business of working with large families even before the term 'family office' existed.' Many wealthy families, particularly the 'legacy' families, hired private money managers to be a part of the family office and manage the family assets in-house. Trust companies had been managing the trust assets since the 1800s, and while both of these situations constituted a 'separate' account managed exclusively for the family wealth, the change that occurred in the 1970s from the family office perspective involved the ability to access professional money managers outside of the family office or trust company (see Exhibit 2.3). This allowed family portfolios to become much more diversified and gave wealthy families access to the best money managers available – the ones who managed the company defined benefit plan portfolios and the portfolios of the family foundations.

In addition, the industry's institutional clients' accounts had always been separate and apart from each other. Because of their large assets, institutional money managers could afford to have a direct relationship with these clients and to give them a more customized service. Before Lockwood's consulting model concept, it would have been impracticable to offer such services to accounts with lower minimums. But under the new consulting model, the managers' only job was to manage the money – to do the thing they did best. So it made sense to open the door to a broader base of smaller assets.

According to Campanale: 'Little by little, we began bringing the consulting process and institutional quality money managers to individuals because, over time, we were able to convince the money managers we could deliver the assets and also take on a lot of the responsibilities for the performance measurement.'[3] Eventually, this access would be opened up to the general investing public, but that did not take place significantly until the late 1980s and early 1990s.

Educating the brokerage community

The next innovative idea was to sell the fee-based business model to the brokers. This was an entirely different and new way of doing business, and the process of convincing brokers of its benefits was slow. The fertile ground at Hutton was the perfect greenhouse, however, and as professional money managers lowered their minimum account requirements to around US$250,000, and in some cases to US$100,000, the attractiveness of 'being on the same side of the table' with their clients, gaining access to a new wealthy individual asset base, and creating a steadier revenue stream gained momentum.

Hutton had also invested the necessary funds to set up the technology systems required to support the new consulting business and the Consulting Group had begun an educational program to apprise other brokers in the firm of the advantages of the new business model. The program began attracting entrepreneurial, top producers and advisors from other firms whose managements were not so forward-thinking.

By 1979, Hutton's advisory force had tripled over a three-year period, bringing the number of brokers close to 6,000. After losing some of their top advisors to Hutton, other firms began sending management teams to Hutton to find out how to implement the new business model for their own brokers. More money managers left banks and insurance companies to establish independent management firms (the asset management businesses described in Chapter 1) that courted Hutton brokers. The attraction of managing more assets without more administrative hassle was strong. Management firms such as Calamos Investments, Brandes Investment Partners, Callan Associates, Rittenhouse, Nicholas-Applegate, and other well-known names were established during this period and as a direct result of Lockwood's brainchild.

Hutton had even formed separate trading desks to handle the smaller order flow size from the increasing number of smaller accounts. The new desks would group the trades together, execute them as a larger block, and allocate them to various accounts at the end of the day. This allowed the smaller accounts to take advantage of the same price execution terms that larger institutional accounts received. This capability added to the attractiveness for money managers.

There was another plus point to the new consulting model. During market fluctuations, the new consultants felt significantly less pain. Early in 1987, Hutton designed another innovative program, Hutton Select Managers, which allowed clients to sign only one investment agreement with Hutton instead of having to sign a separate agreement with each money manager hired to manage their assets. The money managers signed contracts with Hutton to become sub-advisors on the accounts, which helped the firm retain assets regardless of who was managing the money. Money managers began building performance records and databases were constructed to help consultants find the best managers with the best track records and asset allocation focuses for their clients. When the crash of 1987 occurred, the Hutton consultants could not believe the supposed timing misfortune of the launch of their new program, but things turned out better than anticipated, and they began attracting more business than ever. Investors were disillusioned with their commission-driven brokers and, just as they had after the bear market of 1973–74, sought out more advice to help them manage their investments. With the leaps in technology in the form of the personal computer from the late 1980s and the internet from the mid-1990s, the investment consulting business gained sponsorship in practically every major brokerage firm (see Exhibit 2.4).

It was a way to smooth out revenues, minimize litigation problems, and attract higher net worth clients. But the firms had been very slow to catch on and many entrepreneurial brokers who became consultants had fought a difficult battle to establish and grow their

Exhibit 2.4

Influential market-place developments for SMAs

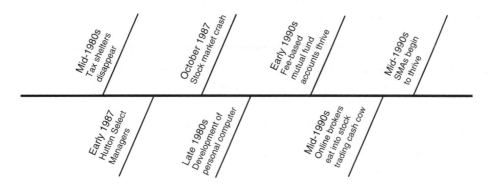

Source: Author's own.

new businesses. These consultants were more interested in serving the needs of their clients than placating the management of the brokerage firms they worked for. When the firms saw the size of the assets the new consultants were attracting, they became more accommodative.

Early operations of the broker/consultants

Many of these pioneering brokers had developed their own profit and loss (P&L) models, separate and apart from that of the brokerage firm. They had proven themselves and their new business models and were now able to operate as separate businesses within the larger firms that housed them. Many developed their own customized technology systems because the firms did not want to invest the money necessary to update their systems to serve the consulting business model. Managements were too concerned about cannibalizing their high-margin commission business, so they had allowed the consultants to operate, but did not give firm-wide support until the mid-1990s.

The pioneering brokers also handled the investment management of small institutions such as small company retirement plans, foundations, and endowments established by wealthy families. This was difficult early on, because account conflicts would arise between the institutional and retail sides of the business. The retail brokers/consultants would not hesitate to fire a money manager if performance was below par or if the managers drifted too far from their stated investment philosophies. But the same managers could easily have institutional money management relationships with the same clients involving much larger assets – a scenario that could create very awkward situations.

Firms that had rejected the retail consulting model in lieu of developing tax-sheltered oil and gas and real estate partnerships came back to embrace it after the mid-1980s tax law changes caused the shelter business to virtually disappear. In addition, many of the partnerships had failed and firms had been hit with a flood of litigation by unhappy clients. The firms began looking for new, more client-centered ways to generate revenue. As firms became more accommodative, more brokers were attracted to the consulting model. Separate organizations were set up by some of the earlier, more enterprising consultants to help educate the new brokers in the consulting process. The two primary organizations – the Institute for Certified Investment Management Consultants (ICIMC) and the Investment Management Consultants Association (IMCA) – merged in 2002 to present a more unified educational effort for the industry.

Mutual funds began to lose assets as a result of the attractive new business model, so they decided to package their own portfolios in a fee-based structure, which was an attractive alternative to independent brokers who had no access to the large systems the brokerage firms had developed. It was also an easier form of fee-based business for those retail brokerage house brokers who were not attracted to the additional service requirements of the consulting model. As a result, the mutual fund business took off during the late 1980s and early 1990s and the consulting business dropped off.

However, the mid-1990s development of the internet led to fierce competition on the transaction side from online brokerages and discount investment houses such as Charles Schwab. Once the return on assets generated by the old commission models of the big brokerages started to diminish, firms again developed interest in the fee-based separate account consulting model. Many firms began adjusting their compensation payouts to provide incentives for brokers to adopt the model. The term 'broker' gave way to more client-friendly labels such as 'financial advisor' or 'financial consultant'. But practitioners who were genuinely focused on providing better service for their clients began to earn certifications to distinguish themselves from their product-selling counterparts. Even today, only 30–38% of practitioners in the retail side of the financial industry have adopted the separate account consulting model.[4] Fewer of those have educated themselves to the point of earning the Certified Investment Management Analyst (CIMA) designation.

Under another type of umbrella, financial services firms are adopting a new account product designed to facilitate integration of mutual funds, hedge funds, private equity investments, and other investment vehicles into one overall account with the fee-based structure previously available only with SMAs. The new umbrella account is called the unified managed account (UMA). Granted, this new product offers a significant step toward integration of various investments with a single manager overseeing all of them, but neither the SMA nor the more recently created UMA provides a complete integrated offering to the wealthy. The missing ingredients are a full understanding of the challenges faced by the wealthy and the services they need, plus education of financial industry advisors in the competent provision of such services.

Conclusions

Exhibit 2.5 illustrates how the two histories reviewed in this chapter and in Chapter 1 converge. By visually placing key aspects of the two chapters parallel to each other, one can see how elements of the histories of both the family office and the financial industry have influenced each other. The seeds of the consulting model were planted by the original family office model, but this model was kept exclusive and private for the wealthy families, especially for the legacy families. The SMA consulting model is based on the same process but has far less depth and integration.

These families valued their privacy highly and still do. However, the evolution of both industries, the increasing costs of the investment business, more complicated governance

Exhibit 2.5

The integrated family office consulting model versus the SMA and UMA models

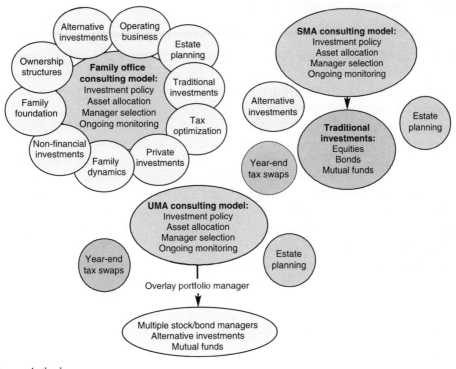

Source: Author's own.

issues, and outdated technology systems have made many family offices more of an albatross than a luxury. And the same is true for the large brokerage firms. In the early 1990s, interest in updating technology systems was low. The systems that were in place were working, so the managements of these firms saw no compelling reason to update them. That changed with the advent of the internet in the mid-1990s. By that time, the technology at the large firms was so old that updating it was a huge task. The discussion of technology and its effect on both industries today is saved for a later chapter, but suffice it to say that the drag in technology adoption by family offices and brokerage firms alike has contributed to the size and scope of the changes both industries are now experiencing.

Coming full circle

The author views the relationship between the family office industry and the financial industry as coming full circle. One was born of the other, saw other ways to profit, became too focused on that profit, and is now struggling to discover its own viable version of the original. Whether that can truly be accomplished is questionable, but the effort is definitely being made; and it is an effort that is being mandated from the investing public and the consultants who see the value of 'doing the right thing' for the client.

The primary problem is one of culture. The early investment industry, which emanated from the need of wealthy investors for professional asset management and the desire of investors with smaller assets to be involved in the equity markets, strayed so long and so far from the original family service model that its product-generating culture is now deeply embedded. A variety of models offering family office style service are being attempted, scrapped, and reattempted in a different form.

The bear market of 2000–03 brought home the value of the consulting model and the imperative to focus on clients' needs instead of concentrating on the hottest product of the day. The after-effects of the most severe market downturn since the protracted reverse of 1973–74 appear to have staying power. Rather than simply looking for alternative asset classes to invest in (which is occurring), clients are also seeking better, higher-quality advice and more integrated investment strategies.

Family offices have offered such integrated strategies for decades. Although the family office model has undergone significant change since the 1800s, it has never lost sight of its purpose – that of serving the needs of the family and stewarding the family's assets. These assets comprise not only investment assets but also the combined human, intellectual, and social capital of the various family members. Today's leading investment management consultants are including these additional assets in their investment approaches. A revolution is occurring that will have monumental results for both industries. An exploration of the significance of this revolution and the range of possible results begins in the next chapter with a closer look at the structure, governance, and service offerings of today's family office models.

---

[1] Much of this historical account is based on information found in LeBlanc, Sydney (2002), *Legacy: The History of Separately Managed Accounts*, Washington, DC, Money Management Institute.
[2] Author's interview with Frank L. Campanale, former president and CEO, Salomon Smith Barney Consulting Group, September 2003.
[3] Ibid.
[4] Percentage estimate by Financial Resource Corporation (FRC), September 2003.

Chapter 3

Family office models: melding old objectives with new structures

Introduction

One of the main changes in the family office service model over the past 15 years has been the emergence of the multi-family office (MFO) – single family offices (SFOs) that either become partners with, or simply open their doors to, other families. The challenge MFOs face is in maintaining the privacy and sense of entitlement to which families are accustomed while providing traditional family office services more efficiently. Although Family Office Exchange (FOX) cites the MFO as the likely model for the future, other models are developing that will fill families' needs in a variety of ways. This chapter examines the ingredients of a family office, service models that have succeeded and failed, the lessons learned from those experiences, and feasible service enhancements to ensure future viability. It will also introduce new models that will enable astute advisors and consultants to offer efficient, high-level services to any of the three markets delineated in the Introduction to this book – the US$5–24 million market, the US$25–100 million market, and the ultra-wealthy. These advisors and consultants will reinvent themselves in an unprecedented fashion. They will become wealth optimization consultants[SM] who will implement the new models, either within the firms of their existing employers or independently, in order to realize the full scope of benefits offered by the wealth optimization consulting concept.[1]

Wealth optimization consultants do much more than manage wealth. They optimize the management and returns of each of the four types of capital possessed by a client family relative to every other type and to the client family's goals and objectives. This new consulting model will be explored in more depth in Chapter 4 and then in Chapter 11, which includes a step-by-step business-building roadmap. This roadmap is presented toward the end of the book to provide readers with the proper foundation upon which to fully and successfully adopt the new business model. The wealth optimization consultant will use the best offerings of both the family office and financial services industries to establish and maintain an unquestionably competitive edge.

The family offices of the future will aim to combine the best of old and new, offering aspiring wealth optimization consultants new opportunities in business and in the marketing of their services. Should they, for example, become affiliated with an SFO, an MFO, or start their own multi-client family office (MCFO)? If they decide to start their own family office business, should they become independent or should they try to establish the business within the umbrella of their existing (or perhaps a more progressive) employing financial services firm? The examination in this chapter of the models currently available and the new models on the horizon will help answer the first question, while Chapter 4 will help answer the second.

As noted earlier, the commonly cited purpose of the family office is to pool the family wealth in an effort to obtain the best in wealth management for the family fortune from generation to generation. Other definitions position the family office as the structure created to conduct the business of the family.[2] In short, the purpose of the family office has been to serve the family in whatever capacity is desired by the family. The focus has been on managing the family wealth, not on developing that management into a profit-generating business. Therefore, most family offices are not profitable, simply because profitability has not been a conscious consideration.

However, families are beginning to realize that they do not have to sacrifice profits for service. With profit becoming more of a focus as families realize the need to manage their wealth as a separate business, new forms of the family office, such as the family investment company, have arisen. These new family office forms, including the MFO and MCFO, have made it possible for less wealthy clients to have access to family office level services. Some 'legacy' families have grown so large that individual members may only have around US$30 million, or even as little as US$10 million to manage. In that sense, as these families have grown in size, they have automatically become a type of MFO. In the financial services arena, the overlooked markets of net worth totaling US$5–24 million and US$25–100 million offer the most opportunity for advisors wishing to exploit the wealth market but aiming to distinguish themselves from competitors for the narrow, ultra-wealthy market.

Owners drive the format of the family office

The actual form a family office takes varies as much as the families they work for, explains Family Office Exchange's (FOX's) Sara Hamilton.[3] She goes on to say that the size of the wealth has little to do with the family office definition:

> There are clear types and patterns of family offices, but they are all driven and built around the goals of the owners. One US$100 million owner may be in a hard-driving, opportunistic, aggressive, performance-generating business mode and want the wealth doubled over the next five years. Another may say, 'No matter what you do, don't lose my principal.' Those are two totally different types of businesses.

Jon Carroll, MBA, CPA, co-founder and managing director of Family Office Metrics, LLC, proposes that a family office creates the opportunity for individual family members, in current and succeeding generations, to pursue personal happiness. Carroll cites five functions that the family office fulfills:[4]

- chief advisor to the family;
- investment management;
- financial administration;
- trustee services; and
- operational (back office) support services.

The chief advisor role is prime among these, as it serves as the liaison to all product and service providers and professional counselors and advisors. In a completely open architecture environment, the wealth optimization consultant is a good candidate for this role. Investment management involves all the elements of the consulting process – formulating an investment policy statement, designing asset allocation, manager selection, and ongoing monitoring. Financial administration serves as the CFO of the family office, optimizing tax compliance, managing projects, implementing financial controls, and performance measurement and reporting. The trustee function offers independent advice, responsiveness, flexibility, efficiency, and security. The family office serving as trustee educates and mentors family members, fosters communication among them, administers the trusts, and guides philanthropic management. The operations management function supports all of the other functions; it collects data, does the family accounting, and reports on all facets of family office operation.[5]

An overview of family office models

The traditional single family office

The first formally structured U.S. family office is said to have been established by the Rockefellers during the break-up of Standard Oil in 1911.[6] Traditionally, the most obvious advantages of the SFO have been in the wealth management area. Large pools of assets can buy the best – the best money managers, access to investments unavailable to other investors, the best tax people, the best attorneys, and so on.

The SFO has also offered privacy – a highly valued commodity – for wealthy families. By hiring advisors and staff that only work for the family, the business of the family remains exactly that and no one else's. The best way to assure a family's privacy has always been to have a single, dedicated family office. Another attraction of an SFO is the integration of services, or what is sometimes called holistic asset management. In an SFO, integration is easily achievable; the family attorney, tax professional, and other advisors are just down the hall from each other, so to speak. This easy access facilitates the process of making sure actions taken in one area of the family's interests will enhance or be enhanced by the management of other areas of the family's interests.

However, the SFO's conduciveness to effective integration of services does not guarantee its success. The following case studies highlight some successful SFOs and some that were not so successful. The first shows how a successful SFO can become a profitable investment management business for the family.

Case study 3.1[7]

The founder of a family operating business offered the family's operating company as an initial public offering (IPO). He then decided to start a private investment firm that would invite other families to invest, along with his US$200 million, but he wanted a specialty investment which would attract these families, so he hired an exceptionally bright, up and coming young money manager to run a hedge fund. The son, daughter, and the hedge fund manager were co-owners in the concern. Meanwhile, the founder continued to invest in private equity on the venture capital side so that his children could be active in an operating business.

This family office became the fertile ground from which sprang a number of entities, including the hedge fund (which grew to US$500 million), a private trust company, and a few start-up businesses actively managed by the son and daughter of the founder and a few employees.

Lessons

Family offices that are managed as business entities and which have successfully educated heirs to accept responsibilities as owners under the tutelage of the family patriarch can become successful business enterprises, increasing the value of the family wealth and serving as a source of satisfaction for all involved. Patriarchs who are willing to share responsibilities continue to benefit their heirs and their employees even after the original family business is no longer under their control.

Case study 3.2

The family office of a prominent family was founded by an attorney, soon joined by an accountant and an investment manager. There were a number of trusts within the family that had existed for years, but the family members had long since stopped asking the sole trustee of the trusts anything about them. They felt they were infringing on his time – he was an extremely busy person and handled the trusts of quite a few other prominent families. So most of the family members were in the dark about the details of the trusts. One family member organized a forum through which the family members could feel comfortable about asking questions and getting the information they needed. This forum, which was actually the family office, in addition to facilitating communication also helped coordinate tax returns. The office faced a number of problems following a transfer of control from the patriarch to his son and subsequently to a sibling partnership. This change from a single-head model to a multiple-head model created communication and structural difficulties. There was a dilution of management control. While family members might have been discontent under the single-head model, the leadership of the family was undisputed; there was no question about decision-making responsibilities.

Family meetings were instituted to facilitate the shift in control to the sibling partnership with the goal of opening up communication channels. However, this was difficult since the family members had previously had no communication channel and were reticent about expressing their views. There were also staffing problems at the office. Years of patience on the part of the family office staff were finally beginning to pay off, when one of the family members became divorced, irreparably throwing off the delicate balance and ultimately causing the office to close.

Lessons

The structure of the office must be sound and must be supported by all family members. Care must be taken to ensure appropriate staff is hired that fits within the framework of the services offered by the family office. Expectations are also difficult to manage in an environment where those expectations are not expressed. Effective organization and communication are essential to a family office's success.

Case study 3.3[8]

A family sold its operating business to a consumer product conglomerate and hired a former money manager from a bank to be the executive of the family office and manage the US$300 million received from the sale of the operating business. The executive hired over a dozen outsourced portfolio managers, which increased the overhead of the office substantially. Since most of his duties were taken over by the outside managers, the executive became bored and recommended that the family start a hedge fund of funds and open it to outside family clients.

The founding family disagreed with this plan and did not understand why the executive was asking for more money to start this fund when the overhead of the office, including the executive's compensation, was eating up almost 3% of the assets. As time passed, the executive kept pushing the edge of the envelope and was eventually asked to resign. Soon after, the family hired an administrative manager who drastically reduced the expenses of the office.

Lessons
The purposes of the family office and its financial goals were evidently not communicated clearly to the original executive. Lack of structure and proper controls allowed a significant portion of the assets to be consumed by unnecessary overhead.

The multi-family office

Although MFOs are becoming more popular, there are some drawbacks. It is practically impossible to have the same level of privacy in an MFO as in an SFO. However, many families with smaller levels of wealth are giving up elements of privacy in exchange for having access to family office services that they might not otherwise be able to afford. The best MFOs create synergies from family to family so that everyone benefits. According to Patricia M. Soldano, president of Cymric Family Office Services:[9] 'If you work for just one family, all you have are the experiences of that one family. With multiple families, everyone benefits from other families' experiences.'

The transformation of SFOs into MFOs is a growing phenomenon. FOX defines an MFO as 'a multi-disciplined firm that offers integrated financial advice to its clients in eight or nine key categories'. These categories include:[10]

- integrated tax and estate planning;
- investment strategy;
- trusteeship;
- risk management;
- lifestyle management;
- record-keeping and reporting;
- family continuity; and
- family philanthropy.

MFOs are being purchased by financial institutions wishing to expand their service offerings to wealthy families. For example, Credit Suisse Private Banking acquired Frye-Louis Capital Management in 2001 and TAG Associates merged with GF Capital Management and Advisors, LLC in 2001.[11] Purchasing an established MFO is a relatively easy way to get into the family office business. Big firms are expanding their previously siloed distribution channels; purchasing an MFO expands distribution and automatically places the institution directly into a profitable market. However, these reasons for purchasing an MFO call into question the longevity of the objective, open architecture aspect of the MFOs acquired by large financial institutions because they are now under the umbrella of a product-oriented system. The following cases provide examples of MFOs that are succeeding on their own.

Case study 3.4
A legacy family's family office developed a specialty for managing the endowments and foundations it founded. The family office followed the pattern of other legacy families and

hired in-house portfolio managers. The office provided such services as tax and accounting, bill-paying, making family airline reservations, scheduling family meetings, helping younger family members find babysitters, and other services. As was typical with legacy families, a good number of trusts were set up and, eventually, the family formed a private trust company.

The size of the family's wealth was staggering since it emanated from the 1920s. Even so, institutional managers did not accept taxable assets of individuals and families to manage, so the in-house portfolio management grew as the family's assets grew. This enabled the family to have a well-integrated investment program, since all the managers operated inside the family office and were aware of each others' holdings and their effects regarding ownership structure, taxation, and other concerns.

As the family grew, its members numbered in the hundreds. Services had to be increased to adequately meet the expectations of so many family members. With the variety of services offered and the number of family members being served, the family opened the office to other families and is now one of the largest MFOs in existence.

Lesson

Prudent management of wealth over many generations, including the willingness to adapt to changes over time, allows the continuation of benefits from the patriarch's original wealth creation.

Case study 3.5[12]

An MFO was founded by a partnership of accountants who were given an offer they could not refuse – an invitation from a family of substantial means to run its family office and bring in the accounting partnership's clients. The three partners had worked together at a prominent accounting firm for 20 years. The accounting firm client who hired them to run his family office was a very prominent businessperson.

Because the public accounting model of the day had accustomed the partners to working with multiple clients of extreme wealth, the three felt it a natural progression to build the new business based on the same operating model. It was one of the first MFOs and, in particular, one of the first to open its doors to family clients who had no relationship with the founding family.

The model was an open architecture, manager of managers model from the beginning. Today, every new MFO has the goal of being an open architecture manager of managers, a concept pioneered by this MFO, TAG Associates. The office outsources all money management as well as wealth psychology, insurance, legal, and estate planning services. In-house, it provides everything from tax planning, asset allocation, and investment strategy design, through to interviewing the nannies.

Eventually, the partners were able to cash in on 50% of their investment, allowing the firm to offer additional services through a merger with another firm as well as to use the new capital to upgrade others.

Lessons

According to the CEO of this MFO, one of the toughest jobs in running a family office is finding and keeping smart people who want to grow the business. Clients want stability and continuity in their advisory relationships, which requires making senior managers partners in the ˜˜m. The MFO is 100% employee owned.[13]

Case study 3.6[14]

An entrepreneur (the founder) grew up in the banking business and found himself (in his late 20s) running the third largest bank in his home town. He then was placed in charge of a significant bank holding company and, through a number of leveraged buyouts, amassed significant personal wealth. That prompted the founder to hire his accountant to set up and run a family office to manage his assets.

The accountant efficiently organized the office and the founder's investments. In 2000, the office was approached by another family to handle its wealth alongside the founder's wealth, and this request prompted the founder to try forming an MFO. By word of mouth, the number of families grew – first to six, then to 12. Today, the MFO has a staff of 21 people and serves 25 families. The firm has never advertised.

Lesson

Consistent, quality service and management speak for themselves.

The multi-client family office

The MCFO is defined as an office started not by a single family that then adds other families, but by advisors, with the sole purpose of creating a business from serving multiple family office clients. The office is owned by the partners with no individual family ownership.

The MCFO is basically a manager of managers that may provide one area of expertise and outsource the other services. It may also provide concierge services and can do as little or as much as family dynamics require. The model facilitates the leveraging of the office's professional talent – in-house or outsourced – while enabling the office to serve multiple need levels for its wealthy clients.[15]

There are many variations of the MFO/MCFO theme. At present, the MFO is the most popular family office concept, both in the United States and abroad, and enjoys the fastest growth. An alternate and increasingly popular form of the MCFO is the SFO or MFO that becomes a family investment company, as in Case study 3.1 above. The key distinction (between the two) is whether it is a family-owned business or, alternatively, a professionally owned business that serves families. The distinction is governed by ownership structure, which in turn determines the focus of the business.

Case study 3.5 above is a hybrid between an MFO and an MCFO. Tax professionals have historically handled private assets for large families, but collectively forming an outside entity specifically for that purpose represented a sea change in the 1980s. It was a natural development for the partners; the public accounting model had many clients, so having the opportunity to build an independent organization to serve many clients was the realization of a dream.[16] This model is still being copied today – sometimes successfully, sometimes not – and is in large part responsible for the explosion in growth of both the MFO and multi-client models.

MCFOs offer many of the same services as MFOs and may be more flexible since there are no ties with a founding family. With MFOs, a family may be offered different levels of services based on the size of its assets or based on the original needs of the founding family. With an MCFO, services are more customized. In other words, rather than having to choose a particular level of predetermined services, families with smaller assets can choose only the services they actually need.

These offices may offer a variety of services such as investment consulting, financial analysis and planning, strategic philanthropy, family education, and tax management. Additional services may include strategic business planning, business continuation planning, succession planning, organizational effectiveness, and governance for family-owned or closely held businesses.[17] Many of the advisors to MCFOs have worked with families before, so they are familiar with the types of services families need.

Another style of MCFO is formed when several families create a family office together without any of the families being a founding or sponsoring family. For example, a group of families with smaller assets may come together, pool their assets, and create a block of wealth large enough to command the services of professional staff, just like a traditional SFO, to perform traditional family office services for them. All families are treated equally; there are no political issues involving the original SFO to cause one family's needs to be weighed against another's.[18]

Variations on original model themes

The private bank

As noted in Chapter 1, private banks migrated from Europe (primarily the United Kingdom) to America as the United States was establishing itself in the 18th and early 19th centuries. They have always served a role for wealthy families. Many private banks began as integral parts of family offices, providing banking services to accompany the individual trust services performed by the trustee, and in some cases teamed with trust companies to offer both services as the early family office model.

Cerulli Associates identifies a bank family office (BFO) as a 'targeted marketing product/service to the higher-end clientele of private banks and brokerage firms'.[19] These services usually are sold as a package of the sponsoring firm's existing products and services customized for the needs of wealthy investors. By creating such a service package, banks can take full advantage of economies of scale, enabling them to accept account levels as low as US$20 million, much like an MFO.

The private bank has long been a source for customized services such as bill-paying, record-keeping, custody, maintaining art collections, and similar services. Today, however, most banks are reticent to offer such full-scale family office services, feeling the risk of losing such large client relationships outweighs the potential benefits of managing the assets. In addition, many of today's private banks are paid to gather assets, so their objectivity may come into question.

Many financial institutions do not find the family office business profitable, so they do not pursue it. Yet, they want to profit from the wealth management aspect of working with families, so many have added limited family office services and adopted the name 'family office' in order to attract the assets of the wealthy. A number of these institutions have also relaxed their minimum account levels for customized private banking services in an effort to accumulate more assets that are less concentrated in one family. Some of these institutions provide valuable services; however, since most of their services revolve around products or service packages, it is difficult for them to offer the objectivity of a true family office. Clients are also uncomfortable with the ongoing merger activity involving banks and other financial institutions. Changes in managers or client representatives are unsettling to any wealthy client. Banks new to family wealth management operations have these significant obstacles to surmount. For older banks more established in family office style services, the story is different.

European private banks are naturally more closely aligned with authentic family office services, since many of them began as early family office models, merged throughout the years with larger banks, and are now forming updated versions of family offices through separate divisions or as subsidiaries. Julius Baer Family Office, Ltd in Zurich is an offshoot of Julius Baer Holdings AG, the largest independent private bank in Switzerland. One European family, the Scotts, formed an MFO, Sand Air Ltd, in 1996 from the sale of its British insurance concern, Provincial Insurance, in 1994.[20]

Some U.S. private banks also have roots as a family office and offer a deeper level of service than financial institutions. As one of the oldest and most representative examples, J.P. Morgan offers comprehensive services from a multi-disciplinary, integrated team that includes a banker, one or more investment specialists, a trust officer, a credit specialist, a wealth advisor who focuses on ownership structure, and a core service team that oversees family client transactions, settlement, and other administrative concerns. Such teams can number from as few as five to as many as 40 people, depending on the complexity of the family's needs, says Amy Braden, managing director at J.P. Morgan Private Bank and head of the Family Wealth Center. She adds:[21]

> The infrastructure of the family itself determines the composition and the role of the team servicing the family. So the role of the team is to support the family office, to be in a position so that the family office can leverage itself by outsourcing selected financial capabilities for the team.

Some of Morgan's clients are MFOs rather than individual family offices. Other clients may not have the resources required for either of these models, in which case Morgan can provide family office style services to fit their needs. MFOs come in all shapes and sizes. For example, MFOs that have an origin in legal practice with a core competency in structuring would outsource investment capabilities. For other family offices, the investment capabilities might be the core competency. They may have started off as a consultant so their core strength is in helping the family develop asset allocation and helping to implement a multi-manager investment strategy. In such cases, Braden explains that the role of the team at J.P. Morgan is to focus on helping the MFO understand and implement the investment strategies they have selected.

In other banks, the family office group may consist of a separate team of bankers with a focus on high-end families, offering both personal and corporate services. Bank of America and Wells Fargo are two U.S. banks that have opened separate family office divisions for clients with net worth of at least US$500,000. Services offered may include banking, investment, and trust management on the personal finance side, as well as loans, lines of credit, equipment financing, and the search for new business opportunities on the corporate side.[22] Other financial institutions may list custody, multi-manager investment offerings, financial administration, and a small selection of concierge-like services as a family office offering.

As many as 20 European banking firms have ventured into family office business. As mentioned earlier, Credit Suisse Group acquired an MFO to jump-start its foray, while UBS recently hired two Merrill Lynch executives to head its attempt at offering family office services, labeled Private Wealth Services and targeting individuals with US$25 million or greater net worth. Deutsche Bank AG of Frankfurt, HSBC Holdings PLC of London, Schroders PLC of London, and Swiss Private Bank Union Bancaire Privée have all formed family office service platforms, although Swiss Private Bank Union Bancaire Privée has since shelved its plans. UBS could also be classified as a large brokerage firm since it purchased PaineWebber, Inc, formerly one of the 'big five' U.S. brokerage houses, in 2001.[23]

The large brokerage firm

The Merrill Lynch family office became an extended family office (MFO) when the family office created for Charles Merrill, the founder of the firm, opened its doors in 1993 to other families, mostly other Merrill Lynch executives. In 1998, the firm again widened eligibility to include families outside the Merrill circle. The office provided no lifestyle or other softer service offerings, but did offer much of its wealth management platform, which included investment banking, estate planning, complicated tax planning, concentrated stock position management, and some general ledger services such as bill-paying.

The firm began the family office in order to capture more IPO business as well as to develop long-term relationships with families. However, as more families were added, more staff also had to be added. The firm discovered that the family office business was a very overhead intensive one, and as more staff were added the profitability of the division decreased. The 2000–03 bear market also took its toll. So the family office was dismantled as a separate entity and its services were folded into the wealth management, trust, and other divisions of the firm.

There are several reasons why providing a full family office service model proves difficult for these firms. Many of them make the mistake of trying to quickly convert a sales-oriented brokerage force into a consultative advisory source for families. Such consultants cannot adequately serve more than about 100 clients who have more complex needs and require higher-level service.

According to Scott D. Welch, managing director at Lydian Wealth Management, banks and brokerages talk at conferences about what they need to do to compete:[24] 'Their problems stem from the fact that they have other lines of business that have higher margin percentages. The wealth management group, the high net worth private client group, the family office, or whatever they want to call it is always going to be competing for resources.' Choosing 12–15% margins in the wealth management group over 30% margins in traditional products is a hard sell to shareholders. It takes courage for corporate executives to risk showing shareholders an earnings hit in the upcoming quarter because a firm believes that three years from now it is going to have the best wealth management organization.

Banks and brokerages will be the most competitive in the US$1–5 million net worth range because that wealth segment is already accustomed to the solutions such firms have to offer. For investors with larger assets, firms are 'muddying the waters' by trying to define the market-place simply because their large marketing and advertising budgets allow them to do so. The confusion arises from the fact that each financial institution is saying the same thing – that it offers an objective, open architecture, integrated wealth manager.

Another problem for financial services firms is the compensation structure for their advisors. Open architecture platforms require hiring people who are trained to deliver that solution, but financial services firms have never hired people with those skills. Despite their rhetoric, Goldman Sachs and Morgan Stanley are effectively getting out of the family office market. The former PaineWebber is trying to bring UBS to bear since UBS has so much product to offer, but that type of program still will not be open architecture. Independent MFOs like Lydian, TAG Associates, and others have no competition for resources and have a business model focused entirely on charging for advice. 'It's always going to be easy to compete against (the big firms),' suggests Welch.[25]

Independent advisors

One of the most successful models, and also one that experts predict will grow exponentially, is the CPA, attorney, financial planner type of independent investment management consultant who specializes in his or her field, then outsources other services to provide families with a completely objective, yet comprehensive advisory service. The accountant model has always been connected to wealthy individuals. The most successful family offices of the future will adopt the manager of managers model, which provides an objective liaison between the family and outside professionals. The manager of managers function can be present in models like TAG's or in any number of individual advisor models, including registered investment advisors (RIAs) who are becoming more and more involved in the family office industry.

Another version of the independent model is the investment-only model. According to Cerulli Associates, this model is also poised for rapid growth over the next several years. As families become more cost conscious, some may opt for outsourced plenary investment consulting and management instead of setting up a full service family office or even going with an MFO. This allows the family to retain more privacy while affording it the advantages of high-quality, open architecture advice. Wealthy families are using the state of flux in the industry to re-evaluate their priorities. The investment-only model offers the dedicated staff, confidentiality, status, and investment management consulting that families are seeking and is a viable alternative to the MFO.[26]

RIAs are in a particularly advantageous position to participate in the family office industry. Because they are independently registered, they are not obligated by a clearing house to use certain products. Many independent investment advisors who are not RIAs conduct their business through an outside platform which may be limited in services and which may not allow the advisors to go outside of that platform. It may also be financially prohibitive to do so, as many of these third party platforms charge as much as US$25,000–30,000 annually for their services. Conversely, RIAs have no such outside allegiance and are freer to be completely objective. Independent advisors (not RIAs) do have many advantages over the large brokerage firms, however, and it is easier for the third party platforms they work through to adopt an open architecture system, so this model may develop more fully over the next few years.

New family office models

New forms of family office models are developing as a result of the changing dynamics and demands of the market-place and the ongoing advancement of technological capability. These new models open the door to greater, more efficient, and more effective choices for optimizing the wealth of client families and, subsequently, wealth optimization consultants' businesses. The following describe some of the most clearly emerging new models.

The 'virtual' family office

Trying to define this model generates similar problems to the MFO label – it means different things to different people. Many firms are saying they are virtual, but there is no firm in existence today that is totally virtual in the sense that it ties together a complete network of outsourced family office advisors covering every aspect of necessary operations. For one, technology is not developed to a point where this can be fully accomplished. Secondly, the masterful creation of synergies between a coordinated team of outsourced professionals to provide the softer services alongside the money management, tax planning, and other services included in a family office is a very elusive process. That does not mean the model will never be possible. In fact, the virtual model will more than likely become an integral part of the family office models of the future, whatever their focuses may be. So, in essence, virtual can mean anything from a paperless office to a network of websites used to foster connectivity and communication between families and their advisors through integrated service offerings on a single platform.

Some even define virtual as a network of relationships with other advisors without sharing compensation. They may have developed relationships with, say, good estate planning attorneys, good tax advisors, insurance professionals, and private travel professionals, but it is not a formalized virtual family office (VFO). From a technological standpoint, the industry is not yet able to tie everybody into a common database of information regarding the client. People say they have done that but it is not widespread in the industry and VFOs have yet to signify a clearly defined model. The author submits the following as a standard definition: a seamless, web-based system linking all facets of investment and wealth advisory in a single, integrated, multi-access platform. Virtual is where the industry is going (see Exhibit 3.1).[27]

For now, however, Carroll agrees that reality, not virtuality, is the way to go. Virtual works best on a project-by-project basis, he says.[28] VFOs may incorporate much of the administrative family office functions, such as aggregation of accounts, document and data management, and fostering communication through secured family websites. Companies such as SS&C, Private Family Networks, and even some private banks offer clients personal family websites that can 'permission' outside advisors to have limited access in order to facilitate and streamline their involvement. The communication aspect can be particularly useful for families with members located nationwide or even globally.

External offerings

Tom Livergood, CFP and founder of Family Office Management, LLC, cites hybrid family office models that are emerging.[29] He defines the appropriateness of each hybrid based on a continuum of self-selection profiling the delegation capabilities of clients. The continuum ranges from the complete do-it-yourself type of non-delegator to the complete delegator who says: 'Here's what I want done, do it.' In the middle of the range is what Livergood calls the validator. According to the continuum, full delegators use MFOs and validators use what are called external family offices (EFOs). Validators are not full do-it-yourselfers; they delegate significant responsibilities but they still like to have some control over the process (see Exhibit 3.2).

For example, a client sells a business for US$60 million. She hires a CFO to help her

Exhibit 3.1

The ideal virtual office structure

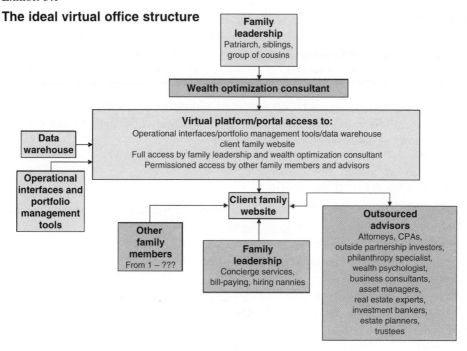

Source: Author's own.

Exhibit 3.2

External family office

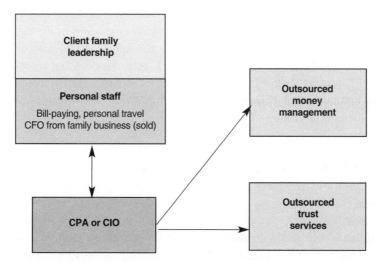

Source: Author's own.

manage the wealth because she wants to buy and sell other businesses. She also hires her personal staff to pay her own bills and set up her own travel. So she delegates things like trust services and money management but wants her database of bill-paying to be integrated with her accountant. 'The external family office comes in on some services but doesn't threaten her or her staff like an MFO would,' says Livergood.[30]

The EFO also involves a manager of managers model; TAG Associates, Lydian Wealth Management, and Tiedemann Trust are good examples of this model.

An external chief investment officer (external CIO) model is basically having a personal chief investment officer to guide and oversee the investment component. Cerulli's investment-only model is similar to the external CIO model.

Family offices around the world

The family office level of services is taking hold around the world, and the U.S. family office model has become institutionalized, according to Barbara R. Hauser, special counsel, Private Client Department, Cadwalader, Wickersham, and Taft, LLP, which has opened the door to competition from financial institutions.[31] It also offers international families the opportunity to improve on the U.S. model.

Europe has experienced the same type of merger, acquisition, and consolidation activity among its banks, resulting in a diminishing number of small private banks. Since the private bank functioned much like the U.S. family office, European families in particular are looking to U.S. models to fill the void. Accountants, lawyers, and financial advisors in Switzerland are researching how their clients can start their own family offices. The French, like the Americans, have a tax focus; Germans are less international in their choice of advisors and the country's financial, estate, and tax planning services are less developed; in England, the emphasis is on privacy and confidentiality; the Japanese are just becoming familiar with the family office concept and are traditionally quite conservative; and Latin American families have a social focus based on family activities.

Many foreign families have multiple-country business and tax concerns, citizenship concerns, and ownership concerns. Hauser proposes a different model that keeps the original focus on the family's needs much more than the financial institutions of the day. Her prototype would consist of a small family staff in an SFO atmosphere. Investment services could be outsourced to large financial institutions, as well as other services that are not feasible to have in-house. This is yet another hybrid of family office models to be explored in this chapter, but it is an efficient and more feasible spin on the original SFO which enables the integrity of the family focus to remain intact.[32]

Measuring value

In the MFO world, a movement is afoot to benchmark their value to their clients. This is an attempt to help clients measure the value of the various MFO models to facilitate decision-making. The problem with setting up such benchmarks is the added human, intellectual, and social capital that is involved in measuring a family office model's success.

Suggested methods of benchmarking include measuring the breadth of service offerings at various MFO firms and measuring the likelihood of wealth transfer scenarios. According to Hap Perry at Asset Management Advisors, there are three basic wealth transfer results: one will show the family very grateful for its founders' foresight; a second will show no one interested; and a third will depict various family members suing each other. The likelihood of any of these situations coming to fruition offers a way to quantify the preparations necessary to produce the desired scenario.[33]

Measuring breadth of service offerings as well as performance of easily measured services such as investment services will help, but the variety of MFO models makes creating measurement tools a challenge. According to Livergood:[34] 'Anyone can call him or herself an MFO or a financial planner. I've been in financial planning for 20 years and we still don't have state regulation. The MFO is where financial planning was 20 to 25 years ago.' This topic runs closely with the debate on creating designations for family office management. But certification and regulation are not nearly as important as making sure the fit is right between the MFO and the client.

Livergood gives an example of two types of MFOs, one that deals with driven, profit-producing entrepreneurs and another that works with fourth and fifth generation families who wish to hold a summer camp on the stewardship of wealth for the family's children. An MFO dealing with hard-charging wealth creators would scoff at any hint of running a summer camp to encourage a participatory governance style. Certification misses the mark in measuring client fit, office integrity, or competency. However, some type of benchmarking is a step in the right direction to help families clear the initial clouds of confusion.

Challenges and issues families face

In the hustle and bustle of firms trying to get in on the family office opportunity, many firms use the label of a family office when they may only offer a few family office level services. Just because a firm works with families as clients does not mean it is a family office. Families go to such a firm expecting an entire slate of services and only receive a few so-called family office services in the wealth management area. They may not know where else to go so they make a decision based on limited information, only to discover later that they have neither the services nor the competency they were seeking.

The models that will emerge as the family offices of the future have yet to be identified, but by examining current models and the improvements that have taken place over recent years and by trying to identify future trends, advisors and consultants will gather important information for developing appropriate business models for their practices.

A round-up of family office models

In conclusion, the family office models now available and those being created are summarized in the following list.

- *Single family office (SFO)*. The traditional model is dying out. Rising costs and the difficulty of retaining top-quality talent are causing fewer families to open individual offices. They are seeking alternatives.
- *Multi-family office (MFO)*. This is the most viable alternative to date to the SFO, although the MCFO is quickly catching up. MFOs are traditionally formed by an SFO opening its services to other families or by several families opening a family office together for the benefit of those families. In this case, the families may or may not open the office to out-

siders. Many MFOs hire high-level advisors and investment management consultants to serve the investment component for these offices. The wealth optimization consultant can serve an expanded role in an MFO.

- *Multi-client family office (MCFO)*. This is a very promising model for aspiring wealth optimization consultants who want to take a few of their best clients and create a more vertical business model of deeper relationships with fewer clients, rather than a horizontal one with a large number of clients with smaller assets and a limited level of services. This model is perfect for a team of consultants wishing to start a family office business with their best existing clients.

- *Family investment management business*. The family investment management business emanates from an SFO that has developed a niche offering such as a hedge fund or private equity fund. Families usually start such businesses after the sale or public offering of the corporate business that created the family wealth. Families hire professionals to be partners in forming an investment firm that provides services that are important to the founding family but which is owned by the professionals. In other words, it is a professionally owned business that serves families, as noted earlier. This can be a very nice situation for a wealth optimization consultant who joins the business as a partner.

- *External family office (EFO)*. Staff and certain advisors from the corporate business may be kept after a sale or merger to continue serving the personal needs of the family, but all other services are outsourced. The wealth optimization consultant can serve as an outsourced provider here.

- *External chief investment officer (CIO)*. An office where the investment component is outsourced, forming a single service family office. In this case, the wealth optimization consultant serves as the outsourced chief investment officer. High-level advisors and investment management consultants also fill this role well.

- *Virtual family office (VFO)*. Virtual platforms will eventually enable full connectivity of all aspects of family office services in whatever form the family office takes. Components of the VFO are available now and will be a vital tool for high-level advisors and investment management consultants wishing to optimize their clients' wealth as well as their own. The VFO is the tool through which enterprising consultants will form the family office models of the future.

---

[1] The terms 'wealth optimization consultant' and 'wealth optimization consulting model' are the marked property of graymatter STRATEGIES LLC.

[2] Author's interview with Amy Braden, managing director and head of the Family Wealth Center, J.P. Morgan Private Bank, September 2003.

[3] Author's interview with Sara Hamilton, founder and CEO, FOX, September 2003.

[4] Carroll, Jon (2001), 'The Functions of a Family Office', *The Journal of Wealth Management*, Fall.

[5] Ibid.

[6] Fleck, Fiona (2002), 'Saving Generations of Wealth', p.2, available at www.loedstar.com/press/wsje-december_2002.htm

[7] Based on Family No. 2 from Beyer, Charlotte B. (1999), 'Family Offices in America: Why the Bloom is Off the Rose', *Journal of Private Portfolio Management*, Fall.

[8] Based on Family No. 3 from Beyer, Charlotte B. (1999), 'Family Offices in America: Why the Bloom is Off the Rose', *Journal of Private Portfolio Management*, Fall.

[9] Author's interview with Patricia M. Soldano, president, Cymric Family Office Services, September 2003.

[10] Hamilton, Sara (2002), *The Multi-Family Office Mania*, PRIMEDIA Business Magazines & Media, Inc, December.

[11] TAG Associates LLC (2002), 'About Tag', available at http://www.tagassoc.com/about/index.html.

[12] Personal interview with Stanley H. Pantowich, partner and CEO, TAG Associates, September 2003.

[13] McReynolds, Rebecca (2003), 'All in the Family', *Bloomberg Wealth Manager,* November, p. 94.

[14] Author's interviews with the founder and the accountant who built the office, September 2003.

[15] Cerulli Associates (2001), *Family Offices*, p. 237.

[16] Author's interview with Stanley H. Pantowich, partner and CEO, TAG Associates, September 2003.

[17] Signature Financial Management, Inc (2002, 2003), *Family Office Services and Family Business Consulting*, available at http://www.sigfin.com/family_business.shtml

[18] Cerulli Associates (2001), *Family Offices*.

[19] Ibid.

[20] Fleck, Fiona (2002), 'Saving Generations of Wealth', available at www.loedstar.com/press/wsje-december_2002.htm

[21] This quotation plus information contained in the next two paragraphs is taken from a personal interview with Amy Braden, managing director and head of the Family Wealth Center, J.P. Morgan Private Bank, September 2003.

[22] McCarthy, Elizabeth (1998), 'Bigger Banks Rediscover the Personal Touch', *Sacramento Business Journal,* 16 February, available at http://sacramento.bizjournals.com/sacramento/stories/1998/02/16/focus3.html

[23] The 'Big Five' included Merrill Lynch, Morgan Stanley, Prudential Securities, PaineWebber, Inc, and Goldman Sachs.

[24] Author's interview with Scott D. Welch, managing director, Lydian Wealth Management, October 2003.

[25] Ibid.

[26] Cerulli Associates (2001), *Family Offices,* p. 235.

[27] Author's interview with Scott D. Welch, managing director, Lydian Wealth Management, October 2003.

[28] Author's interview with Jon Carroll, MBA, CPA, co-founder and managing director, Family Office Metrics, LLC, October 2003.

[29] Author's interview with Tom Livergood, CFP and founder, Family Office Management, LLC, October 2003

[30] Ibid.

[31] Hauser, Barbara R. (2001), 'The Family Office: Insights into Their Development in the U.S.: A Proposed Prototype, and Advice for Adaptation in Other Countries', *The Journal of Wealth Management* (Fall), pp. 20–21.

[32] Ibid.

[33] Wilmott, Andrew (2003), 'Multi-family Offices Try to Measure Value', *Fundfire*, 4 August.

[34] Author's interview with Tom Livergood, CFP and founder, Family Office Management, LLC, October 2003.

Chapter 4

Facing the emerging realities

Introduction

The financial services industry's concentration on products and profits makes it extremely difficult for it to foster the kind of environment necessary for high-level advisors and investment management consultants wishing to optimize their clients' wealth. Although some financial industry firms have membership in family office industry organizations such as the Institute for Private Investors (IPI) and have attempted to set up specifically designated family office level services, the pressure from shareholders and the firms' concentration on producing short-term profits have significantly compromised the development of this environment. As a result, many high-level advisors and investment management consultants (and their teams) are considering going out on their own to develop the type of business that will allow full, unbiased optimization of their clients' assets.

According to Charlotte B. Beyer, founder and CEO of the IPI, financial services firms still focus on products and not enough on process. Too often, advisor training emphasizes the products and technical aspects of wealth management at the expense of teaching professionals how to interact with, as contrasted with sell to, an investor. However, Beyer believes that financial services firms still have the opportunity to refocus themselves:[1]

> Financial services firms have been very successful at reinventing themselves over the past 90 years and I don't see any reason why they can't keep reinventing themselves. It was only in the 1920s that the whole idea of investment advisory came into being, so the industry is in its infancy. When you see that Salomon Smith Barney has Goldman Sachs Asset Management on its open architecture platform, you know something's going on here.

That reinvention is predicated, however, on firms' willingness to educate shareholders in new and better business models and to educate their advisors in deeper skills. Beyer adds:

> There's a hub (in the family office model) and the spokes go out to a whole slew of different advisors. (Firms' reinvention) is only limited by the firm leadership's willingness to be more holistic in its approach. But that requires a far broader technical and interpersonal skill set than many firms are prepared to teach their advisors.

Regardless of firms' willingness to reinvent themselves, aspiring wealth optimization consultants have that option, and this chapter will explore the choices advisors have for accomplishing this. It will examine trends in the family office and financial services industries, both overt and underlying, the most likely scenarios for the next several years, and how advisors/consultants should position themselves to take the best advantage of industry cross-currents to create the most rewarding practices possible.

54

Landscape of the financial services industry

The first step from the viewpoint of financial services industry firms in educating advisors in these skill sets has been the offering of separately managed accounts (SMAs) to individual, retail investors. The problem with financial services firms today is their focus on that first step as a primary solution for client needs. Sales of SMAs have jumped from US$4.3 billion in 2001 to an estimated US$14.5 billion in 2003.[2] The SMA fee-based business structure is finally gaining a stronger hold.

In 2001, some firms packaged the SMA like a product and initiated a great debate – was the SMA a process or a product?[3] Certainly the most important part of the SMA equation has been the process its evolution brought to bear – the consulting process. Whether the SMA was a product or a process was a worthwhile discussion, but it was not the important point. The important point was how the consulting process was giving advisors a way to serve their clients on the clients' terms. It was giving them a way to be paid for their advice rather than for the products they sold.

A huge segmentation is evolving in the financial services industry that will become more apparent over the next few years. Large financial institutions are embracing the SMA as a new and better way to do business, but they are reticent to completely abandon the profitability of the product-based environment or to commit fully to the comprehensive, integrated wealth management mandated by the very target market they are seeking to attract. SMAs are available to the mass affluent – defined by the industry as US$500,000 to US$1 million in net worth,[4] as well as high net worth and ultra high net worth clients – but the ability to use money managers outside the firm's pre-approved list is limited. The consulting process has been superficially incorporated into the SMA offering, but most firms offer little in the way of internal education to their advisors who would be consultants. Many advisors who have taken the cue from their firms to adopt the fee-based compensation structure have done so with minimal training, especially in the most critical component – basing their advice on client needs and building and strengthening relationships.

The financial industry has been looking to the SMA as the model of the future. The SMA model is even being expanded to include multiple managers (the multiple strategy program or MSP) and to include other investment vehicles such as hedge funds and mutual funds in one overall wrap program called a unified managed account (UMA). These expanded SMA platforms usually have what is called an overlay portfolio manager (OPM) to oversee all of the sub-accounts within the MSP or UMA. These account models will be attractive to the wealth markets as tools with which to accomplish their objectives, but no form of the SMA-based model alone will be enough to attract and retain the assets of wealthy families. There remain many missing ingredients needed to serve these clients adequately and no product alone can fulfill them. At the advisor level, even early adopters of the SMA-based consulting model will need to reinvent themselves and their businesses to remain competitive.

The financial services industry view of consulting

Beginning in the 1990s, financial institutions began seeing a decline in their return on assets (ROA) for the transactional side of the business. The limited partnerships and tax shelters of the 1980s had disappeared and the consulting side of the business was gaining ground. Firms that had fought the fee-based approach because it slowed down the sales process began to see that it was a good way to do business. It was better for clients, less litigious, and a way for the institutions to counteract their deteriorating ROA.[5]

So firms began to offer incentives for advisors to switch from transaction-based to fee-based business. Consulting was presented as a multi-step process centered around gathering information from the client, producing an investment policy statement based on that information, designing an asset allocation, choosing money managers to implement it, and then monitoring the portfolio on an ongoing basis to ensure the managers perform as promised. Advisors implement this process with varying degrees of commitment, from simply gathering enough information to fill out the form on their computers and allowing the software program to do the rest to spending significant time with clients, getting to know them, their families, what motivates them, what they want their assets to accomplish for them, and what those accomplishments will mean to them and to future generations. Most financial services industry advisors do the former, while the latter is more fully aligned with the needs and desires of the wealthy.

The examination of the financial institutions' move into family office services in Chapter 3 brought to light some of the problems large firms are having in trying to enter the market. Elements of the consulting process mirror elements of the family office industry. For that reason, firms have thought they could adequately serve wealthy families and win larger assets simply by taking the fee-based services they already offer and adding select services on the soft side. However, there was much more involved than they had expected. In order to provide family office quality services, additional staff had to be hired as assets increased, so dreams of added profit from significant new assets began to fade. The additional staff was necessary to fully accommodate requirements demanded by a significant number of families. There is also a cohesiveness to serving families well that is difficult to emulate from a product-based culture.

As a result, most firms have adjusted their models to focus on what is now being called 'private wealth management', offering higher-level, hard, technical services without addressing clients' softer service needs. Approaching family office wealth management has been a trial and error process supported by a large investment of funds with no emergence of a clear, viable model. Based on a 2003 IBM Institute for Business Value analysis,[6] firms' efforts to effectively address the wealth market seem to be undermined by poor execution of strategies, ineffective organizational design, and fragmented operational effectiveness. In an effort to offer the most services for the least cost, firms seem to be lumping the broad and inhomogeneous needs of the wealthy into one basic, all encompassing product design, failing to recognize that even the lowest level affluent have taken on many affluent and ultra-affluent characteristics, causing firms' focus to be off track.

Although large firms are working toward a focus on the client, they find that total open architecture is an unprofitable, unscalable business. The solution so far has been a compromise between total product sales on the one hand and total open architecture, client-focused consulting on the other. As with single family offices (SFOs), there are as many combinations and forms of this hybrid as there are firms. It can result in offerings ranging from packaged wrap programs to working on a higher level with a personal advisor. However, advisors are limited in the extent to which they can practice a full-scale, objective consulting model.

Firms may offer a variety of choices, but those choices still reside primarily within the firm. The fact that sales incentives for advisors are still offered sends a message diametrically opposed to the broader 'do what's right for the client' message issued by the powers-that-be, and the limited training available is still primarily focused on product knowledge and awareness.[7]

Investors have not needed to rely on advisors for information for years. With that need more than adequately served by various media, investors seek out advisors for objective, high-quality advice. They feel overwhelmed by all the information available and need professional guidance in discerning its trustworthiness and, much more importantly, its relevance to them. But advisors at large firms are frequently locked into just one area such as asset management or asset allocation, overlooking clients' other needs such as risk management, integrated management programs, and philanthropic advice.[8]

All wealthy clients, from the mass affluent to the ultra-wealthy, expect high levels of service, especially as regards advice. But financial institutions' focus is rarely completely client-centered.[9] With a fixation on margin retention, firms are trying to gain the greatest return possible from their lower-margin dollars, and, to an extent, their preoccupation is understandable. The pressure to appease shareholders is great and, unfortunately, takes precedence over the invaluable long-term planning that would be most beneficial, both to the firms and to their clients. The other missing ingredient, according to the IBM analysis, is that the wealth management business has not been fully analyzed at these firms and their approach to the market has not been fully evaluated.[10]

The consulting process fostered by financial services industry firms falls far short of comprehensively serving wealthy families' needs. At the *Institutional Investor* 2003 Integrated Wealth Management Forum in New York City, Jean Brunel, CFA and managing principal at Brunel Associates, LLC, agreed that there are missing ingredients in firms' approaches. Brunel cited two major gaps in the consulting process used at major firms. One is embedded in the fact that the SMA consulting model derived from the institutional consulting process. The model worked well for institutions, so it made sense to adapt it to individuals – except that individuals have radically different concerns to those of institutions. A primary difference is tax status. Individuals need tax-efficient investment strategies; institutions do not. There are many other problems arising in relation to performance reporting as a result of newly proposed Association of Investment Management and Research (AIMR) performance reporting standards for SMAs,[11] but taxation is the primary concern from the investor's point of view.

The other gap cited by Brunel is little or no integration of asset allocation and behavioral finance, emphasizing that an appropriate allocation for a wealthy family based on information input into the system may be completely at odds with what the family is willing to accept emotionally. Industry advisors have been taught to advise clients to separate their emotions from their investing and to focus on long-term results. However, money is such a highly emotional factor, especially where family dynamics are concerned, those instructions are much simpler to iterate than to actually deliver. Relative to family wealth, emotions and family dynamics must be considered in investment management; however, day-to-day gyrations in a portfolio resulting from emotional reactions obviously do not serve any client well. Lydian's Scott Welch adds:[12]

> In the institutional model, there was a consistency of purpose but a high turnover of members looking at the portfolio. In families, you have exactly the opposite – you have a consistency of members and a high turnover of purpose. The ideal is to create portfolios that are quantitatively valid but emotionally and behaviorally acceptable.

Successfully doing so requires more time to get to know the dynamics of the family, which is a time-consuming process that can only be fostered by a long-term business planning view.

Therefore, firms' shortsightedness regarding their business models may eclipse their ability to truly offer what the wealthy and super-wealthy demand and what would ultimately allow them to maintain their market share. Neither individually nor collectively have they seen enough value in the long-term approach to facilitate effective change. This is evidenced by the number of alliances which were formed to provide wealth management services on a large scale, then rescinded because they did not produce the desired results.[13]

Some advisors who see the value are taking it upon themselves to create the practices they want and to get the education they need. These represent the top 10% or so of advisors, who have far surpassed the capability of their firms to provide what clients are really seeking.

The writing on the wall

Granted, the larger the firm, the longer it takes to implement change. But the large firms are historically slow to accommodate change, especially if the old way of doing things is still working. For example, as technology was making huge strides in the late 1980s and early 1990s, firms made do with the systems they had, upgrading only enough to accommodate the addition of mutual fund wrap business. The advent of the internet in the mid-1990s caused many firms to undertake major upgrades to their systems, but those upgrades were not enough. Current systems are still tied to the legacy systems of earlier years, making it difficult for today's advisors to be adequately equipped to conduct the kind of business mandated by wealthy clients.

If the large firms continue on their current paths, they will lose a great deal of their market share to firms and qualified consultants who, rather than try to cling to elements of a disappearing yet still very profitable environment, are seeking to build a practice that is focused only on the client and his or her needs. Simply from a technical, business point of view, conflicts between open and closed systems eventually resolve themselves with the closed systems on the losing end.[14] At the other end of the spectrum, product-based services, whether sold on a commission or a fee basis, will become more commoditized and advisors who sell them will become higher-level salaried employees. Most of the services offered today will become commoditized in the same way that trade execution became commoditized when online brokers entered the scene.

Third party platform providers and financial software programmers already have systems that can automatically process the basic components of consulting. Client profiles, investment proposals, investment policy statements (IPSs), asset allocations, manager research and selection, and review functions can all be created electronically from a basic set of input information. According to Frank L. Campanale:[15]

> Custody, performance measurement, evaluation programs – even manager research to some degree – is a commodity. There are different levels of quality, but it won't be long before (individual investors) will be able to get qualitative research from some source that allows them to buy it directly; then, it too will become a commodity.

The online firms that survived the bear market of 2000–03, such as E*Trade, have teamed up with firms like Ernst & Young to provide online advice.[16] Charles Schwab and Co. now offers everything from trade execution to lending, financial planning, and portfolio consultation. It also offers educational articles on a variety of topics, including investing to reach clients' goals and a choice between one-time advice and ongoing advice.[17] Competition in the wealth market is growing, and, as happens in all industries where competition becomes acute, consumers and the economy are forging irreversible change.

Most components of today's financial industry services will metamorphose into a supermarket of services, including SMA services. Campanale predicts that consultants will see the supermarket atmosphere of the big firms and decide they do not really need the support of such firms any more. Many will begin to wonder about the value the firm offers them from the 65% of their payout that is withheld. They will decide to go out on their own and use that 65% to help pick and choose services from a variety of providers. More and more consultants will be managing their own functional profit and loss (P&L) statements instead of being part of a big firm's P&L. Consultants will have control over their own practices and will have the tools and support they need to offer whatever level of service they wish.

The concept of consultants having their own P&L is not new. The earliest adopters of the consulting process in the late 1970s and early 1980s persuaded their firms to allow them to have separate P&Ls for their teams. They developed their own technology systems because their firms' systems were not sufficient for them to conduct the new, fee-based consulting business. Even consultants who began consulting in the early days will find the need to reinvent themselves, if they haven't already. Family office industry experts feel strongly that financial industry firms will always be influenced by their product-based cultural history. The accuracy of that prediction remains to be seen, but, regardless, consultants will have decisions to make as choices become clearer.

The family office view of consulting

In the context of the family office, consulting is a much deeper process than the financial services industry version. It is a meticulously customized, seriously thorough process that begins with the elements listed in the financial industry description above. By placing the two consulting methods side by side, the differences can be more easily compared and the gaps that need to be filled become more apparent.

Creating the investment policy statement

In a family office there will usually be more than one investment policy statement (IPS) since there are a variety of portfolios with different purposes. These portfolios are also integrated with each other to meet the overall objectives of the family. For example, the family foundation may have one IPS; the family may have several trusts with different objectives; and there may be several taxable accounts outside of either the trusts or the family foundation.

There should also be an overall IPS governing the investment and objectives of the assets as a whole. As mentioned in Chapter 3, wealthy families have four types of capital, and each source of capital must be a component of the overall IPS, as well as for those of each individual account. This requires a much deeper information-finding process than is normally undertaken by advisors undertaking SMA business at large firms. Psychological factors come into play, and family demographics, legacy preferences, and the needs of other family members must also be considered. Business sales or succession plans and the ownership structures of non-financial assets also factor into the mix. This part of the process is the most important, as it affects every aspect of managing a family's wealth.

The IPS serves as a blueprint for attaining clients' investment objectives. Wealthy families expect a blueprint to reach the objectives for their overall wealth, including their human, social, and intellectual capital, and they need 'sub-blueprints' to achieve the objectives of each individual portfolio. By approaching wealth management in this fashion, clients reap the benefit of making the sum better than just a combination of the individual parts.

Asset allocation

Family wealth usually involves a broader range of asset classes than stocks, bonds, and cash. Multiple homes, boats, planes, commodity investments, art collections, various venture capital and private equity investments – all must be considered in designing the asset allocation for each portfolio. The ownership structure of all of the assets may also influence allocation, as well as the purpose of the portfolio, its time horizon, and many other factors.

Ultra-wealthy families tend to have a greater understanding of correlation because of the diversity of their assets. Many are involved in more than one business, which makes them more knowledgeable about private equity investments. They are familiar with private hedge funds and other non-traditional investments that, until recently, were not accessible to investors with less wealth. The family may have valuable art collections, significant real estate holdings, or other non-traditional investments. These assets must be taken into consideration when planning an overall asset allocation. Correlation of assets is key to protecting financial assets. This is a critical missing link in asset allocation programs at large firms, which primarily focus on diversification among traditional asset classes and sub-classes.

Financial industry advisors are not educated to explore correlation factors and the effects of non-traditional investments on investment portfolios. The vast majority of advisors stick with stocks, bonds, and cash, even limiting the equity side to large cap portfolios. This is primarily due to the lack of availability of other asset class choices. Some firms are beginning to offer equity style portfolios other than large cap in their SMA programs, but the numbers are still few and are still within the equity asset realm. Firms do not seek out the types of investments that offer the most valuable diversification properties. As a result, clients who think they are diversified find out in rude fashion during market downturns that they are not. Their diversification is typically contained within a single asset class, which is usually equities.

The importance of having equities in a portfolio is not up for debate. But limiting diversification to the sub-styles of any single asset class is an invitation for disappointment. Over-diversification can undermine performance; diversification without considering correlation, geographic, interest rate, and other risks can lull clients into a false comfort zone.

Manager research and selection

One of the purposes of having a family office is to enable the family to access the best managers, regardless of minimum account requirements, by pooling the family assets. This factor ensures that the search process for managers operates at an entirely different level.

Most financial advisors either use the approved money manager lists issued by their firms or, in the case of those with their own P&Ls, have their own systems from popular vendors through which they research managers for their clients. In the SMA world, however, only managers who are willing to handle SMA business are available. Since SMA business is not highly profitable and technology is slow to make it so, some of these managers have ceased to manage SMA money for individuals.

The open architecture format allows consultants to choose managers from any asset management firm in their known universe, not just from a large firm's approved list. It also opens the possibility of gaining access to institutional level managers who have chosen not to participate in SMA business. Quality of management is a huge issue in the management of great wealth. Open architecture allows the quality needs of the wealthy to be met.

The term 'open architecture' is often used, but with no precise meaning attached. The best definition the author has seen is as follows: 'Open architecture can be broadly defined as a system that adapts to the needs of the client rather than requiring the client to accommodate the limitations of the system.'[18] Such a definition covers all areas of wealth management, including the ability to find the best custodial, transaction execution, reconciliation and other services, as well as freedom to choose the best asset managers.

Ongoing monitoring

Obviously, wealth management consultants working exclusively for a family in a family office are able to monitor not only the financial assets, but how the management of other assets is affecting the financial assets. This gives the family as well as the consultant a significant edge over the financial industry advisor in the sense that the 'inside' consultant can more adequately serve the family's comprehensive wealth management needs. Wealth management consultants in other family office models can also accomplish this since they are more familiar with the family's overall situation.

The monitoring process conducted by financial industry advisors is primarily confined to funds invested at the firm or, in the case of a consultant, to the assets they have under advisement, regardless of custody. Other assets of the family may or may not be known – it depends on the depth of the relationship the consultant has developed with the family. A consultant may advise primarily on institutional accounts with only a few individual accounts that are sizable enough to merit his or her attention. Even in this scenario, the assets under advisement are usually the only assets monitored on an ongoing basis.

What the wealthy are seeking

The caveat to creating cost-efficiency and/or profits for these families is the sacrifice of certain amounts of privacy to which they have been accustomed. The family office industry has converged sufficiently with the financial industry to cause families to rethink their wealth management business models in order to combine the best of both worlds. The rethinking process from the family office perspective is different than the process from the financial industry perspective. Families want the advantages of multi-family offices (MFOs), but they also want the level of privacy they had with their SFO.

There is a subliminal shifting in an effort to balance both needs efficiently and adequately. Like the financial industry, families have not yet found the ideal model that achieves the right balance. Unlike the financial industry, the very nature of family wealth management opens the door to customized, individual solutions to the challenge. The nature of the financial industry is innately antithetical to the nature of family wealth management, giving the financial industry more to do than families who are seeking to increase cost-effectiveness and maintain their highly customized service solutions. Wealthy families like having the best of everything. They enjoy being catered to and they feel they have earned the right to such privileges. The point at which they are willing to give up part of that privilege determines the basis of the model that is right for them.

Enter the wealth optimization consultant

According to FOX's Sara Hamilton, hundreds of families each year are going through some type of financial transition that causes them to wrestle with questions like, 'What kind of provider do I need? What are my real challenges? Where should the kids go to school? What do I want to do with my philanthropy?'[19] Families are searching for customized answers to these and other questions. They need help picking advisors who will guide them toward the solutions they need. FOX, the Institute for Private Investors (IPI), and a growing number of smaller firms are offering networks and educational programs aimed at locating advisors who may be the right fit for them. Advisors who meet the required qualifications can become members of these organizations, giving them a more direct channel to the type of clients they are seeking.

Unlike the 1980s, when 80% of families started their own SFOs, Hamilton says: 'We're moving into a period in the next decade where 80% of families will not start their own offices.' Too many viable alternatives are materializing. Families can save money by outsourcing, or by hiring only the services they have the time and staff to supervise, while outsourcing the rest. The crystallization of these choices over the next three to five years will create a window of opportunity for consultants. In Hamilton's view:

> We're in the midst of a dramatic paradigm shift in terms of what the (family wealth) owner is willing to recognize and to pay for. Owners are coming to recognize they need to pay for independent, objective advice. The question is, will they be smart enough to pay enough to sustain a revenue model that will attract the smart people that work in the business?

According to Frank L. Campanale:[20]

> Consultants wish to provide a menu of services that is not only personal to the client, but that's also personal to their particular styles of business. The fee for a high-touch, high-feel kind of consultant who spends a lot of time sitting down with the client, helping them decide whether to lease or buy the car, whether to refinance the house, listening to them complain about their children's problems, and hopping on an airplane once a month to go through an entire reporting package with them is going to be higher than for the consultant who only sees a client twice a year and talks to them every other quarter.

Hamilton believes that families are becoming educated on the need to pay higher fees based on the quality of advice they seek. 'The markets have helped them realize that it's more difficult to manage the wealth process than they had thought,' she explains. They are giving discretion to their advisors in ways they did not in the 1990s when they felt 'it couldn't be that hard to manage money'. Now they are saying, 'I need a professional to oversee this process. I'm going to give him or her permission to make decisions on my behalf and I'm going to pay more for that advice.'

At the big firms, the top consultants are seeing the need for change and many are realizing that the firm may not allow them to accomplish their goals. According to Sara Hamilton:

> The reason professionals move into the wealth advisory world, the family office being at the high end of that, is because they are able to work with less than 30 clients and do a much more comprehensive wealth planning process. They are tired of doing a lousy job for a large number of clients; they want to do really well for a small number of families.

FOX and IPI are not the only channels opening up for consultants. New organizations, such as the Family Wealth Alliance, which was recently created by Family Office Management, and firms such as Lydian Wealth Management, and MFOs like TAG Associates offer opportunities for consultants wishing to form a different kind of practice.

The Family Wealth Alliance is an independent organization that provides education and guidance to wealthy families to find the best wealth manager 'fit' to achieve their goals. In doing so, it considers the four types of capital which make up the family assets as well as the integrity and competency of the wealth manager. Other companies specialize in the financial asset management of philanthropic organizations and include in their offerings many of the softer services such as family event planning and education. Lydian Wealth Management offers back office solutions to consultants wishing to provide a completely unbiased, open architecture service model to their significantly wealthy clients. TAG Associates is an example of how advisory specialists such as CPAs and attorneys can build a business by providing high-level family office services to multiple clients.

These organizations and firms highlight the new opportunities becoming available to consultants. These consultants will reinvent themselves and, rather than simply managing investments for their clients, they will turn to optimizing their clients' entire portfolio of assets – including human, intellectual, and social assets – in order to serve their clients' needs comprehensively, optimally, and efficiently. As such, these consultants will adopt a new description for themselves – that of wealth optimization consultant. The specific characteristics of this new type of consultant will be explored in Chapter 11.

Who are the wealthy?

Financial industry firms have targeted the mass affluent and the low-end affluent, thinking they can gain critical mass by offering private wealth management services. These levels are relatively underserved in the area of private wealth management. It is a wealth level that may well be served by the commoditized offerings of the large firms, which may in turn serve firms' desire to maintain or increase margins and cut costs.

The wealth segment is also well served with the SMA model, but the wealthy and ultra-wealthy are looking for more and this is where high-level consultants will find opportunity. Hamilton identifies the US$25 million level as the point where the complexities of managing wealth change dramatically:[21]'It gets more complicated (at that level) because there's money that will be going to the next generation and there's enough to think about a foundation.' Tax and ownership issues also become more complicated at higher wealth levels. But the complexity is not just driven by the level of wealth. 'It's how complicated you want your ownership structures to be, how aggressive you decide to be in your tax planning, how diversified you want to be in the investment of the asset pool, and how comprehensive you want to be in your family's philanthropy,' she explains.

For the big firms, the way ahead lies in a redefinition and narrowing of their target markets as well as catching up with the rest of the industry in adding efficiencies through technology. Granted, SMAs have many variables and special considerations that the rest of the industry does not, but firms' tardiness in addressing these concerns has contributed greatly to the problems they are currently facing. By undertaking deeper marketing research to identify the segments of the mass affluent and low-level affluent markets that will be most attracted to their service offerings, they can avoid the false assumptions that have guided their activities to this point and turn their focus to more conducive segments. Generalized, one-size-fits-all approaches simply do not work in today's world. Yet, there are ways to scale certain aspects of large firm services to increase efficiencies while still providing a modicum of customized service. Doing so would free up other monies to provide at least some of the more customized, soft services the wealth market demands. But large firms have a lot of hurdles to overcome before they reach this point.

The technology, education, venues, and mindsets that will foster the wealth management models of the future will be discussed across the remainder of this book.

---

[1] Personal interview with Charlotte B. Beyer, founder and CEO, IPI, November 2003.

[2] McKinsey and Co. Financial Research Corporation (FRC) (2002), *Separately Managed Accounts: Overview and Perspective*, PowerPoint presentation Slide 4, June.

[3] Reinhart, Leonard A., and Whipple, Jay N. (November 2001), *2010: A Managed Account Odyssey*, Lockwood Advisors, Inc.

[4] According to McKinsey & Co. Financial Research Corporation (FRC) (2002), *Separately Managed Accounts: Overview and Perspective*, PowerPoint presentation Slide 7, June.

[5] Author's interview with Frank L. Campanale, former president and CEO, Saloman Smith Barney Consulting Group, September 2003.

[6] Desai, Shyarsh, Latimore, Dan, and Robinson, Greg (2003), *Technology is Not the Trump Card in the Mass Affluent Wealth Management Game*, IBM Business Consulting Services, p. 6.

[7] Ibid, p.6

[8] Ibid.

[9] Ibid.

[10] Ibid.

[11] Gray, Lisa (2003), 'Will Standards Kill SMAs?', *On Wall Street,* March.

[12] Author's interview with Scott D. Welch, managing director, Lydian Wealth Management LLC, October 2003.

[13] Desai, Shyarsh, Latimore, Dan, and Robinson, Greg (2003), *Technology is Not the Trump Card in the Mass Affluent Wealth Management Game*, IBM Business Consulting Services, p. 3.

[14] Mrak III, Joseph (2003), 'Open Architecture and the SMA', *Waters,* February, available at http://www.placemark.com/WatersFeb.03SMA_web_print.pdf

[15] Author's interview with Frank L. Campanale, former president and CEO, Saloman Smith Barney Consulting Group, September 2003.

[16] Brick, Michael (2000), 'Ernst & Young, E*Trade to Form Online Advice Firm', *The Street.com,* May.

[17] 'Schwab Advice and Research', available at http://www.schwab.com/SchwabNOW/SNLibrary/SNLib122/SN122mainMiniHome/0,4525,505,00.html?dest=m%2Broverview&orig=planningoverview&pos=topnav&ebmk=acquisition

[18] Mrak III, Joseph (2003), 'Open Architecture and the SMA', *Waters,* February, available at http://www.placemark.com/WatersFeb.03SMA_web_print.pdf

[19] Author's interview with Sara Hamilton, founder and CEO, FOX, September 2003.

[20] Author's interview with Frank L. Campanale, former president and CEO, Saloman Smith Barney Consulting Group, September 2003.

[21] Author's interview with Sara Hamilton, founder and CEO, FOX, September 2003.

Part II

The basics

Introduction to Part II

Service definition is no longer dictated by the providers of services; it is dictated by the clients they serve. This change in control has major implications. The first and most important implication is the necessity on the part of high-level advisors and investment management consultants to adopt a different mindset regarding business focus and compensation structure. These aspiring wealth optimization consultants must change their previously autonomous, protective business outlook to one of collaboration with other consultants, advisors, and the clients they serve. Choosing a market tier to focus on is a critical component of the wealth optimization consultant's success; that choice will dictate the range and depth of services to be provided, both from in-house and outsourced resources.

In order to make the most appropriate choice, the available tools and essential ingredients for providing services to any tier of wealth must be examined. Only then will the wealth optimization consultant be able to clearly define the proper balance between the service level to be provided, the resources available, and the level of profitability sought by that consultant.

Chapter 5

Creating efficiencies through collaborative networks

Introduction

Forward-thinking financial services industry firms are providing unprecedented support for team development. Entire divisions have been set up to teach advisors how to form teams, how to iron out partnership agreements, and how to delineate team compensation and operating parameters. But to truly provide wealth optimization to wealthy clients, consultants need not only to build team relationships with like-minded colleagues, but also relationships with other advisors involved in serving their clients. 'How do advisors effectively develop those relationships?' is an old question that prompts a range of misguided answers. This chapter will explain the reasons for developing these relationships, the benefits such relationships hold for consultants and their clients, and a method for developing them that really works.

Family offices have operated as teams from the start. With such a well-developed team mentality, family offices offer the highest levels of integrated services and collaboration on the parts of advisors for the family's benefit. Top consultants are following this lead. They have adopted a team philosophy and have had their own functional P&Ls for years. Some of these teams work through brokerage firms (firm teams); others have established independent practices. Firm teams hire their own staffs, construct their own technology on top of the firm's systems, and develop their own distinctive brand. They are governed by firm compliance, but they are allowed to create their own names, much like a subsidiary, within the firm. Templates for these names include examples like 'Smith Investment Group at XYZ Firm', 'Smith/Jones Consulting Group at XYZ Firm', 'Premier Consulting Group at XYZ Firm', or the 'Chicago Consulting Group at XYZ Firm'.

This revolution at large financial institutions has been mandated by advisors and consultants wishing to create an assignable value to their practices. These consultants are adopting business structures and creating detailed business plans in addition to controlling their own P&Ls. The shift to the team structure also empowers the advisors and consultants who form them. They have more control over their careers and also over the level of service they give to clients. It also gives consultants a salable enterprise with which to leverage an exit when they are ready to retire or start a new venture.

The most successful teams undertake a combination of retail and small institutional business. In many cases, these teams have developed some type of specialty such as managing the assets of healthcare organizations, or endowment fund or foundation assets. More and more, teams are focusing on offering family office level services to the wealthy. Although firm teams operate within a large firm structure, they have trimmed their client bases to make it possible to give clients the one-on-one care they need.

Teams can build a strong presence by focusing on clients' needs and communicating that focus through wise business and marketing planning. The most successful teams have a unique component. They have identified a target market that is associated with leisure interests or they may enjoy working in a particular segment of wealth management. Regardless, they are active in that market's interests. They know that market so well that their reputation alone draws clients to them. They have become more than investment management consultants; they have become wealth optimization consultants.

Successful teams have chosen to sacrifice short-term success with smaller assets for long-term success with larger assets and multi-generational relationships. They have made a conscious decision to conduct business on their own terms, to get paid for advice instead of for selling products, and to provide clients with the services they want.

The team structure functions more efficiently, rounds out service to clients, and attracts more assets than advisors working alone. Many partners invest their own money to adequately fund their staffs and the levels of service they wish to provide. The return on investment is one of the best available. Many established teams regularly receive lucrative offers from other firms. But instead of evaluating what other firms can offer them, they are beginning to evaluate being with a firm versus going out on their own. Teams do a greater amount of high-quality business. They have more control over their own destiny.

Building an effective team is difficult and may involve some trial and error. It can take time to find the right people with the right backgrounds and the right objectives to make the team function as it should. It can take even more time to iron out agreements that are workable and acceptable to each partner. Teams encounter issues and suffer problems similar to those of small business start-ups. Partners can be added and, after several months, not work out despite the original care given to their selection. Staff may be hired and fired before a cohesive support group can be found. Funds can be slim and new teams may need to borrow money in order to pay the staff and buy the systems they need until the business becomes established. At various points in its growth, a team may need to hire outside business and marketing coaches to get to the next level. With all of these initial drawbacks, what value do advisors see in forming a team?

Team dynamics and the waves of change

Entrepreneurial spirit is a significant factor in the development of these partnerships, but there is also a growing industry trend of advisors wishing to create measurable value for eventual sale. As the financial and family office industries go through one of the most definitive changes in their histories, advisors are preparing themselves, knowingly or unknowingly, to reap the benefits. Earlier in this book the histories of both industries and the underlying currents that have brought each to the point of such monumental change were reviewed. The ways in which the two industries are converging and how each is borrowing ideas from the other were highlighted. Teams have become the prototype of each industry's future.

The family office 'team' is receiving a dramatic facelift, while the financial industry has only recently begun to encourage team formation within its firms. Merrill Lynch and UBS have taken the lead by establishing 'team specialists' who guide advisors on structuring, identifying roles and responsibilities, and goal-setting and achievement.[1] Team formation is also a result of different industry dynamics compared with the family office industry, which is simply streamlining itself to create greater efficiency while sacrificing as little as possible of the personal service and privacy to which wealthy families have become accustomed. The financial industry, on the other hand, is struggling to find a feasible way to adequately serve a wealthier market in order to remain viable.

There are several ways in which the team concept fits well with the changes now occurring in both industries. One of these is integration of services. No matter what type of business model teams of the future adopt, they will be heavily involved in the 'intimate integration' of services for their clients. Family office clients have always demanded this; now, increasingly sophisticated clients outside the family office are also demanding it. Simply stated, 'intimate integration' of services means considering the results of each investment action on every other aspect of the client's portfolio. This includes hard assets such as collectibles and real estate as well as private equity, venture capital, managed futures, and other alternatives. It also includes a consideration of the client's overall tax liability – both regular income tax and liability to the alternative minimum tax (AMT). Estate planning, trust structure, and long-term financial planning are also included in the mix.

When financial industry consultants speak of integration, they primarily mean integrating the investment of the assets over which they have control with such services as tax planning and estate planning, with little consideration of the other types of assets, their structure, or the advisors who control them. For example, a client family may have US$8 million in various types of equity investments, a US$12 million bond portfolio, US$6 million in private equity, US$7 million in hedge funds, US$8 million in energy partnerships, and another US$9 million in real estate (a primary residence, two vacation homes, and some undeveloped family property). This family may also have a US$10 million foundation and another US$50 million-worth of the operating company's stock in trust for their two children. Perhaps it also owns a private jet, a 30-foot yacht, and a ranch in Texas where cutting horses are bred. Such a family is likely to have its own single family office (SFO) with estate planning, real estate, and tax attorneys; CPAs; investment consultants; and staff to handle bill-paying and other concierge services.

Significant activity in this family's assets such as monetizing a block of company stock (not 144 stock) would need to be within the guidelines of both the overall investment policy statement (IPS) and the IPS for that group of assets, as it could affect the tax liability of the family as well as the overall asset allocation. Ownership structures would need to be considered as well any public relations ramifications.

Although clear distinctions can be made with cases involving smaller assets, a US$10 million client with a US$3 million block of company stock, another US$1.5 million in company stock options, US$2 million in other equities, US$2 million in bonds, and US$1.5 million in hedge funds will involve several of the same considerations as the US$110 million family above. This client would need integrated management of these holdings in order to take advantage of continual tax optimization, to maintain an appropriate asset allocation, and to effectively manage risk. The hedge funds would need to be in strategies other than long/short funds – perhaps a balanced blend of non-equity and equity strategies other than long/short in a hedge fund of funds. Regular income tax and AMT implications from the equity, bond, and hedge fund investments would need to be coordinated and optimized, and public relations management could still be needed if the client decided to exercise his stock options to invest in non-correlated investments. State income taxes would also need to be considered as well as charitable contributions.

On an even smaller scale, a client worth US$3 million might have a US$1 million stock portfolio, US$500,000 in municipal bonds, US$400,000 in a 401(k) retirement account, a US$600,000 house, and US$500,000 in hedge funds. Activity in this portfolio would need to consider regular and AMT tax implications, state income tax, and asset allocation guidelines as well as estate planning considerations.

Keeping in mind the entire portfolio of assets while managing any single part of the assets is important to any client. It can make a difference in multi-year tax optimization, cost controls – both in fees and in opportunity costs – and risk management. Unfortunately, most clients outside of a family office atmosphere do not receive such comprehensive consideration of their overall assets. Even if firm teams work with clients' outside advisors, such intimate integration of assets can be difficult. However, a team of wealth optimization consultants can take a leadership position with a client's CPAs, attorneys, and other advisors to facilitate such integration. This is where collaboration becomes important.

Team collaboration with outside advisors

Obviously, it is impossible to create the level of integration clients are seeking without collaboration among all advisors. Autonomous activity by a client's attorneys, CPAs, investment counsel, and other advisors is quickly giving way to a more collaborative attitude. Clients become frustrated by in-fighting among these advisors and end up not knowing what to do. All are trusted advisors; all are giving conflicting advice.

Teams and outsourced advisors of the future can be expected to be more cognizant of these conflicts and the confusion they produce for clients. They will become more willing to sacrifice ego and total control over one aspect of the client's financial life in order to work collaboratively with other advisors for the overall benefit of the client. This is how quality advice should be working, but what should be and what is can be quite different. The marketplace is demanding collaboration and intimate integration. Like asset allocation, integration within one segment of a client's assets does not accomplish much if investments in assets outside that segment negate the integration benefits. Yet one segment – the segment they manage – is often the solitary focus for financial advisors.

Not until (and unless) all non-beneficial barriers have come down between various advisors, product availability, and service limitations will the financial industry be capable of truly competing with the family office industry. Higher-level teams within large firms are still limited on product availability. Higher-level producers are given access to a limited number of outside vendors, but such limited availability cannot assure the client is getting the best product for their needs. It is unreasonable to demand that an advisor search through the myriad of products available to find the very best one for each individual client; however, it is reasonable to realize that a list from a limited number of well-known product providers and a list compiled from a majority of product providers, including some lesser-known but possibly higher-quality ones, may offer clients two entirely different solutions. Such open architecture may temporarily increase competition for the larger providers, but healthy competition presents the best results for clients and consumers.

Financial advisors have also had an extremely difficult time forming relationships with CPAs, attorneys, and other advisors. Most often, their attempts at building relationships turn out to be token referral exchange programs, which do not have much appeal to any of the parties involved, simply because none of the advisors wants to give away business to another advisor. A financial advisor cannot approach a CPA or other outside advisor and expect a quality relationship to be formed simply by agreeing to exchange referrals. Developing these relationships takes time; it also requires a different approach.

If a financial advisor approached a CPA and asked him or her what services the advisor has that might benefit the CPA's business, a wider door to a relationship would automatically be opened. Richard Joyner, CPA, CFP, CIMA, and president of private wealth management at Tolleson Wealth Management cautions advisors to do some homework before going to talk to a CPA or other outside advisor:[2]

> I find it very disturbing that many investment consultants don't want to take the time to learn about other types of businesses. A consultant at a big financial services firm, for example, might make broad and sweeping assumptions about how my business works. But the first and most important step to getting into (the CPA) market is to understand it. Don't assume that every single business is alike. Ask questions to understand what drives that particular business model, what creates revenue, what types of things that particular firm thinks it does well and doesn't do well – most firms will be honest with you and about those things. Then, try to figure out where the fit is, as opposed to working the other way around and assuming you know what the fit is on the front end. The latter approach is so pervasive and it's really incredible … When I was at a CPA firm, they would come to me and assume everything I did was tax. They'd say, 'Well, I know how tax returns work, yeah. I understand what you're after!' Well, they never bothered to ask and their assumptions were incorrect most of the time.

This is a good time for developing CPA relationships according to Bradley K. Walton, CPA, PFS, CFP, and a shareholder in Signature Advisors Group, Ltd:[3] '…40 to 60% of public practicing accountants have the capacity to offer non-traditional services such as investment advice, financial planning, retirement plans and even insurance.' CPA firms are incorporating these services in a variety of ways. Some are forming strategic partnerships with wealth management consultants; others are educating themselves and other firm partners to provide the services; and some CPA firms are either acquiring financial services firms or being acquired by financial services firms. So the climate for developing mutually beneficial relationships with CPAs is extremely favorable, although the actual expansion of services is difficult to implement. Disruption of long-term client relationships is the primary concern in transitioning a CPA practice to include the new services.[4]

A good way to start a relationship with CPAs looking for strategic partners might be to simply share ideas for a while. This allows each advisor to become familiar with the other's business and service objectives, the way the other cares for his or her clients, conducts their current business, and the level of each person's integrity and ethics. If conducted well, this step lays the groundwork for the next level of trust, which might be working together on a few mutual client situations. If the relationship deepens through this process, a partnership conversation may be broached. This method of developing trust on a series of deeper levels can lead to long-lasting, high-quality, mutually beneficial, and mutually profitable relationships.

A recurring theme in developing higher-level practices for financial advisors is the time required for development. This investment of time can be viewed as a significant hurdle for advisors. However, an advisor with high-level goals will see the value of such an investment.

Enhanced efficiency and profitability

One prohibitive factor in both the family office and financial industries is mounting costs and inefficiencies – for practitioners, firms, and their clients. In the financial industry, these problems are larger simply because of the massive scale involved. Diminished assets result-ing from any market downturn always highlight costs, but the severity of the 2000–03 bear market has exacerbated the effect of costs on portfolios. The author submits that such con-siderations will not be abandoned after the recovery and that attention to costs will continue as clients seek better returns in a market and economic environment that may not be as giving as the 1982–99 bull market. Therefore, efficiency and profitability will continue to be important factors in both industries.

Teams have an opportunity to exploit these two factors to their significant benefit. But first, practitioners should look at the various costs and inefficiencies involved in managing wealth. These costs involve more than actual dollars; they also include time and opportunity costs, which ultimately translate to actual dollar costs. For the client, actual dollar costs involve:

- transaction costs;
- management fees;
- flat advisory fees or billable hours;
- embedded costs in various products such as mutual funds; and
- profit-sharing costs as with hedge fund and managed futures managers.

For advisors, basic costs include:

- office equipment;
- staff salaries;
- technology investment;
- travel expenses (either to visit clients or to attend educational or trade conferences); and
- outside educational and coaching fees.

Even if advisors work for large brokerage firms, they have these same costs. The 60% or so taken by the firm pays for basic office equipment, technology, and staff. Teams may have to pay more out of their own percentage to upgrade systems and add more staff than the firm is willing to provide.

Time costs for clients include:

- meeting with advisors – especially if the client owns an operating business;
- meeting with partners and family members;
- looking over performance and other reports;
- keeping an eye on all advisors who manage facets of his or her personal and corporate business; and
- development and assessment of advisory relationships.

Time costs for advisors include:

- meeting with clients;
- phone conversations with clients;
- business and marketing planning;
- meeting with staff;
- overseeing their practice, its functions, and its service provision;

- generating new business;
- attending educational or trade conferences; and
- earning recognized credentials.

Opportunity costs for clients lie in:

- inappropriate asset allocation relative to risk tolerance;
- lack of overall risk management;
- not being able to meet cash flow needs; and
- minimal, once-per-year tax consideration with no consideration of other years' tax implications.

For advisors, opportunity costs lie in:

- attracting the wrong clients;
- not having access to the right tools and/or training/education;
- not keeping up with industry trends and technology development;
- lack of business and marketing planning;
- neglecting to examine staff or partner talents and abilities sufficiently; and
- maintaining relationships that take time away from more important business generating activities that could produce more beneficial relationships.

The costs cited in any of these areas – actual dollars, time, or opportunity costs – can become expensive. Actual dollar costs garner the most attention, but the other costs can be much greater than they may appear. Ignoring them usually translates into increases in actual dollar costs. When this happens, measures are usually taken to control the actual dollar costs when they may not be the cause of the added expense at all. In examining actual dollar costs, the impetus behind a rise in costs must be examined and properly assessed. By correctly identifying the source of the added costs, misdirected use of funds may be avoided. Actual dollar costs can be easily exacerbated by trying to remedy the wrong source, wasting dollars without solving the problem.

Efficiency through state-of-the-art technology and streamlined, effective business processes solves the cost problem in all three areas. Effective efficiency requires intimate integration in an advisor's business and in client wealth management. Proper integration of services eliminates duplication and oversight of important tasks or of small problems that can become large ones; it automatically creates efficient time management.

How to create efficiency and reduce costs

If time efficiency is added, costs are reduced and profitability is automatically enhanced. Viewing an advisory practice as a business is essential to incorporating the structure necessary to enhance efficiency. A well-organized team of collaborative relationships among advisors who have the same objective (working for the benefit of the client), the right qualifications, and agreement on basic business tenets can create efficiency in all areas of a practice. A properly organized, motivated, focused, and educated team with a similarly organized, motivated, focused, and educated staff has no limit to its opportunity. The correct processes will be in place to maximize each person's abilities; service delivery will be prompt and effective. Clients will sense the high quality in the atmosphere of such an organization; they will feel the benefits through the level of service and individual care that is produced.

Like most worthwhile endeavors, this ideal tends to be easier to describe than to put into practice and maintain. The important focus is on the business systems put in place by a successful team; not on achieving perfect results. Here are some examples of how teams can work in real life if they have detailed planning and proper focus. The examples are based on actual practices but have been expanded to show how teams can realistically function if they maximize efficiency and minimize all three types of costs. Although these examples may sound 'ideal', they are achievable in existing environments. As an important preface to the examples, in each case the following has been accomplished.

- The partners have taken the time to really get to know each other's motivations, career goals, and the reasons they are in the wealth management business.
- They have agreed on how they want to operate their new business, including revenue-sharing arrangements, clarifying responsibilities, and incorporating an exit strategy in case the partnership ceases or they decide to sell the business.
- They have extensively interviewed their staff so that they are fully aware of each person's capabilities, establishing solid communication with each during the process.
- Partners have been willing to put in the time required because each partner feels their long-term goals merit such extensive preparation.
- They have developed a habit of regularly reviewing their processes to determine adjustments that may need to be made.
- They have accomplished this preparatory planning by outsourcing a marketing consultant who has experience in their business and is credentialed in wealth advisory skills.

Example 1

Two advisors have decided to form a team. They have 600 client relationships between them and wish to trim that total to 100. They have both been trying to build relationships with outside advisors but have yet to be successful. They decide to increase their service platform to include trust, estate planning, tax planning, philanthropic counsel, and wealth psychology services. One partner specializes in retirement planning and the other specializes in business succession planning. They feel that adding the other services will help them attract wealthier clients so that they can further cut their client list to 60 highly serviced, highly customized relationships.

The partners want to keep overhead as low as possible so they spend time determining how much staff they will need to coordinate not only the services they provide, but also the five extra service areas. They can access three of these service areas within the large firm that houses them, and they plan to outsource the other two. Their goal is to provide complete manager of manager services, so they decide to slightly overstaff to make sure they can provide that service fully. Because the partners work within a brokerage firm, they cannot share revenues with any of the outsourced advisors. But they feel they can increase their fees slightly toward the high end of the spectrum to cover the manager of managers services they plan to provide with their staff.

As they hire staff, they keep their business and service objectives in mind as well as the abilities of each person they hire. During the hiring process, they spend a lot of time with each candidate learning what motivates them, where their strongest abilities lie, and the type of work they most enjoy doing. Afterward, the two partners meet to organize the use of everyone's abilities as fully as possible without overloading any one person unnecessarily. They set up a cross-training program to avoid any gaps in service when someone is out of the office.

They fully explain their service and business objectives and provide incentives for delivering quality service and for working well together, aiming to produce an efficiency-minded atmosphere within the practice. Ideas from the staff for improvement are welcomed and fully considered; the best ideas are incorporated. This is how the partners envision putting their business together. But six months into the new set-up, a licensed staff member who has worked with one of the partners for nine years and is critical to the practice becomes pregnant and decides she can no longer work and care adequately for her growing family. Another advisor friend of the partners wants to join the team, but with such a critical staff member leaving, the partners are unsure about adding anyone else at this time. In addition, the relationship the partners were forming with a mutual CPA friend has taken an unexpected turn (after a time investment of eight months) and they decide to no longer pursue it. After five more months, they find another CPA who shares their service and business goals more fully. They go through four different hires before finding the right replacement for the original staff member.

Meanwhile, their service reputation has flowed through the two outsourced advisors. One is on the board of a large, prominent, non-profit organization in which one of the partners is active. Having been actively involved in the organization for three years and having accompanied the outsourced adviser to various committee meetings within the organization, this partner has built trust with some of the board and committee members, who subsequently approach him to learn more about his team's services. The second outsourced advisor often asks the partners to speak at family meetings she moderates. Some of these families have expressed interest in hiring the team to manage certain of their portfolios.

After four years of sticking to its plans, the team has trimmed its client base to 75 relationships, has increased assets under management to US$600 million (up from US$200 million originally), has established new relationships via the two outsourced service areas, and is ready to add another partner.

Example 2

A two-partner team with 70% of its business involved with institutional clients and 30% with retail clients advises on US$8 billion worth of assets. Its staff includes four performance analysts, two technical analysts, two consultants, and three registered assistants. It decides to expand its ratio of retail clients, which consists primarily of investors worth a minimum of US$30 million. It hires another partner/consultant with a focus on family wealth management, revamps its business and marketing plans, and decides to offer family office level services, beginning with an educational program for its current retail clients on the new services it has decided to offer. The team begins deepening the relationships it has developed with the outside advisors of its original retail client base, and offers to help these advisors by sharing with them the team's newly outsourced resources in wealth psychology and philanthropy.

The team uses its firm's in-house trust department to round out its internal services. After five years, the team's client ratio is 55% institutional and 45% wealth management for retail clients. It has increased its assets under advisement by US$2 billion and has added 20 retail relationships to the original 30. The team's average retail client net worth has increased from US$30 million to US$50 million.

Example 3

An independent firm begun 15 years ago by four advisors has a staff of six and subscribes to a third party technology provider with a highly sophisticated platform of services. It has 120 clients and advises on US$650 million in assets. The firm works primarily with individual investors. Services offered include financial planning, investment management consulting, and retirement planning. It has developed state-of-the-art technology systems, which have been enhanced by the services of the third party platform. This team decides to expand its service offerings to include more family office level services. It decides the best way to do this is to become a multi-family office (MFO). It takes its top 30 clients (average net worth US$15 million) and hires a CPA with whom it has a multiple-year relationship to work in-house. The CPA brings 10 ultra-wealthy clients with her. The firm decides to outsource other services as needed. With the 10 new clients brought in by the CPA, the firm has 40 clients with an average net worth of just under US$24 million and advises on US$950 million in assets.

The firm has developed direct relationships with money managers over the years and uses the third party provider as a source of back and front office services. However, its services are limited to the offerings of the third party provider and as the third party provider adds new services, the services become more expensive. The firm prefers to offer different services than the third party provider and is currently reviewing that relationship.

These case studies illustrate some of the challenges that must be overcome in establishing effective team relationships, within and outside of the internal team structure. By being aware of these challenges and taking steps to either circumvent or manage them well, wealth optimization consultants can realistically plan their success.

A new version of the team model

As technology advances, basic financial services, including elements of separately managed accounts (SMAs), will become commoditized. This will allow wealth optimization consultants to focus on the most valuable aspects of their businesses – building and managing relationships. Business models of teams will make a dramatic shift as basic service elements will be organized and performed by technology systems, reducing the number of operational staff needed for the practice. Technology consulting companies provide objective counseling to practices on the technology solutions that will best fit their service models. There are no product-based compensation structures; the consultants are paid by fee, just like the wealth managers they are advising. They base their recommendations on the talents of the team and the functions they are setting up.[5]

There are other technology companies providing flexible platforms for SFOs and MFOs that can be customized to meet the office's specific needs. These companies offer secure websites to families to facilitate communication and integrated counsel among members and advisors, as well as front and back office services to facilitate operations. These websites enable what are called 'virtual' family office services. No technology solution offered today provides complete, seamless services with absolutely no human intervention (also known as straight-through processing or STP). So a complete virtual offering is not yet available; it is, however, quite close to becoming a reality.

Fast-forwarding to the day when such an offering has become a reality, the teams used in the above examples will undergo significant changes. These changes will level the playing field in favor of wealth optimization consultants. To see how this leveling may occur, each example is updated to the future.

Example 1

The two advisors who formed a team, initially trimming their 600 relationships to 100, are in the process of re-evaluating their need to work within a large firm. The team now has three partners, 60 client relationships, and has increased its US$600 million in assets to US$800 million. The team has investigated a number of technology companies offering family office level platforms that are completely open architecture, totally web-based, and are flexible enough to accommodate full customization for each client. The team picks the platform that will meet their needs today and over the next five years. Its next step is to leave the brokerage firm at which the team started.

The technology platform they have chosen allows the team to search for services with specific criteria in mind. The team creates its own lists of service providers and performs a layered due diligence process that takes less than a week to apply to each service they plan to offer. Since the team is no longer at the firm, they have total discretion over which providers to use. The technology platform also allows the team to set up communications with client family members and service providers located around the globe. The team holds family meetings online. The building of their manager of managers service and reputation along with increased technological and communications connectivity has allowed them to serve client families as a totally objective consultant, serving on the family office council, and helping the family obtain the best advisors, regardless of location. The team coordinates all activity provided on behalf of the family and essentially serves as a virtual family office for its clients. Its services are streamlined and cost-effective, yet retain the caring, personal touch desired by wealthy families. The team has coordinated all of its services among a variety of providers through its application service provider (ASP) platform, greatly reducing technology costs. The detailed organization of the business plus the freeing of human, social, and intellectual capital previously chained to 'overhead-laden activities'[6] enables intimately integrated, comprehensive service to each client family. It has also helped the team position itself uniquely in the market-place.

Example 2

The two-partner team with combined institutional and retail business successfully increased its retail component to 45%. It, too, found it could do more on its own with the 60% it was paying the firm rather than by continuing to sacrifice such a large portion of its payout for a lower service level than it wanted to offer. Since the commoditization of services previously requiring hands-on involvement, the team hired a technology consultant to assess the systems it had acquired and built on its own relative to what it would need to operate independently to offer the level of service its clients desired.

The technology consultant created a customized platform of service capabilities for the team which comprehensively met the unique needs of its clients.[7] The team decided to retain its former employer firm to provide some of the institutional services that met its quality and service standards, but all other services were outsourced to a variety of providers who were able to coordinate their service efforts over a private, secure communication system on the team's website. Each of the team's families now has its own private, secure website as well, fully equipped with permissioning functions to allow various advisors access to limited areas and allowing the family as well as the team to look at the entire portfolio of assets. Each family site also facilitates governance through its online meeting and secure website capabilities; each site has a fully integrated tax module that considers regular income tax rules as well as AMT liability; and each family has access to a system with layering and aggregation methodologies for partnership allocation, performance measurement and attribution, trust accounting, and other complicated reporting services.

As a result of eliminating the firm in the team's business model, the team has developed direct relationships with money managers, which allows it to realize greater profit margins without having to raise fees. The firm now makes the most of its money by providing out-sourced services to virtual family office staffs.

The team is now able to monitor all systems and services on the internet, to run its business on its own terms, and to offer truly objective advice and services to its clients. The efficiencies created by fully integrated technology systems allow the team's business and marketing plans to be implemented cost-effectively and seamlessly. There are system alerts that let staff know when a particular client's portfolio needs attention based on criteria input during the initial phase of the consulting process.

The demographics of the baby boomer generation have benefited the team's healthcare focus, allowing it to increase its institutional and retail businesses to maximum capacity. The team purposely limits the number of clients it takes on so that it can give the level of personalized service its clients – both institutional and retail – demand. Yet asset levels keep climbing.

Example 3

The independent firm has abandoned its third party platform provider in favor of a totally open architecture system created by integrating the best of the technology systems originally developed for private banks and third party separate account platform providers.[8] These companies have agreed to integrate their systems with the systems of any number of companies that are members of a consortium that requires a certain level of service quality, capability, and flexibility. The consortium helps member firms market their services to family office advisors looking for high-quality service providers. All consortium members offer complete web-based ASP access to their own services as well as web-enabled interfaces with other family office service providers.

Due to the internet, the independent firm can afford the best in technology services because no infrastructure is required. The firm has also been able to meet client demand for broader service offerings and a 'knowledge' manager to help clients assess the value of information to their particular situations. This is a significant departure from the services offered by the third party platform provider they previously outsourced. The firm's consultants can now use their intellectual capital to provide highly customized service to clients.

Through the CPA partner it hired, the firm has successfully enhanced its in-house wealth management services. All other family office services are outsourced and integrated into the wealth management services for each client. The firm's asset base has grown exponentially from US$950 million to US$2.5 billion. Its client relationship base has grown from 40 to 100, the maximum number of clients allowed by its business plan. The firm is considering adding to its mix an attorney with whom it has developed a relationship. This person is a long-time associate of the CPA and would round out the tax planning services offered by the firm. The way the independent firm is set up is also quite attractive to the attorney, whose practice will become a subsidiary of the firm, allowing the integration of wealth management and family office services with the estate and tax planning services the attorney has provided for 18 years, and for which he previously billed by the hour.[9]

What technology can and cannot do

These examples show the value that outsourcing can provide in areas beyond the scope of advisors' and consultants' expertise. The investment made is more than recouped via gains in operational efficiencies and the extra effectiveness of the organizational structure.

This chapter has provided an initial glimpse into the family offices of the future. Business models will take many forms, but technology will allow firms the freedom of developing highly customized models – customized both to fit their business focus and their clients' demands.

Clients expect an integrated approach to wealth management.[10] The focus on delivering such integration has been on technology. But intimate integration goes much deeper than technological capabilities. Wealthy families and investors will continue to want the very best in services across every facet of their needs, and will continue to make huge demands on the time and resources of advisors/consultants. Technology only serves as a support tool in fulfilling that mandate. Advisors must educate themselves to be investment management consultants, while investment management consultants must educate themselves to be wealth optimization consultants. Clients want knowledgeable, credentialed advisors. Today's designated consultants will have to continue to distinguish themselves through their ongoing education and their objective advice.

Effective teams have adjusted their focus in order to work collaboratively with each other, with their clients, and with their clients' other advisors. There is no better way to accomplish comprehensive service to the client and maximum business growth and profitability for the wealth optimization consultants. Although financial services industry firms have adopted a team focus, they do not offer the unbiased, fully objective environment necessary for wealth optimization teams to function effectively and efficiently. If financial services industry firms are to retain their brightest and most productive talent, they must shift their focus toward total, objective, open architecture environments that will allow wealth optimization consultants to thrive.

---

[1] Konig, Susan, and Chapelle, Tony (2003), 'The Challenge of Teams', *On Wall Street,* August, p. 30.
[2] Author's interview with Richard Joyner, CPA, CFP, CIMA, president of private wealth management, Tolleson Wealth Management, September 2003.
[3] Walton, Bradley K. (2003), 'Growing Pains', *Insight,* September/October, available at http://www.insight-mag.com/insight/03/09/col-9-pt-1-MoneysWorth.asp
[4] Ibid.

[5] Author's interview with Jon Carroll, co-founder, Family Office Metrics, LLC, September 2003.

[6] Horn, Greg, and DeAngelis, Steve (2000), 'Facing the Technological Revolution', *Trust & Estates,* June.

[7] Author's interview with Jon Carroll, co-founder, Family Office Metrics, LLC, September 2003.

[8] Author's interview with Mike Cagney, president and CEO, Finaplex, September 2003.

[9] Horn, Greg, and DeAngelis, Steve (2000), 'Facing the Technological Revolution', *Trust & Estates,* June.

[10] Casey, Quirk & Acito (2002), *Six Themes for 2002 and Beyond*, Casey, Quirk & Acito LLC, Darien, CT, p. 4 (May).

Chapter 6

Harnessing the power of information management

Introduction

High-level financial services advisors have long been enamored of technology and its business enhancing potential. However, many of these advisors have unwittingly made technological tools the focus of their practices, depending, for example, on impressive slide shows and multi-media presentations to attract new business. The role of technology in wealth optimization is that of a critical, but completely supportive tool. Granted, it is powerful and can create greater efficiencies and service capabilities than ever before, but technology is also a commoditized offering and, as such, it is not designed to provide what wealthy clients are seeking. Only consultants who expand their businesses to optimize a client's wealth will fit the right profile, and this chapter examines how technology will help them achieve this.

Today's advisors have more technological capability than their predecessors ever imagined. But any appropriate discussion of technology relative to those who would provide exceptional service to family wealth owners must focus on its meaning and usefulness to that purpose. Unfortunately, technology can easily become a sales tool or impressive gimmick used – wittingly or unwittingly – to mask a target of gaining assets under management.

Technology's place in the wealth management service module of tomorrow will be of great importance, but increasingly from a behind-the-scenes standpoint rather than as the key to developing a client relationship. The adoption rates of the technology tools available today vary widely across both industries. As more solutions become web-based, adoption rates will increase. Web-based systems will be more cost-effective, will increase the efficiency of doing business, and will enhance service provision at all levels. However, discerning clients who have been dulled by sellers of investment products and scarred by the 2000–03 bear market are looking not only for serious technological capabilities but also for top-quality service, in-depth knowledge, and genuine interest in their welfare.

The next 'big frontier'

The family office and financial services industries have their own quests. The family office industry is looking for ways to streamline costs, effectiveness, and operations; the financial services industry is looking for ways to boost profit margins and to keep its top producing advisors.

The web is the next big frontier for these industries as family offices and large financial services firms both still rely mainly on legacy systems that were never designed to import or export the large amounts of data processed by today's firms or perform real-time processing of vast amounts of information.[1] Legacy systems at single family offices (SFOs) or smaller multi-family offices (MFOs) may not encounter such capacity problems, although family

83

offices and large institutions do have many technology needs in common. The key differences lie in how each side uses its respective systems.

Both industries require state-of-the-art performance reporting, but family offices have more of a need for account aggregation – including bank accounts, credit accounts, and others – than is normally included in the aggregation services of financial services firms. Family offices also have different communication needs. Connectivity is critical between the various family advisors, the family office staff, and the family itself, especially if family members are located in different parts of the world.

For the financial services industry, past technology concerns were associated with distributing the firm's investment products through siloed (single-focus) marketing channels. As profit margins have narrowed and siloed distribution has faded to black, the technology focus at these firms has shifted to the disparate and clumsily aligned functions of back office operations.

With the complexity of technology increasing and industry dynamics at work, it is useful to outline technological developments within each industry so that wealth optimization consultants will be able to discern the best business model for their particular needs.

New technology mandates

An increase in software applications and web interfaces is introducing greater efficiencies into financial technology that cannot be ignored. Like it or not, family offices of all sizes and service platforms, as well as large financial services industry firms, are being forced to contend with the technology hurdle that the archaic legacy systems have created. On the family office side, such hurdles have more to do with cost containment and streamlining communication and governance functions. The financial services industry faces more extreme consequences – the retreat of money manager involvement in separately managed account (SMA) business because of the increased costs of having to work with outdated technology.

The SMA platform, and now the unified managed account (UMA) platform, has been viewed as the Holy Grail solution[2] to declining revenues at large firms caused by the squeeze on profits and the battering of portfolio values during the 2000–03 bear market. UMA business only complicates the matter from a technology standpoint, adding the different accounting and record-keeping requirements for mutual funds, hedge funds, multiple style managers, annuities, and so on to the mix.

It will be much easier for smaller family offices to upgrade to web-based systems because of their size, as the only infrastructure needed is basically a PC and a high-speed internet connection. Costs may be another matter. SFOs may not feel their needs warrant complete upgrades, although weighing the benefits of completely web-based systems will increasingly come into play.

The conversion to web-based application service provider (ASP) platforms may be disruptive to both industries and will not happen overnight. However, as more and more third party vendors convert their services to the ASP model, those services will have to be assimilated into the operations of financial institutions. Although large MFOs with over 100 client families may have a more difficult transition, they still have the advantage of being smaller than large financial institutions. They also have only a few branches as opposed to several thousand for a large financial services firm and will have generally made wiser technology investments over the years, making adoption much easier. However, both industries have a

84

hurdle to surmount that has nothing to do with technology itself; this hurdle is the reticence of firm and family office executives to take the plunge into new technology. Concerns about security are primary with family offices; concerns about investing ever more money into technology against a background of diminished profits reign at financial institutions.

Functions such as processing data needed to perform back office tasks are already occurring at the third party providers' large data centers that then push the information to thin clients (web browsers) on a global basis. According to Greg Horn, CIMA and CEO, and Steve DeAngelis, CIMA and president of ADVISOR*port,* a fully integrated investment consultant platform and a subsidiary of PFPC Worldwide, Inc, state-of-the-art technology in 2000 allowed legacy systems to be integrated into a single system with common access by users through a web browser.[3]

Today, firms like ADVISOR*port,* Finaplex, and SS&C Technologies, Inc can remove the interfaces of the older systems, substitute their own web interfaces, and wrap aggregation and other services – including those from outsourced providers – into a flexible, integrated system accessible to all advisors involved in serving the family's needs. The system then points to the firm's database to seamlessly interact with a family office's general ledger, portfolio accounting, performance reporting, tax analytics, and other functions provided by a number of other application modules.

This type of integration highlights the difference in service needs of the family office from those of traditional financial services industry accounts. Family offices have multiple layers of family members and underlying investors involved in the overall family portfolio. A composite view of these layers is necessary in order to provide the best wealth management advice bearing in mind the ownership structures, the various types of accounts, and the transparency required over the entire group of assets.

The 'virtual' family office

The pooling and transparency of information is critical on many levels, but particularly from a tax management standpoint. The effect of the multiple layers of accounts and the owners involved create complexities rarely faced by financial services advisors. This is where the 'virtual' family office concept comes in. A virtual family office (VFO) is basically a website-based network set up exclusively for the management, governance, and communication needs of a family's wealth. The site is controlled exclusively by the family and its chief advisor who grant access to certain areas of the site by other advisors involved in the business of managing the family's wealth. Other family members who may only need access to certain accounts or areas of the business of the family wealth are also given permissioned access to the limited areas in which they have an interest.

The virtual capability also allows easier assessment of costs and other efficiencies. Regarding web capabilities, security issues have been of primary concern to smaller industry players; however, ADVISOR*port*'s DeAngelis confirms that the web is 'a much more secure and failsafe environment than a firm's own computer in an internal network'. This security translates not only to confidentiality of information, but also to the data redundancy necessary to provide adequate disaster recovery capabilities. And there is no question that the web enables significant streamlining of access and communication costs between various advisors and family members.

Family governance is also facilitated and expedited, adding further efficiencies to family office functions. Today's families have service needs encompassing investment management, tax optimization, trust and estate planning, banking services, insurance and risk management, various concierge services, philanthropic services, web-based capabilities, trustee and fiduciary functions, legacy concerns, and family meeting coordination. They basically have three choices for obtaining these wealth management services:[4]

- become a client of a large financial institution;
- join an MFO; or
- establish an independent family office.

MFO start-ups find it impossible to compete with larger firms in offering such services to their clients; therefore, outsourcing has become an attractive alternative. By outsourcing the services of attorneys, CPAs, banks, consultants, and technology vendors, the VFO can function much like a traditional SFO but with added efficiency, fewer costs, and better communication between the involved entities.

Third party virtual platform providers offer highly integrated capabilities including scheduling of tasks, family meetings whether virtual or in person, and confirmation that those tasks and meetings have been accomplished. Staffing requirements consist of only two or three people and fees charged by the VFO platform providers are much lower than other third party platforms. Automatic efficiencies such as fewer salaries for family office staff and timely accomplishment of tasks and meetings regardless of the location of the individuals involved make VFO services extremely attractive, not only to MFOs but also to individual families wanting to start their own offices on an effective, yet cost-efficient basis.

The VFO will also become a primary resource for wealth management consultants who wish to set up their own firms similar to the multi-client family office (MCFO) structure outlined in Chapter 3. Although there is no complete system available to include VFO services plus back office operational services, the availability of such a system is only a matter of time. According to DeAngelis: 'It will get too difficult to compete in the market-place unless you can operate your business highly efficiently and effectively – that's the nature of any industry as it matures.' Competitive pressures resulting from the increased adoption of web-based or virtual services will force more advisors and firms to convert their systems.

A concept called straight-through processing (STP) is the goal of the financial technology industry. Simply stated, STP means that a transaction or function moves through any number of stages – all contributing to that transaction or function – without human intervention of any kind. In the financial services industry, STP is most often encountered in the front-end transaction side of the business. In the family office industry, STP encompasses an entire range of service operations including front-end and back-end functions.

Most disconnects (ie, most points that require human intervention) remain on the back office operations side, which affects both industries, although in the financial services industry the gaps are small-scale. On the family office side, STP extends to allocation of investment activity all the way down the line to all family members, the underlying investors, to the various K1 tax forms for the portfolio of family businesses, and even to the family website. The website might actually be comprised of a separate batch file that is populated into a website, with the website functionality taking over after the data has been incorporated. So, although every element of every function may not be exactly straight-through, today's more complete integration capabilities bring processes very close to the STP goal.

Functional overlap between the industries

Some (although not the majority) of the large financial services industry firms have realized the efficiencies web-based platforms can offer and are spending money to interface to web-based systems despite the inordinate amounts spent on earlier systems made archaic by the advent of the internet. Smaller SFOs may not see the need to convert to such systems; however, family offices and smaller financial services firms can be extremely agile in terms of the development and implementation of new technology.

The paradox lies in the shared functions required by both industries in order to serve the needs of today's more sophisticated clients (see Exhibit 6.1). These functions center around the investment management component, which, in turn, involves traditional front and back office functions such as trade execution, reconciliation, custody, performance reporting, and portfolio accounting. Then, each industry has its own additional functions that differentiate the levels of service they provide.

The advancement of web-based functionality is facilitating the commoditization of services mentioned in Chapter 4. The market-place is becoming more sophisticated and demanding, and the level of relationship management capabilities must rise to match these demands. Both the family office and financial services industries are facing large-scale technology challenges and, interestingly, each industry has a different take on the real capabilities of the other. In the following two sections we examine the processes currently under way on each side and take a look at how the challenges of each are being addressed, which helps illuminate the bridge being built between the two industries. More importantly, this examination highlights the viable choices open to advisors in determining their business models for the future.

The state of technology in the financial services industry

The financial services industry has been struggling with connectivity and operational gaps in technology for several years. Add to that the changes occurring in the industry

Exhibit 6.1

Comparison of overlapping and non-overlapping functions

Family offices
- Risk assessment
- Lifestyle goals
- Wealth transfer goals
- Investment goals and policy
- Philanthropy goals
- Cash flow and liquidity management
- Financial consolidation
- Partnership accounting
- Foundation compliance
- Gifting and grant making
- Trust and partnership structures
- Family member education
- Family member involvement
- Family governance
- Tax planning and compliance
- Bill-paying and record keeping
- 100-year goals

Overlapping functions
Operational interfaces
Portfolio management
- Trade execution
- Reconcilliation, custody
- Performance reporting
- Portfolio accounting

Consulting process
- Information gathering
- Investment policy formulation
- Asset allocation
- Manager selection
- Ongoing monitoring

Financial services
- Considers financial assets only
- May or may not include risk assessment
- Little attention to tax planning
- Process limited to basic four-step consulting process
- Little consideration of financial asset investment on other assets
- Little financial planning
- Short-term goals

Source: Author's own.

87

regarding methods and requirements of service and the emergence of new products or updated forms of products and the mix becomes complex. SMAs and UMAs have their own technology complications which separate them from the institutional counterparts from which they were originally developed. For ease of illustration, mostly the SMA will be cited in the following discussion.

On top of these challenges, the commoditization of information and technical services is a tsunami-like movement impossible to circumvent. The plethora of data and complex operational and reporting requirements demanded by the SMA business compound the problems. To exacerbate them further, many firms have abandoned or limited open architecture efforts because of the following.

- The money crunch caused by the 2000–03 bear market.
- Open architecture is not as immediately profitable as the current closed systems.
- Some firms are not even familiar with the open architecture concept.[5]

The key points of interface that the SMA industry revolves around include portfolio accounting systems, money manager models, client data, securities data providers, and trading systems.[6] Many of these interfaces are still subject to manual intervention such as sending information by fax or manually inputting data. Sponsor firms require managers' systems to communicate with their proprietary systems. A manager can do a trade in one stock over the scope of all of the portfolios he manages, but then will have to break down each account's portion of that trade and reconcile the necessary information to the proprietary system of each sponsor firm contracted. Each system is different; each has manual 'holes' in different places. Expenses go up because of the extra work involved and the errors generated by human intervention.

On the other hand, the market-place is demanding these services and sponsor firms have no choice but to provide them. The advent of virtual platforms will force sponsor firms either to revisit open architecture or allow most of their services to become fully commoditized with salaried sales and service people constituting the majority of their employee base. Sponsor firm profits will then come primarily from the provision of services to financial advisors who have long since established independent firms and are simply outsourcing the services of their former employers.

Regardless of the way financial services industry firms evolve, a standard protocol for completing STP between front-end transactions and back-end operations will be necessary to connect the data held by the legacy mainframe systems to the web-based applications available both now and in the future. A standard protocol is one of the last hurdles to complete web-based platforms. As Steve DeAngelis explains: 'You have to get the data out of those closed legacy systems once it has been processed and into an open architecture environment. Once the information is in that open architecture environment, serving it up on the web is quite easy.'

Currently, the inefficiencies on both the sponsor and money manager sides have forced sponsor firms to limit their product offerings to those of the platform vendors' choices of managers, trading firms, and custodians at the same time as they are trying to attract the markets that require broader services. The industry is at such a crux point that firms' ability to collectively establish such standards will determine their very survival.

A force that has brought this fact starkly to light has been the issuance of new Association of Investment Management and Research (AIMR) performance presentation standards (PPS) for separate accounts. AIMR has long been the standard bearer for the institutional side of the business and recently turned its attention to the fact that the performance reporting of separate accounts was based on the institutional account performance, not the actual separate accounts owned by individuals.[7]

The costs associated with these cumbersome processes are ever increasing against a backdrop of diminished sponsor firm profits and increasing fee pressure from the marketplace. The AIMR mandate served as a wake-up call to the financial services industry, which is successfully addressing those problems, led by the efforts of the Money Management Institute (MMI) which has recently developed standardized business notification procedures that should have been put in place years ago. However, in this respect the MMI is helping the SMA side of the financial services industry catch up.

The state of technology in the family office industry

As in all industries, the state of what is available from a technology standpoint and the degree to which applications have been adopted and systems have been updated are two completely different things. Although the needs of each industry have been different, more and more overlap of the functions necessary to adequately serve high net worth clients is occurring. In addition, there is a new technology client on the horizon – the wealth management consultant – who will require the same capabilities as traditional technology clients, namely large firms and sizable MFOs. What has previously been considered unattainable from an individual advisor's or an advisory team's perspective is now becoming affordable.

As technology improves, costs come down. Also, adoption rates of new technology can be slow at the beginning but start to pick up speed as the new efficiencies and performance advantages begin to be recognized. In the family office industry, many of the back office needs are the same as those of the financial services industry, and obviously so, since SFOs and MFOs use advisors at some of the large firms to manage the investment component. However, some of the newer technology firms which provide family office level capabilities also provide capabilities for large firms. The most efficient model currently available is a web-based platform for front-end services that interfaces with either single or multiple outsourced back-end service providers. The following sections provide some examples of how this combined service platform can work. These are certainly not the only firms that offer viable solutions, but they provide good illustrations of what is available in today's technology market-place designed to provide top service to the wealthy.

SS&C Technologies, Inc[8]

SS&C's family office technology was a natural offshoot of its hedge fund systems from the perspective of the complexities required for information flow. 'Where (hedge funds and family offices) differ is in the legal structures and in the allocation of investment activity out to family members,' explains Ward McGraw, senior vice president of the firm's hedge and family office vertical. For example, if there are 55 family members who each have an interest in an account, the technology must be able to pass account information through to all 55 family members' underlying accounts. In addition, these family members wish to see a statement that shows their share of this account and the percentage of their entire portfolios that it represents. At tax time, this type of information must be compiled from every account of every family member.

The information needed may include data from private equity K1s, hedge funds, interest and dividend activity, etc. In an MFO, these needs are multiplied significantly.

A typical sequence in an SFO or MFO is as follows: trade execution, reconciliation, custody, performance reporting – all of these functions are performed on the investment side of the family's assets just as for the client of a financial services firm. Added to these services are the custodians from which feeds must be obtained and the vast amount of information that must be captured. Downloads from various trust companies, custodians, prime brokers, investment managers, the general ledger, and investment dividends must all be passed through and allocated to the accounts of the various family members. From there, the information may need to be passed through to a variety of K1 and other functions and into the core books and records systems.

The system takes in all of this information from an omnibus level and 'bursts' it out into the granular pieces that are needed based on the complex structures of ownership that sits on top of the omnibus account. According to McGraw:

> Our systems were built to deal with what we call partnerships within partnerships. Let's say at the very top you have a partnership that invests in marketable securities and at the end of the day, you do a valuation of those securities and derive the NAV of the partnership. One of the investors in that partnership may actually be another partnership. We structure that internally in our system so that as you value the securities from the top, that value automatically flows down pro rata.

This bursting process eliminates the necessity of manually valuing each entity across the board.

All of these processes are fully integrated. Positions, market valuations, performance measurement, and other investment functions are integrated with the general ledger in the form of debits and credits. There is a fully automated check disbursement process so that bill-paying and other non-investment related functions can be incorporated as well. Integration into the tax module, aggregation for partnership allocation, and many other functions are also available from a single platform. As McGraw explains:

> Our systems are aware of the interdependencies of the various transactions. If you have to reverse a trade, a screen pops up alerting you to a variety of dependent transactions that may be affected. There may have been a capital gain from that trade that has already been allocated to investors, or a wash sale, or other income that is affected – you can still unwind the trade but the system will let you know that there may be a dozen other things that may be unwound as a result of this trade reversal.

All of these services are integrated with SS&C's virtual offering as an outsourced resource. The virtual platform folds the fully integrated information from the outsourced platform into the communications and other functions it provides.

Finaplex[9]

Finaplex has built a technology platform around the fullest definition of the process of wealth management, according to CEO Mike Cagney, which is the basic process of prospect identification, information capture, proposal generation, customer acquisition, execution, reporting, and reassessment combined with the special needs of the family office client. Rather than piecing together a variety of applications from a variety of firms to create the complex capability needed to service family office level clients, Finaplex has created a platform consisting of four different components: a boundary layer, a data layer, an application layer, and an interface layer.

At its incorporation in 2000, the new company realized that the advisory community was extremely underserved from a technology perspective. So it created a platform that could take any amount of disparate data, consolidate it, and build entitlement around the data so it could be easily disseminated for any number of purposes such as portfolio accounting and trust and estate planning. The data is then disseminated to the desktops of financial advisors, clients, administrators, and others. The dissemination facilitates data and workflow continuity throughout the complex technological structure of family office service. As Cagney explains:

> A lot of this back-end infrastructure exists within any market segment. We do work for some of the very large wirehouses but we've also had a lot of attention from the RIA and family office communities. They want the same functionality as the wirehouses. So we've extended this capability to RIAs and others who are starting family office type businesses. Finaplex starts with the third party data repositories and builds client infrastructures around those sources.

The boundary layer comprises the set of connectors into the back office brokerage processing systems and service bureau systems. That helps a registered investment advisor (RIA) or family office clear through multiple custodians and have the capability to pull data from a variety of sources into one spot. Finaplex can wrap in other types of functionality such as value analytics, market data feeds, security master information, and any other content that might flow through the application.

The data layers smooth out the data received, which dramatically reduces the time spent reconciling accounts. According to Cagney: 'It's like a real-time data mart. We drive broker desktop information from it and also heavy duty analytics from it.' Information from private equity, real estate, art collections, jewelry, and other non-financial investments along with tax, trust, and other information is combined into what is called an entity relationship model through which an extensive number of people can access the data they need. 'We set the entities up through systems of entitlement and inherited entitlement. You can create a trust that has a group of accounts and have a pro rata share of that trust attributed to a set of dependants – second and third generations or whomever – or you can allocate the assets arbitrarily and manage them that way,' he adds. The dependants can then log into the application and see the information they're entitled to see. CPAs, attorneys, investment managers, and other family members have the same set-up. The flexibility of the virtual data framework facilitates the service functions for all advisors and family members involved.

The next technology piece is the application layer, which includes business components such as performance reporting, portfolio accounting, trust and estate analytics, and other modules wrapped in from outsourced providers. The interface layer is 'stripped off the application layer' so that it can be customized to create an individualized user experience.

In summary, Finaplex provides full integration of front and back office functions along with a virtual platform that can be customized for each user. A financial advisor using the system can have access to complete client profiles, proposal generation, investment policy, asset allocation, and manager search applications. The system also provides a variety of analytic functions from which the advisor can create efficient frontiers, projected returns, and goal assessment. The advisor can create multiple proposals, analytical reports, investment policy statements (IPSs), and information gathered about the client, and store it all in a document repository accessible from their desktops. Even information about non-financial assets can be stored in the repository along with outside accounts and other information.

Any of this information can then be accessed on an entitlement basis. It can be used in family meetings by setting entitlements for all of the attendees so that everyone can log in and see the information concurrently. This is a prime example of how the VFO can facilitate communication between advisors and family members located all over the globe.

Finaplex also has a multi-currency application which holds all investments in their native currencies and automatically performs the conversions necessary when appropriate. Another part of the system sends liquidity alerts such as a bond that is about to be called or market alerts such as ratings changes. This allows advisors to manage clients' cash flows, monitor task fulfillment, and perform other time saving and service enhancing functions.

Summarizing the technology platforms

These applications are not exclusive to SS&C or to Finaplex or any number of other financial technology firms.[10] ADVISOR*port,* Integrated Decision Systems (IDS), and many others have similar applications, but few financial technology firms that previously have not catered to the family office market have the continuity or extensive capability of firms such as SS&C and Finaplex. That may seem like an obvious statement, but its importance lies in the fact that outside firms are beginning to work with more and more family office clients; therefore, their need to develop family office level applications is pressing.

On the financial services side, financial technology firms have concentrated on the financial services business, providing little incentive or capability for consultants to address the needs of wealthy clients outside of the traditional boundaries of that industry. But things are changing, and the need for such technological capability is becoming more urgent. As it stands, firms such as SS&C and Finaplex have a very attractive window through which to attract aspiring wealth optimization consultants and their firms. Meanwhile, the tech firms on the financial services side are preparing an effort to catch up to such broad capability, although the goals for bridging the gaps are only beginning to be focused upon, and the scope of services that those goals will encompass is not yet known.

On the financial services industry side, IDS provides the most comprehensive portfolio management solutions. Founded in 1981, the firm offers automated portfolio management, accounting, performance measurement, online compliance, and trading systems both domestically and globally. IDS supplies a broad cross-section of firms including investment banks, brokerage firms, mutual funds, money managers, securities lenders, and SMA sponsors. Its modular and scalable models facilitate connectivity for both large firms and small niche businesses. The firm offers a single database solution to provide STP and automation.

IDS' portfolio management interfaces include STP services, information services, custom interfaces, and general ledger services. Tax optimization and multi-currency applications are ideal existing service offerings for family office level wealth management. The firm is positioned across most financial industry market segments and could incorporate a complete range of family office capabilities either to provide a seamless solution or to become an outsourced solution through the services with which it interfaces. Thus, the firm believes it is a leading potential bridge from the back office application side of the financial services industry to the family office service arena.[11] Rival CheckFree Investment Services is also preparing to address the family office market and has built a stronghold across the financial services industry by acquiring such pioneering legacy firms as Security APL and Mobius to create a well-rounded offering.

ADVISOR*port* is a front-end platform designed specifically for investment consultants, and its services are designed around the consulting process used by top financial services industry consultants (tomorrow's wealth management consultants). Its platform is web-based and its clients are primarily premier banks, independent and regional broker/dealers, trust companies, and small advisory firms. The platform can be private labeled for any client and has a wide range of service offerings for investment consultants on the financial services side.[12]

Firms such as IDS, CheckFree, and ADVISOR*port* are each recognizing the need to address the family office level of service offerings. Some of their current clients are family offices and with families looking to set up new SFOs and MFOs, and advisors beginning to start MCFOs, the next logical distribution channel points in the direction of family wealth management. However, companies such as SS&C and Finaplex have a definite edge in the family wealth arena. The next few years will be intriguing to watch as the development of firms addressing these markets proceeds. Brokerage firms, private banks, regional firms, and investment boutiques all want a share of the family wealth management market.

Each of these firms provides valuable offering for the wealth optimization consultant; however, no one firm provides everything required. The family office focused firms have the advantage of being a portal through which all services can be accessed, if not actually providing all of those services themselves. There has been more development on the side of firms wishing to address the needs of family office advisors than with technology firms catering to the financial services industry's needs. As the two industries converge, savvy technology firms will begin addressing the needs of the other market, which would be an ideal development for wealth optimization consultants from the standpoint of gaining access to the entire slate of services quicker and through a more seamless structure.

Another facet of this convergence of services is represented by firms like Family Office Metrics, LLC, that serve as impartial technology consultants to build a customized, seamless offering. There is a plethora of smaller firms that specialize in one particular service segment or another and who are well-suited for such offerings. They compete by not trying to be all things to all advisors, but instead offer higher, more specialized quality. Performance reporting is a particular area that is receiving great attention and, as Lydian Wealth Management purports, can be an easy marketing entrée for wealth optimization consultants.[13]

However, effective use of this tool can only be implemented against the backdrop of delivering quality advice and guidance. This point is aptly made by Ron Surz, CIMA, and president and CEO of PPCA, Inc, a performance measurement and attribution firm:[14]

> The craft of delivering advice and guidance (by consultants) has been evolving quite nicely…. The deliverer of advice has progressed from report schlepper/salesman to trusted advisor. In many ways, the consulting industry has compensated for its lack of advancement in the quality of advice by significantly enhancing the delivery of that advice. Now, it's time for clients to get the quality goods.

Surz goes on to cite that the predominant evolution of consulting within the financial services industry has occurred, particularly in light of the revolution in technology, in efficiency, but not in the value provided to the client. Lower fees may be the only exception to this lack of evolution in provision of value and quality advice. 'The frontline consultant appears with a kit of the same old packaged solutions,' adds Surz. His comments complement those of Frank L. Campanale's below and Jean Brunel's (see Chapter 4) in identifying the huge gaps and misplaced focus in today's consulting model. According to Campanale:

> I see an awful lot of financial consultants hiding behind technology. They try to dazzle clients with multi-colored graphs and charts and the clients a) don't understand what they're seeing and b) don't really care about understanding it. If you want to use technology because it helps you manage the portfolio better, that's terrific. But if you're using it just to razzle dazzle the client, that's not a good thing.

Surz predicts three possible paths for the combination of investment advice backed by technology. The first will 'provide the best advice and guidance to the masses as a commodity'. The second will preserve the highly customized, cottage-industry focus on custom tailored solutions for the unique needs of individual clients or client families. The third will be extinction of firms and advisors who remain stuck and who refuse to see the opportunities before them.[15]

Technology case studies

A type of financial technology assistance that may be more directly helpful to wealth management consultants is the technology consultant. Firms such as Family Office Metrics, LLC are much like open architecture investment consultants – they are completely objective and have clients' needs firmly in focus. Explains Jon Carroll, Family Office Metrics co-founder:[16]

> We work with families to provide solutions for them. We have to see what their objectives are, not only in the current timeframe but also looking out three to five years so we can get them up the curve quickly on the range of solutions from the standpoint of technology and process. If they have people issues, we can also help them define roles and responsibilities.

Basically, the firm identifies the current situation of the client and recommends a technology platform based on the client's vision of the future. Once the possible solutions have been identified objectively, the firm leads the implementation project and fine tunes the platform to fit the client's specific needs.

Family Office Metrics also advises wealth optimization consultants wishing to enter the family wealth service arena. Carroll points out the additional technology needs for such consultants and the best way to use them in setting up service components designed for wealthy families. For example:

> There's a whole separate piece of accounting that goes along with the trust, trustee support, and administration aspects of trust accounts. Trust accounting is essentially a requirement that you separate income and principal cash. There are two types of beneficiaries – one to the principal income and another to the principal cash. And those can be two different people in two different periods of time.

By the very nature of the fiduciary responsibilities inherent in managing trust accounts, conflict can easily arise. The trustee must be accountable for all cash flowing from the trust in the forms of expenses and gains, realized or unrealized. This can be a frequent point of contention between family members and must be dealt with by the wealth management consultant. Trusts are quite common in the family wealth business; having the proper technology to perform these important trust functions is essential to any consultant working with family wealth.

Many families question the need to upgrade if their systems are adequately serving the needs of current family members. Factors such as resentment of the governance system that absolutely must be in place in order to maintain organization within the business of managing the family assets can raise questions regarding cost and staffing requirements. 'Why does it cost so much? Why do we have to have these people? Why do you want to upgrade that?' are frequent questions Carroll encounters with family office clients.

Family Office Metrics has no platform; it builds the best platform using the best technology software and services available relative to the needs of the client. 'The model for a family office is really the small business model,' adds Carroll. 'It's mom and pop doing things on the side – that's the way they've always done it – and it's all in their heads rather than institutionalized like a business.' Carroll's work focuses on the procedures end of the office since the customization segment centers around those functions: 'We help them understand what it's costing them to do things and how that compares to what they'd have to pay if they just went out and bought those services in the market-place.' As noted above, a discussion of technology without tying that discussion to high-quality client service would be fruitless. The following case studies offer an in-depth illustration of the technology/quality service connection.

Case study 1

A case in point involves a patriarch who has always been in total control of the family's assets. He is getting older and is concerned that no one else in the family knows how to carry on what he has been doing. This patriarch is the center of all family wealth activity. He likes being in control and does not really want to share information with anyone else. But he also realizes the procedures he has been performing must be institutionalized if they are to continue after his death.

Carroll's first recommendation was for the patriarch to hire a chief investment officer (CIO) for the family: 'We had to establish procedures so that other people could handle the wealth as he had.' From an investment standpoint, the patriarch had multiple concentrated positions resulting from the way he built the wealth in the first place. He would grow companies, then sell them at the right time to larger entities, increasing the value of his own stake in the original company. This process created the concentrated positions, which any prudent CIO would immediately sell in order to provide diversification for the portfolio of assets.

Such a move can be of significant importance to the family office, creating huge tax, asset allocation, trust, and other ramifications. A CIO had to be found who would be able to coalesce the data so that it would make sense to the rest of the family while the patriarch was still alive and so there would be some continuity after his death. The patriarch needed better controls over reporting and better interfacing of information for outsourced advisors, all of which leads to data aggregation. Non-financial assets such as partnerships and art collections were entered into the system after the various brokerage statements and investment, tax, and other information was entered. This enabled the creation of a consolidated statement for the entire portfolio of family assets.

Next came the automation of bill-paying and keeping the general ledger. Explains Carroll:

> We used Pertrack to set up the investment process to capture, file, and document all the information. The data from Statement One (used to aggregate the data) was then extracted along with the information from Pertrack and fed into QuickBooks. QuickBooks was set up as the general ledger, which automatically paid the bills. The patriarch had multiple bank lines of credit that he had used throughout his life, houses, boats, planes – there was all kinds of stuff.

In this case, simple tools were used and the process was the focal point rather than the technology, but the technology provided the backbone for setting up the systems and organizing the family office. This reorganization enabled the family to enhance the work done by the financial advisor, the CPA, the attorney, and all other advisors involved.

Case study 2

In another case, Carroll helped a family convert to more integrated software. Family Office Metrics undertook the data conversion and set up the websites for the MFO so that its clients could access all of their reports online. The software provider did most of the actual work, but Carroll's firm operated very closely with the MFO to make sure the procedures were implemented effectively and fine tuned in order to provide complete support for the MFO's needs and business objectives.

Case study 3

This case involves a financial advisor wishing to become an outsourced chief investment officer. 'In such a case,' says Carroll, 'the advisor has no interest in doing bookkeeping, record keeping, or even hand holding – they want to outsource all of those services and really just be the CIO to the family office.' Carroll says there are a number of 'handshakes' that must be accomplished in order to smoothly fit the services of the CIO into the family office structure.

Obviously, the family had been dealing with a number of brokers up to that point as well as with managers of illiquid investments. The new CIO must develop a grasp of the entire asset portfolio as solidly as that of the family office's. As a new member of the team, care must be taken to ensure that the CIO receives all of the information required to do his or her job. The family office may initially put up barriers to including the new CIO as a fully fledged team member, compromising the CIO's ability to perform successfully. A triangular relationship automatically exists between the new CIO, the family, and the family office. Effective and appropriate communication is key to the CIO's success.

'A family member may wish to see his positions every Monday morning. If the CIO says reporting is only done on a monthly basis, then that's a disconnect right there,' says Carroll. So there are significant challenges for the wealth management consultant who wants to be an outsourced CIO encompassing communication, reporting, data and information flow, and a host of other factors. Family Office Metrics facilitates those 'handshakes' by systematizing them for wealth management consultants wishing to enter the outsourced CIO function. This function is appealing to wealth management consultants who want to focus on providing CIO services but who do not wish to become involved in a fully fledged family office.

Case study 4

Lastly, there is the wealth optimization consultant who wishes to create a multi-client family office. This case study borrows somewhat from the future, but that future is close enough to address as a realistic option. The consultant may wish to take her 60 top client relationships and open an MFO to provide a deeper and broader level of services for these families. Initially, technology is key. The platforms chosen must be cost-effective, yet must provide the depth and range of services required by an MFO, with the wealth management consultant serving as chief advisor.

The consultant can (a) hire a technology consultant such as Family Office Metrics, (b) use a virtual web-based system and outsource back office functions through firms such as SS&C or Finaplex, or (c) become part of a smaller MFO which has already developed its technology platform and through which the wealth management consultant can outsource other services such as philanthropic advice, wealth psychologists, trust services, estate planning, and tax optimization.

Option (a) obviously exists currently and may be a viable choice for consultants who have already set up a functional profit and loss (P&L) within their large financial institution employer. In most cases, such consultants (and their teams) will have purchased and (over a period of years) built their own systems fully customized for the services they provide to their clients. A technology consultant can review those systems and recommend the most appropriate technology services to fill in the missing parts.

Option (b) whispers of the VFO. Firms such as SS&C, Finaplex, and others[17] can currently provide an almost complete suite of services, and will be the first to offer comprehensive STP of the broad range of services required for involvement in the family wealth management arena. Private banks such as J.P. Morgan, some large financial services industry firms, and other technology firms have such platforms available with a variety of outsourced resources to provide what their platforms lack. This model makes it possible for an individual or a team of wealth management consultants to go out on their own, have total control over their practice, develop it into a viable business model, and distinguish themselves according to their particular niche or specialty.

Option (c) may also be very attractive, as it gives consultants control of their businesses but within a framework that they did not have to spend time or money setting up.

Preparing for future success

The aim of this chapter has been to create an overview of technology in both the family office and financial services industries. The purpose of such an overview is to obtain a better perspective on how technology is helping to shape the future of each industry, how the industries are moving toward each other in a variety of respects, and how the astute and forward-thinking consultant can take best advantage of the opportunities ahead. The case studies provide clear examples of what is possible now and how implementing the right technologies can serve advisors and consultants well as they transform their businesses.

The internet is enabling the development of a much more efficient and cost-effective platform of services to wealthy clients. It is also fostering better and more timely communication between family members and between the family and the advisors who serve them. Old legacy systems are still viable, but only in the function of developing and housing the data being used to provide financial services today. The family office industry looks at web-based technology in the same way, but on a much smaller scale. The need to purchase massive new systems and a plethora of software programs is past; better connectivity, communication, service provision, and operational capacity are vital offerings of web-based ASP delivery. The capabilities of web-based systems will not be fully available for several years, but the capabilities that are available, such as virtual communication and connectivity, are already helping today's aspiring wealth optimization consultants to build feasible services models that will differentiate them from the competition.

---

[1] Deloitte & Touche for The Money Management Institute (2002), *Operational Interfaces in the Separately Managed Account Industry*, p. 2 (August).

[2] According to Chris Davis, executive director, Money Management Institute (MMI).

[3] Horn, Greg, and DeAngelis, Steve (2000), 'Facing the Technological Revolution', *Trust & Estates,* June.

[4] SS&C Technologies, Inc (2002), *The Virtual Family Office*, February.

[5] Mrak III, Joseph (2003), 'Open Architecture and the SMA', *Waters*, February.

[6] Ibid.

[7] Gray, Lisa (2003), 'Will Standards Kill SMAs?', *On Wall Street,* March.

[8] Author's interview with Ward McGraw, Senior Vice President, SS&C Technologies, Inc, September 2003.

[9] Author's interview with Mike Cagney, CEO, Finaplex, September 2003.

[10] See Appendix for a list of firms that provide various technology platforms.

[11] IDS information obtained from www.idsnet.com and a personal interview with John Simpson on 11 September 2003.

[12] ADVISOR*port* information obtained from www.adviserport.com and a personal interview with Steve DeAngelis in September 2003.

[13] Author's interview with Scott D. Welch, managing director, Lydian Wealth Management, October 2003.

[14] 'Investment Consulting Craft Trades Up to 21st Century: Update', by Ron Surz, CIMA, president and CEO, PPCA, Inc, *Senior Consultant,* January 2004.

[15] Ibid.

[16] Author's interview with Jon Carroll, MBA, CPA, co-founder and managing director, Family Office Metrics, LLC, September 2003.

[17] See Appendix for a list of firms that provide virtual platforms.

Chapter 7

The feasibility of the new family office models: costs and how to manage them

Introduction

What will it cost to stay ahead of the competition in the new environment? What is the best business model to adopt based on the market tier and the platform of services to be provided? Answers to these questions are an essential part of the wealth optimization mix. If high-level advisors and investment management consultants are to expand their services to optimize the wealth of their clients, they must also be able to optimize their own wealth and resources. The two sides of the equation must balance for both entities to profit. An accurate assessment of the costs is best accomplished by examining the expenses involved in setting up and running the versions of the business models wealth optimization consultants choose to employ. The employment of the models outlined in Chapter 3 can be highly customized. Just as there are as many single family offices (SFOs) and multi-family offices (MFOs) as there are families, there will be as many wealth optimization consulting models as there are consultants. Therefore, the most pragmatic information this chapter can provide is an outline of the costs and feasibility of the specific services available rather than a specific cost comparison connected to each type of model. The outline will be based upon the service costs, the compensation structures, and the operational capabilities available today. It will be up to the consultant to choose the best combination for his or her needs.

The trend of increasing wealth management costs is no secret, and there are several factors behind this rise. With asset levels diminished as a result of the 2000–03 bear market, expenses have received much greater attention. This explanation runs true across both industries. While investors were receiving the exceptional 30% and 40% returns of the late 1990s bull market, such expenses were virtually ignored. With those returns brought down to earth during the 2000-03 bear market, expenses were suddenly paid much more attention. But there are many other factors at work, including the demand for a broader range of services, the higher costs created by gaps in straight-through processing (STP) on the technology side, costs of upgrading to web-based systems, costs of trying to keep and attract top-level practitioners, and the multiple layers of advisors employed by the family office.

Operating a full service SFO can easily run to US$1 million per year, which, on an asset base of US$100 million, translates to 1% of assets in addition to fees paid to money managers. Such costs are a major factor in the growth and popularity of MFOs. According to TAG Associates' Stan Pantowich:[1]

> Having this incredible depth of infrastructure that supports many people makes us more cost-efficient. Costs decrease based on the size of assets, so there's no question we can be more efficient than an SFO because we spread our costs across a broader asset base.

For that reason, families have become willing to sacrifice at least part of their privacy in order to gain family office services at a price they can afford. And for SFOs who have opened their doors to other families, great economies of scale can be realized by sharing the services the family office provides, even if more staff must be hired to adequately serve the additional client families.

For financial services industry firms, fees on separately managed account (SMA) business began at 3% in the late 1970s. The fees for the money managers ranged from 50 basis points to 1%, while the fees for the advisors ranged from 1–2%. As technology advanced and online trading became available, commissions from the bread and butter transaction business of financial services industry firms suffered severely. Industry firms turned their attention to SMAs and asset-based fees as they realized the commission-based cash cow's days were numbered.

From the investor perspective, asset size makes a big difference. Most institutional accounts pay 40–75 basis points for equity management and around 25–40 basis points for fixed-income management. Those are direct charges to the clients with no added fees for sponsor SMA programs. Individual investors with smaller assets may pay as much as 200–225 basis points depending on asset size and the level of service they demand. There is not a lot of spread from one manager to another. Fees may range from 2–2.25% for professional management combined with the fees for the services offered through the sponsor firm's SMA or unified managed account (UMA) program. Accounts with larger assets usually pay lower combined fees on a declining scale.

A significant portion of these costs have been due to the technology gaps in STP. Those costs will be reduced as solutions for those gaps are found, but such solutions will be implemented in stages, not all at once. The important point is that this is indeed happening, as evidenced by the recent announcement by CheckFree APL[2] regarding its Galaxy automated transfer of execution prices among managers who use CheckFree APL systems and DTCC's announcement of better work flow connectivity in SMA account set-up.[3] These new services represent a direct hit on the high operational costs that have plagued the SMA side of the financial services industry. The wake-up call by the Association of Investment Management and Research (AIMR) (see Chapter 6) expedited efforts to create such services and also expedited the development of a common protocol. In the same DTCC press release, Money Management Institute (MMI) executive director Christopher L. Davis states that DTCC will operate as a new hub for processing and communications and will be using the new business notification procedures standards recently developed by the organization. DTCC's wide reach throughout the industry makes it the only logical choice to serve in such a capacity.

The MMI has led the way in addressing the technology gaps that have plagued the SMA side of the financial services industry. The most immediate difference will be in the amount of time it takes to set up an SMA account. Because of the hundreds of accounts handled by SMA sponsor firms, it previously could take up to two weeks to get all the information entered, accounts set up at both the sponsor and money manager firms, and trades executed. This cumbersome process was not only innately costly, it was costly from a market opportunity standpoint for investors wishing their asset allocations to be implemented. With the streamlining of operations made possible by these new services, that time gap will decrease significantly, eliminating errors and other costs related to human intervention and eliminating duplication between sponsor and portfolio manager. Such developments are obviously important factors in service provision and margin enhancement possibilities for sponsor firms.

These cost savings will feed through to the family office industry as well, enabling staff reductions on the financial services industry side, which will translate into lower fees for family offices. Investment is still the largest and most costly component of the family office service platform. These announcements from CheckFree and DTCC will also facilitate the commoditization of services already occurring in the financial services industry.

Family office industry advisors and professionals most commonly get paid for their advice, not for product. The financial services industry compensation model is the exact opposite. But as services become commoditized, financial services industry professionals will increasingly look for ways to be paid for the advice they provide instead of for the products they sell.

Considerations in setting up a new family office practice

It is important to remember the different types of assets comprising the family wealth and the services required to optimize them. The combination of human capital, social capital, intellectual capital, and various forms of financial capital are intimately intertwined with each other. Therefore, treating any one of them autonomously is an inadequate approach.

A family's human capital encompasses all family members, the family office staff, and all the advisors, including the trustees and boards of directors. These are the sources of capital needed to organize, manage, and monitor the balance of the assets.

A family's standing (social capital) can have a great effect on its success and the influence it can wield in its local, state, national, and even international communities. Despite the possibility that family operating businesses may have a checkered history regarding the way they built their wealth or the manner in which they treat employees, companies such as Dupont, Ford, Forbes, Microsoft, and others also have affected people's lives in any number of positive ways. Perhaps in an effort to emulate the Rockefellers' efforts to change the tainted image that building the wealth created, their founders' philanthropic efforts have helped find treatments and cures for disease and created hopeful possibilities for people who had none. People of such standing run for office and are influential in legislation that can affect the global population as well as the national. Universities name buildings after people who donate sizable sums for their projects; hospitals name wings; cities name libraries and streets.

Intellectual capital underpins the financial capital that is created; it, like the social and financial capital, gets passed on to heirs and its continuance and growth depends upon how it is managed and put to work by each generation. New ideas or new takes on old ideas are the fodder with which entrepreneurs create wealth. The growing popularity of leaving the major portions of inherited wealth to charity could also contribute to the creation of new companies through the intellectual capital of ambitious heirs.

Assessing each of these types of capital is invaluable to the successful management of family assets. The key to working with ultra-wealthy clients is to be concerned first and foremost with *their* needs, not with what advisors or consultants can provide for them. All industry advisors are on a quest to find the right mix that will attract the ultra-wealthy, and the quest may or may not be rooted in fertile soil. As a result, many family office models and semblances of family office models are springing up. Each tries to send clients the same message: 'We provide the comprehensive, integrated services you are looking for.' Brokerage firms, private banks, independent advisors, and various entities promoting themselves as MFOs are collectively going after the same market – the ultra-wealthy. With more entrepreneurs creating successful businesses and with the greatest wealth transfer in history already in process, that market appears even more lucrative than in the past.

For those who wish to become wealth optimization consultants, the number of options becoming available from a cost standpoint are increasing daily. As mentioned in Chapter 4, many early entrants to the SMA side of the financial services industry spent inordinate amounts of money building their own systems because those of the firms they worked for were inadequate to serve the more customized needs of their clients. In developing their own technology systems, many of these entrants mirrored the proprietary nature of the systems of the large firms that housed them. As a result, these consultants will have to do their own technology upgrades in order to maintain the level of customization they have traditionally provided for their clients.

Early on, these consultants subscribed to the same software system vendors now used by the large firms: Zephyr Associates, Inc for performance analytics; CheckFree's Mobius for manager search capabilities; and Ibbotson for asset allocation programs, sector analysis, and other basic tools.[4] As these services become commoditized, these 'pioneer' consultants will have ever more streamlined and efficient services at their fingertips.

Technology advances and the commoditization of services will place new entrants into the wealth optimization field on a level plane with their pioneer colleagues. Set-up for a new practice will become easier, faster, and will have lower initial costs as well as lower ongoing operational costs. But the most important aspect of these developments will be the change in the way consultants are paid. These consultants will be able to use state-of-the-art financial services industry technology and services, but will be paid for their advice and the service they provide to their clients, not for the products they use in their SMA programs. They will increase assets under advisement and will realize economies of scale through increased assets, not necessarily an increased number of clients.

Costs of becoming an independent wealth optimization consultant

The costs of setting up an independent practice today are much lower than they were two or three years ago. Also, independent advisors and consultants have many more service options available. In the recent past, third party separate account platform providers such as Lockwood Advisors, Inc, Brinker Capital, or ADVISOR*port* offered complete service platforms including front and back office capabilities such as asset allocation software, manager search assistance (or, most often, a pre-screened list of managers), and proposal generation programs. Such offerings would cost from US$25,000 per year upwards. Of course, the actual cost is based on the level of services provided and the US$20,000–25,000 price level has been fairly cost-effective considering the access, products, and services these independent advisory offices receive.

On the family office industry side, companies like SS&C and Finaplex offer the same front-end and back-end services plus the plug-in website communication services discussed in Chapter 6 for either the same or much lower prices – again, based on the level of service subscription. According to Finaplex's CEO, Mike Cagney:[5]

> You can look at Morningstar's Portfolio Xray which has some uptake among independent advisors and which offers a subset of the services our platform provides. It also has some things that live

outside our platform, so it's not a direct apples-to-apples comparison, but they have a price point of between US$2,000 and US$4,000 per year per user.

Such a price point is affordable to enough registered investment advisors (RIAs) and independent advisors to make it a feasible offering for Morningstar says Cagney:

> For the same kind of technology platform, a company like SEI will charge a little more than the Morningstar fee but they charge per advisor rather than for the total relationship. So if there are five advisors in the firm, you may be looking at US$20,000 or so per year. But you also may have other capabilities available.

Cagney says that price points within the industry are still difficult to identify specifically due to the range of service capabilities available and the traditional margin gaps that have existed between providing services to large firms with billions of dollars in assets and providing services to small RIA firms that can only afford to pay a few thousand dollars per year for fewer services. That picture is changing, however, and developments such as CheckFree APL's new electronic trade execution price service and DTCC's account opening and maintenance services will rapidly decrease the costs in these areas.

According to Cagney, Finaplex can provide an independent advisor with all the set-up services needed for US$5,000–10,000 depending, of course, on the range of the services subscription. And as he pointed out earlier, some of the larger third party providers may have other services they provide at the US$20,000 or greater level.

> For example, if we have a critical mass of users, we can go to someone like PFPC [a major pooled investment services provider and recent acquirer of ADVISOR*port*] and ask to distribute their funds directly through our platform. However, we can potentially provide a much less expensive, more direct medium for the end-user to have access to product – and open architecture product, not from just one company like PFPC.

Cagney continues by illustrating the costs of going to other distributors who charge 25–40 basis points for access to their product and service platforms: 'By reaching critical mass with your service platform, you have a wonderful product distribution capability that's consistent with complete open architecture that individual advisors want.'

The key to profitability in both industries, says Cagney, is to build long-lasting, high-multiple subscription revenue. Such consistent revenue increases forecasting ability and a consistent business model, which is significantly more important to service provider firms today than the enterprise licensing revenue focus of the past. From that standpoint, firms like SEI and other third party platform providers are beefing up corporate strategies toward capturing the independent, family office focused market.

For wealth optimization consultants, this is good news. More focus on providing family office level services will enhance service provider choices and lead to the commoditized 'pick and choose' control being handed to consultants who wish to go out on their own. Cost efficiency will continue to improve and consultants will be able to charge more for their expertise and advice as clients realize the value they bring and the quality of service they will receive.

ices available to consultants

ces for wealth optimization consultants include technology and operational con-
Family Office Metrics, LLC, which helps firms create customized, cost- and
ient platforms from the variety of applications and resources available. Since the
firm is so familiar with the needs of the family office, it provides a more robust consulting
offering to help wealth optimization consultants maximize their entry into the family office
service segment.

Services offered by the Family Office Exchange (FOX) include the Buyer's
Exchange, which is a consortium designed to help family offices and their advisors find
'best of breed' service providers and offer a discount on their service fees. The services
available include a hedge fund database, a cash management resource, tax-efficient index
portfolio management, private placement life insurance, and discounts on a variety of
family office software packages.

Financial services industry technology vendors such as IDS, ADVISOR*port,* CheckFree
APL, and others (a list is provided in the Appendix) are also looking to address the family
office market. Some of these firms are focusing on the private banking aspect of family
wealth management, while others (like IDS) are opening their services to the growing independent RIA market.

Total control

It seems clear from this review that wealth optimization consultants will soon have the ability to totally control the cost-efficiency and service offerings of their businesses. Most importantly, they will have access to the same level of services previously exclusively offered by
large financial services industry firms. The continuing development of web-based applications and service offerings will make the virtual family office (VFO) a more realistic and
comprehensive platform through which wealth optimization consultants can function as chief
advisor for the family, wealth manager for the family and for wealthy individuals, single service provider for families, or any number of other service combinations they choose. As technology develops to eliminate the bottlenecks that currently besiege the money management
service component – which is why these announcements from CheckFree APL and DTCC are
so important – wealth optimization consultants can look forward to substantial capability
enhancement over the next five years.

The capability for wealth optimization consultants to serve as an objective, overall team
leader for the range of advisors needed by wealthy families will be facilitated by the ability
to outsource any services consultants do not wish to provide. This means that consultants will
have the capability to provide investment or wealth management services from an open architecture perspective, retaining objectivity in working with outsourced advisors and service
providers, and leading the entire advisory team, staff, and family members to the overall benefit of the family.

Meanwhile, Jon Carroll of Family Office Metrics advises sticking with the realities
of today:[6]

> If you want to build this kind of business, the cheapest way to build it is in reality, not virtually.
> Virtual is convenient and can be very project oriented, but if you're looking to build an ongoing

relationship business over the long term, it needs to be based on the old typical management employee and not virtual.

Carroll adds that virtual capability has more to do with delivery systems than relationships: 'If I'm a family, I have to be able to count on you to do whatever I need you to do, when I need you to do it. Otherwise, you're just another name in the phone book.'

Virtual means outsourced. The model detailed in Chapter 3 will eventually be able to streamline its operational costs, but other costs will need to be addressed. The fees charged by outsourced consultants such as wealth psychologists, philanthropy specialists, art and museum curators, and others must be factored into the overall service costs for the family and for the wealth optimization consultant. For example, prominent wealth psychologist Lee Hausner bases her fees on a daily consulting rate: 'I don't charge as a percentage of assets. I charge on a project basis. I figure out how many days the project will take – for example, if an assignment looks like it will require 10 or 11 days, I base my fee on that number of days.' Those 10 or 11 days may or may not occur in succession – most often, they do not. So consultants like Hausner can inform a wealth optimization consultant of the total fee for her services and the consultant can help the family plan appropriately to incorporate this into the overall cost structure of their family office services.

CPAs and attorneys have typically been paid on a billable hours schedule, but these advisors are also beginning to charge for their advice rather than for their time. So, as these fee structures change, it becomes possible for the wealth optimization consultant to set up a workable and feasible service program for clients, customized for their specific needs, using no more of the services of these outsourced providers than is needed.

Monitoring costs and creating a business

Detailed costings for setting up the various models of practice are admittedly difficult to pinpoint. According to FOX's Sara Hamilton, FOX is conducting customized studies around the cost issue through research with wealth advisory firms and owners to attempt to 'pattern out what that cost structure will need to be. We'll be able to sustain the boutique model by educating families about paying higher fees for advice and the value of a completely objective process. But it's going to take another three to five years for all of that to sort itself out.'[7] Articulating the value of the objective service process will determine the profitability of these boutiques. Hamilton continues:

> A lot of technology providers are currently looking at the question of what they need to build to become the back office for this type of advisor. For the first time since wealth management became a hot part of the market, these firms are indicating the market may be big enough to merit their attention. Over the last 10 years, we haven't had enough people building good integrated software tools.

That situation is already changing. More firms are looking at the wealth management market and are developing the tools needed to obtain their share. Meanwhile, established advisors are working at becoming more profitable and decreasing costs exponentially over the long term. The VFO is a start in this area. Today's practitioners will be helped to reinvent their practices as formal business entities with an assignable value (Chapter 11 explores this facet of practice reinvention in greater depth).

[1] Author's interview with Stanley H. Pantowich, partner and CEO, TAG Associates, September 2003.
[2] 'CheckFree Investment Services Launches New Galaxy Functionality For Automating and Simplifying Transfer of Execution Prices Among Separately Managed Account Sponsors and Managers', press release dated 10 November 2003.
[3] 'DTCC Plans Launch of Separately Managed Account Service', press release dated 27 October 2003.
[4] Author's interview with Rod Hennek (2001), managing director, Morgan Keegan & Co, Inc, July 2001.
[5] Author's interview with Mike Cagney, CEO, Finaplex, September 2003.
[6] Author's interview with Jon Carroll, MBA, CPA, co-founder and managing director, Family Office Metrics, LLC, September 2003.
[7] Author's interview with Sara Hamilton, founder and CEO, Family Office Exchange, September 2003.

Chapter 8

Family dynamics and governance

Introduction

This chapter focuses on understanding how demographics and generational attitudes and outlooks affect family office structures and functions. In any kind of financial or wealth management, operating in a vacuum without considering the effects of family attitudes, traditions, governance structures, ownership of the assets, decisions made regarding those assets, and the results of those decisions can cause more problems than solutions. Add the new dynamics of growing wealth creation by women and other minorities, particularly Hispanics and Asians, and the challenges financial advisors and consultants face today take on an entirely new dimension.

Temporarily setting the influences of women and ethnic minorities aside, consider the following scenario. A financial services advisor meets with a prospective client who has US$8 million to invest. Today is the third meeting with the prospect and the advisor has been asked to organize all the necessary paperwork. The time for the meeting arrives and in walks not only the prospective client, but also his wife and their two children. Ten minutes after the meeting commences, the wife and children are in conflict with the prospect about the way this money should be invested. The wife wants to put US$3 million in trust for the grandchildren; the daughter wants US$2 million to go to a charity in which she feels the entire family's involvement is important; the son wants US$2.5 million for a new business venture. The original prospect wants to invest the money with a variety of money managers in a sound investment program to ensure his legacy. With so many seemingly disparate objectives for the money, nothing gets signed and the family leaves without having made any productive decisions.

Obviously, our financial services industry advisor received a stark lesson on the impact of family dynamics, requiring here a fundamentally revised approach to the prospect and his family. Unfortunately, however, this case is quite typical, with the client's investment objectives considered relative only to financial assets, not to the family business or the roles other family members may play in decision-making and other important family functions. Non-financial assets and other non-correlated assets are rarely considered in asset allocation decisions; few consulting questionnaires ask how the manner in which accounts are set up may effect the client's overall situation or other members of the family. Professionals wishing to work with the wealthy must overcome this and other critical types of disconnect.

How family dynamics shape family office structure

Because family dynamics play an integral role in wealth management, a consequence is that family offices are organized and shaped according to the dynamics of the families they serve. Also, recent decades have seen service requirements become more and more complex as a result of prolific technological development, the creation of more sophisticated investment instruments, and the exponential realization of family wealth through initial public offering (IPO) and mergers and acquisitions (M&A) activity.

A huge array of choices emerges through such liquidation, creating complex considerations for the family.

- Should the money be dispersed among the family?
- If so, which family members get how much?
- Should the money be invested collectively?
- What about family members who want to take a large segment of their portions in cash now?
- How will that affect the founder's legacy?
- If invested collectively, how much 'say' does each family member have in investment decisions?
- Should the founder continue to carry the weight in decision-making until he or she is ready to pass the torch to the next generation?

Such choices, along with the growing number of family members, the increase in divorce rates threatening unplanned wealth dispersion, and the increase in the costs of services mean that many families are finding it more and more difficult to set up family offices.

Family dynamics play an integral role in every facet of the family office – its set-up, its functions, its governance, and its resulting success or demise. These dynamics are rooted in generational demographics. Whether it is the current generation, a combination of several generations living at the same time, or the legacy of a preceding generation, the governing generation's values, management styles, and outlooks on life rule the family and, therefore, the way the family business is conducted. The industrialists who created the initial wealth of the 'anchor' families of today and the post World War II generation (often called the GI generation) have until recently ruled family management. Now, the baby boomer generation is beginning to experience the largest wealth (and control) transfer in history in the midst of more choices than ever, more family members than ever, and a heavier management burden than ever.

Two population segments – the baby boomers and the millennials (also called generation Y) – hold the keys to the future of the family office. Baby boomers still have the greatest influential sway, but as they migrate from middle age into senior status, the millennials (born between 1982 and 2002) are bringing their own attitudes and outlooks to bear. The number of millennials exceeded the number of baby boomers in 1998, although their share of the total population still does not match the boomers' at the same age.[1] In fact, the rate at which the under-18 population is increasing has steadily diminished each year since its peak in 1990, falling by 17% by the end of 2002.[2] However, millennials are certainly not to be discounted. On the whole, this generation looks to be better educated, more affluent, more community minded, and more ethnically diverse than preceding generations.[3]

In the days of the industrialists, things were much simpler. There were only the immediate family, the parents, and siblings. There was only one controlling generation and it had only one 'boss' – the founding industrialist who had made the money in the first place. As subsequent generations were born, grew up, and began to take an interest in what the family wealth held for them, the founder sought to keep control to assure the money he had worked so hard to accumulate was not simply frittered away. But as the original generations passed on, heirs began to take control and multiple generational influences began to have impact. Today, as the baby boomers contemplate plans for their own legacies, there are many more family members to consider, many more issues to address, and a much greater need for qualified advice.

Significant changes in accepted roles of family members, life concepts, and what people can or cannot do at specific ages have naturally spilled over into family dynamics. As family members have grown in number, the wealth has grown in size, and investment options have become more numerous, the issues for families have created a greater need for structural guidance in the form of family governance. Issues surrounding the psychological aspects of wealth abound: whether to leave a full share of the wealth to less competent heirs or more to an heir with greater needs, how much to leave to family foundations and how much to leave to heirs, whether to include spouses of heirs at family council meetings, and so on.

The increasing influence of women and ethnic minorities is adding new dynamics, as these are the fastest growing wealth segments in global society today. Highly successful women entrepreneurs and women who inherit wealth through a spouse's death or a divorce are growing in number; ethnic minorities are also building assets quickly and may have different family traditions that influence the optimization of that wealth. Such complex issues have expanded the advisory list from the single trustee of the wealthy merchant to a trustee, bank, attorney, CPA, insurance specialist, investment advisor, philanthropy specialist, wealth psychologist, concierge, and other specialists – including cultural diversity counselors.

Indigenous generational dynamics

Exploring generational influences on the dynamics of the family and, simultaneously, the dynamics of the family office will help provide a picture of some of the neglected areas that need to be addressed by wealth optimization consultants.

The GIs

By far the largest and most powerful of past generational influences (before the baby boomers) were the GIs. They were, according to Howe and Strauss,[4] 'the confident and rational problem-solvers of twentieth-century America, the ones who knew how to get things done'. Members of the GI generation were between 17 and 34 years old when the Japanese attack on Pearl Harbor took place. The GIs were the children of the 'lost' generation – the generation most affected by the Great Depression – the wealthiest of whom were able to invest in the economy despite their wealth being cut in half (eg, John D. Rockefeller, Jr.), thus planting the seeds for the great wealth being passed on to the baby boomers. As the immediate benefactors of this wealth, the GI generation arguably gave new spirit to the United States with a 'never say die' attitude toward solving problems and an unprecedented collective energy. They contributed U.S. presidents from JFK to George Bush, Sr. – the longest domination of the White House by a single generation. The power and influence of the GI generation transformed every stage of life it encountered. But it often did so in a rigid fashion in an effort to secure the well-being of its progeny according to its own standards, thereby planting the seeds for the rebellious attitudes of the boomer generation.

GI generation influence

The GIs brought specific values to bear in the management of family wealth. In the context of the limited investment options available for individual wealth in the 1940s to the 1970s,

109

wealth management was relatively straightforward and uncomplicated.[5] The GI generation was accustomed to being in control without question. They were the leaders of the free world; the saviors of the world from Nazism. This 'unquestioned' control created family dynamics where children were kept in the dark about family wealth management. Family governance was in the hands of the patriarchs, who left everything in the hands of the trustees, who, as noted in Chapter 1, were not subject to very much accountability.

The silent generation[6]

The GI children, often called the 'silent' generation, came of age during the McCarthy era and around the beginning of the Cold War. It was given its name by a 5 November 1951 *Time* magazine cover story. The silents were a generation of outward conformity, afraid to overtly express their own views due to the impact of McCarthyism and the fear instigated by the nuclear threats of the Cold War. Early on, they followed in the footsteps of their GI parents, but later they would become more influenced by their baby boomer children, establishing the foundations for the social disruption of the 1960s and 1970s.

David Foot, another generational historian, calls the silents the most successful generation, citing 1938 as the most successful time to be born, reaping the benefits of the abundant employment opportunities created after World War II and contributing some of the great musicians and thinkers of the time. On the other hand, the silents were the only generation that did not produce a U.S. president.

The silent influence

Coming between the two strongest and most influential generations, silents have been torn between the influences of both the GIs and the baby boomers, which makes it easy for advisors to pigeonhole their attitudes and philosophies into either the GI or baby boomer camp. However, making such assumptions can cost advisors valuable relationships with the silents. As with any prospective client they meet with, advisors must put aside any preconceived assumptions and intently listen to the needs and objectives that silents will express regarding their wealth. Their 'silence' does not negate the fact that they are indeed individuals.

The baby boomers

The GIs overpowered their 'silent generation' children who were too young to participate in World War II and too old to be subject to the Vietnam draft. Then came the baby boomers, who strongly opposed the idea that any particular set of values was more valid than another.[7] The baby boomers came along with optimism and a determination to live life according to their own terms. Because of the size of their population segment, boomers received more attention than their GI predecessors regarding their changing attitudes, social mores, and outlooks on life and wealth.[8]

Members of the boomer generation have witnessed the effect that mammoth inheritances have had on some of their peers. Despite their self-absorption, generally rebellious attitudes, and the desire to do everything on their own terms, many baby boomers who have become the stewards of the family wealth focus more attention on the effects their wealth might have on their children and grandchildren. This new focus is driving the growing interest in philanthropy, which promises further changes in approaches to governance issues and advisory involvement in the education of future generations. The family foundation is becoming a type of training ground for family members as young as eight years old and parents are seriously pondering the wisdom of unconditionally leaving their vast wealth to their children and grandchildren.

The boomer influence

Boomers live much more fluid lives than their GI, linear, age-defined parents. But they are also more educated and experimental than their parents, so they are more willing to try new things. They are more directly involved and more tolerant of others' ideas. With medical advances extending life expectancies, the boomer generation will continue to be the major influence on the life stages through which they pass. Many are entrepreneurs who have started second businesses after leading successful careers at big companies. They are picking up where their GI parents left off, but putting their own stamp on the legacy, changing the meaning of retirement and seeking to remain vital and active for the remainder of their lives.[9]

The millennials[10]

Ironically, the formerly free-wheeling boomer generation has put into place the structure of greater responsibility that is shaping the potentially powerful millennial generation. This generation is generally optimistic and focused on doing a better job than their parents and grandparents.

As baby boomers march ever closer to senior status, the millennials are coming of age. The first millennials were 20 years old in 2002. Howe and Strauss propose that a new constellation of generations is formed every 22 years, creating a different view of life as it is being experienced during that time period. This constantly changing constellation of generations is making its own contribution to the sea change now occurring in the family office and financial industries.

The millennial influence

The millennials tend to be focused on teamwork, achievement, modesty, and good conduct. Rather than becoming spendthrifts with generous allowances, they are making more joint purchases with their parents and having greater influence on their parents' buying decisions. There were 76 million millennials at the end of 2002, one-fifth of whom had an immigrant parent. Including future immigration projections, they could be the first 100 million member generation, the most ethnically diverse generation, and the first truly global generation.[11] This blending of cultures will spill over into family office structure as greater portions of ethnic populations become more successful and as the millennials become the youngest generation yet to accumulate great wealth.

Millennials are the first generation since World War II to be confronted with higher academic standards than the generation preceding them and to show early signs of meeting those standards. They feel they have few adult role models and say that is one of the biggest challenges they have to face. They are civically inclined as a result of the listing of community service on high school graduation requirements, they volunteer at the library, and are getting increasingly higher SAT scores. Howe and Strauss predict: '... over the next decade, the millennial generation will entirely recast the image of youth from downbeat and alienated to upbeat and engaged – with potentially seismic consequences for America.'

111

The family governance ingredient

The need for structure is more acute amidst the sorts of change and upheaval discussed in the previous section. Businesses need governance, and when a family's wealth becomes large enough to be managed like a business, it also needs governance. Andrew Keyt, executive director of the Family Business Center at Loyola University Chicago, defines family governance as 'the systems, processes, and procedures that are put in place to provide accountability to the leadership of the organization'.[12] Governance also concerns decision-making – ie, who is to be involved in making decisions and who is not.

Lists of 'must haves' in governance structures have been widely touted in the family wealth industry, but families have different needs, along with different generational, relationship, legal, and ownership structures. Not every family needs a board of directors, an advisory board, and a family council. Some need one or two of those entities, others need all of them, others need none of them. But all families need some form of governance, if only to help keep family members informed. The waves of converging influences, generational forces, and the short-term crises that can result require internal strength for families to weather them well, and appropriate organization of family affairs and structures offer that strength.

Family governance can be as simple as having family meetings twice a year to discuss family issues, or as complex as having an entire representative governance structure including a board of directors, advisory board, and a family council. Family governance obviously has different components compared with corporate governance, and it also requires more flexibility in order to accommodate the differing needs of family members. A family may have goals and objectives other than managing the family wealth, such as perpetuating a legacy of philanthropy or certain educational traditions.

In its simplest form, family governance is the structure through which family decision-making occurs. Exactly who makes the decisions (a single person such as the founder, the family as a whole, or various levels of representatives for different family branches), and through what process, comprise the basic issues addressed by family governance. Barbara R. Hauser, special counsel to the Private Client Department of Cadwalader, Wickersham & Taft in New York, likens the various types of family governance structures to political structures: dictatorships, communal or consensus governments, and representative democracies. Translated into family governance, dictatorships are symbolized by the founding wealth creator or entrepreneur, communal or consensus governance is likened to a partnership, and a representative democracy is patterned after the representative democracy in the United States, with representatives chosen from family branches instead of autonomous states.[13]

The need for governance is based on a number of things: how well a family works together, how complex the ownership structures are, how many family members are involved in making the decisions, and what assets are considered communally owned (the family airplane, the yacht, multiple homes all over the world, etc). Family governance can be much more complicated than corporate governance because emotions, feelings of entitlement, damaged relationships, and other subjective factors are involved.

The type of governance needed is much more dependent on the complexity of the family and its assets rather than on the size of the family. If certain family members have a partnership in a family business, some family members are not as competent as others, or the family has 200 to 400 members, a more formal governance structure can add efficiency and objectivity to the operations and optimization of the family wealth. As Keyt explains: 'You can have a US$10 million estate that is extremely complex – more complex than a US$30 million estate for somebody else.' Other factors to consider in determining governance structure are the age ranges between family members and the addition of spouses and the determination of their roles.

Governance is not only about adding structure to the business of managing the family assets, it is also about fostering connections between family members. Family members on opposite ends of the age spectrum will have different views on life and different understandings of family dynamics. Several decisions must be made.

- Spousal involvement – should a spouse be included in making family decisions and if so, which decisions?
- How do other family members feel about including the new spouse?
- What management abilities and beliefs does the new spouse bring to the family?
- What role should an ex-spouse play in family decision-making, if any?
- How old should the children be before they are included in the decision-making process?

These are just some of the situations and questions that arise in determining family governance. Governance puts into place the structures through which the family communicates, decisions are made, and family business is conducted. It also sets up guidelines regarding such basic administrative functions as scheduling meetings and performing necessary but perfunctory tasks. There is an art to the process of determining the right governance structure for a family and that determination is usually made by the family leadership with perhaps one or two outside advisors. Keyt recommends families also talk to other families with successful governance structures in order to determine the best fit for their family. With only one-third of family wealth surviving each generational turn, an appropriate, sound, yet flexible governance structure becomes extremely valuable.

A certain amount of flexibility should be built in to any governance structure, corporate or family. Flexibility allows the freedom to make the quick decisions required to handle short-term crises – which are inevitable for any family or corporation – within the overall guidelines of the family structure. The intricacy of balancing such a complicated set of variables stemming from the number of generations in a family constellation, the legal structures of the assets, and differing goals and objectives of the family as a whole mandate the ability to adapt within an overall foundation of strength and continuity.

Concerns regarding governance

Regardless of governance structures, it is up to the family to guard and protect the family assets. This requires careful weighing of actions taken both during the lifetime of the family leadership and after. There are two methods of 'passing the baton' of control to advisors or succeeding generations: (a) delegation during the control of the current leadership; and (b) transfer through trusts when the time comes for handing off that control permanently. Effective governance is involved in both. Proper delegation and anticipation of unforeseen possibilities created by the method of transfer can affect the preservation of the wealth for as long as 100 years.

From the inside view of the family, establishing appropriate governance is not a simple task. The founding entrepreneurs may have a 'take charge' approach to management – that's

113

how they built the wealth in the first place. If they are still at the helm, it may be difficult for them to let go and allow delegated authorities to take over appropriate functions, even if those delegated authorities are family members. Younger family members who feel reticent to participate in family management until the founding entrepreneur is no longer at the helm miss the opportunity to learn under their tutelage, creating more problems for managing the wealth through successive generations.

Again, looking at the experiences of other families can help; it serves as a useful outside influence, placing their personal situations in perspective. By looking at the mistakes and successes of others, families can more effectively see how their decisions may affect their family's future. In addition, input from trustworthy outside advisors can help families see more clearly the talents of following generations. A movement for better education of family members at an earlier age also holds hope for assisting future generations in managing and preserving the family wealth. The wealth management issues families face today are the natural inheritance of the attitudes and actions of individual family members in the past. The new focus on education and a new openness to the feelings and talents of younger family members hopefully promises change for the better.

The objectives will be: preservation of the existing wealth, as well as additional wealth created by heirs; better use of that wealth toward the benefit of society as a whole; and better benefits for the heirs themselves. Every entrepreneur wishes his or her progeny to benefit from the wealth and station of life that has been created for them. Knowing which family members and outside advisors can be trusted with which delegated tasks and which tasks should be delegated in the first place can prevent problems down the road. Here's an example of what families can face as a result of improper delegation:[14]

> An entrepreneur has successfully turned around an inherited business and created significant wealth from it. His widow is elderly and the four siblings are in constant conflict with each other. One-third of the wealth is directly invested in eight privately owned companies as a result of the entrepreneur's primary interest of investing directly in other enterprises. He developed controlling interests in four of the eight companies and minority interests in the other four. A management team sits on the boards of six of the companies, and at least one of the siblings also sits on those boards. There is a lack of trust among the siblings, making the other three uncomfortable with the single sibling's presence on the management team. Despite their conflicts, the siblings do care about each other, which further complicates the situation. After much consideration, three of the siblings decide to extract their holdings from these companies over the next three years. The one sibling can stay involved, but will not be allowed to do so with money belonging to the other three. The original entrepreneur's attorney has been apprised of these plans, but the management team has not. How can the siblings inform the management team and effectively 'spruce up' the assets for sale without precipitating the team's departure?

According to Kenneth Kaye and Sara Hamilton, the problem in this situation lay in too much delegation to the siblings with too little choice about their involvement. There was no investigation of the siblings' skills or interests, which exacerbated the distrust among them. By including the siblings in the process early and getting to know each sibling's feelings about the family businesses, these problems could have at least been better managed, if not avoided altogether.

Siblings' capabilities also need time to be tested. The baby boomer generation is seeing the benefit in setting up training programs by establishing junior boards for family foundations. They are also trying to be more open to younger family members' opinions, and although baby boomers may not be 'getting there' just yet, they are making a sincere effort. Patience and cooperation among family members and outside advisors to whom certain tasks have been delegated are having a positive effect on upcoming generations. The positive attributes being developed by the millennials indicate the effort is working. How well all of this translates into the actual lives of millennials as adults remains to be seen, but the early evidence is quite encouraging.

The growing role of philanthropy

Philanthropy is an important issue for the families of today, and it affects the entire family office structure, from governance to education to managing the family's wealth. As stated earlier, the baby boomers have seen the folly of their peers who inherited massive funds and led empty, non-productive lives. As a result, more focus is being placed on educating younger family members about the value of wealth, how it should be used, and the place it holds in their lives.

Stanley H. Pantowich, a partner at TAG Associates, says he is seeing more and more clients considering leaving amounts as small as US$10 million to their children and giving the rest to charity.[15] Pantowich believes that people are coming to the conclusion that US$10 million may be enough, feeling that amount gives heirs the advantage of having money so they can buy a nice house and invest the rest, but also the incentive to go out and achieve more as a result of their own efforts.

This trend has been in place for about a decade (although US$10 million is hardly a typical figure), and for society as a whole it has the implications of changing the view of wealth and the people who have it. If huge portions of wealth are given away to worthy charities, it can benefit society at large and the world as a whole. Bill and Melinda Gates, Ted Turner, George Soros, and others are in the news regularly for the philanthropic choices they make.

But is limiting the wealth passed on to succeeding generations the proper way to accomplish this? With better education and training of upcoming generations as well as the family leadership, succeeding generations will be more capable of making wise decisions as adults. This need not preclude the emphasis on philanthropy, but questions arise: in some sense, do the heirs not have a right to the family wealth and do they not have a right to do with that wealth what they wish? Giving succeeding generations the option of philanthropy and good management after equipping them with the necessary tools to choose wisely is preferable to the sort of arbitrary path emerging with this trend. Predetermining heirs' lack of ability or interest by limiting the amount of wealth transfer is unfair and can foster ill feelings. A wiser choice might be to strengthen the relationship with these heirs so the patriarch's assessment may indeed be well founded rather than pre-emptively judgmental. Obviously, this is a question that must be explored by each individual family. But the tools of appropriate governance based on family dynamics and individual needs can be powerful aids in that exploration.

The family foundation is a very effective training ground for the younger generations, says Lee Hausner, Ph.D., an internationally recognized clinical psychologist, business consultant, and family wealth advisor and partner at DoudHausnerVistar Advisors. As she explains:[16] 'I like my families to practice with the next generation. They can collectively make decisions and they can create a model for decision-making within the context of philanthropy before having to handle decisions for the family business.'

115

Such training also allows the current generation to see the true capabilities the future family leadership may possess, helping them make wiser decisions about future governance and avoiding undue burdening of family members who do not want the responsibility. Philanthropy obviously carries the moral aspects of 'doing good' for others who are less fortunate and of properly positioning the meaning of wealth in future generations' eyes.

The wealth optimization consultant's role in governance

As an unbiased resource for investment management, service integration, and other wealth management services, the wealth optimization consultant is a prime candidate for membership on the family council (see Chapter 9). Advisors who are employed by large firms are most often viewed as having a bias toward the firm's products and services; as such, these advisors are typically not good family council members, although they may be asked to report regularly on the state of the portion of the family wealth under their advisement.

The growing influence of women and minorities

Along with the baby boomer generation came the civil rights and feminist movements. The civil rights movement laid the foundation for the multi-cultural society we have today, the influence of which on the family office will increase as the millennials become more involved in the family wealth. The feminist movement instigated slow but steady change in the way society and the corporate world view women. Women and minorities are now the fastest gainers in income, entrepreneurship, and spending.

Although the women's movement of today is less flamboyant than in the 1970s and 1980s, the percentage of women involved in the workplace, owning their own companies, and building significant wealth on their own is increasing. The portion of the U.S. female population in the workforce grew from 18.8% in 1900 to 59.8% in 2002. Today, women are the CEOs of two Fortune 500 companies – Hewlett Packard and EBay – while the percentage of Fortune 500 companies with female corporate officers has doubled since 1995. The establishment of women as a prominent component of the working population today allows women to place greater focus on their accomplishments and how those accomplishments open doors for, and influence the career decisions of, women all over the globe.[17]

This trend is important to high-level advisors and investment management consultants wishing to address the family wealth market for the following reasons.

- Women comprise 1.3 million of the top wealth holders in the United States.
- The combined net worth of those 1.3 million women approaches US$1.8 trillion.
- Women outlive men; therefore, they stand to ultimately inherit the US$41 trillion wealth transfer boom over the next 50 years.

For these reasons, women are being considered a target market by more and more advisors. However, women approach investing differently from men, although they have many of the same goals as men, and they want to be treated fairly and respected for their business acumen and investment knowledge.

In the case of ethnic minorities, the sheer number of these segments, their growth rates, and their desire to manage their newly acquired wealth wisely and in line with their personal objectives offer astute advisors and consultants yet another differentiating opportunity. The following factors are forcing, or soon will force, businesses, including financial services and family office businesses, to offer services directed toward ethnic markets.[18]

- The rate of growth for Hispanic wealth is greater than the rate of growth of wealth for the general U.S. population.
- The number of Hispanic households earning more than US$100,000 annually has risen 126% over the last decade.
- The majority of Hispanic businesses are family owned.
- There are approximately 3.7 million wealthy Hispanics in the United States, whose buying power is projected to be US$292.4 billion by 2006.
- The Hispanic population in the United States has increased by 57% since 1990.
- South Asians are the sixth largest growing population segment in the United States.
- Of that segment, over 200,000 are millionaires.[19]

The influence these minority markets will wield in the investment arena in the coming years is undeniable. Some independent advisors already target business women or women going through divorce or widowhood as a major market for their services, while a few large brokerage firms target the growing Hispanic and Asian markets. Many more will be compelled to follow their lead.

Conclusions

The purpose of this chapter has been to outline the influential factors (and their origins) that underlie all investors' motives, attitudes, and philosophies. These factors are the bedrock of every investment decision investors make. However, they are the most often ignored aspect of wealth management today.

The generational influences are summarized below.

- *The 'GIs'* are today's seniors. They are accustomed to being in control and may have kept the rest of the family in the dark about a variety of aspects of the family wealth, including the amount, its form, and other vital information. They view their values as the values of primary import and want control over their legacies through multiple succeeding generations.
- *The 'silents'* have been influenced by both the GIs and the baby boomers, creating a confluence of philosophies (sometimes diametrically opposed) and a lack of overt expression. This generation needs to be carefully handled. They may not volunteer the information wealth optimization consultants need in order to serve them appropriately; therefore, consultants must gently and skillfully open the door for them to express the needs and objectives they wish to be addressed. Careful attention to the dynamics of this generation within each individual client family can contribute valuable insights for consultants wishing to work with multiple generations within a single client relationship.
- *The 'baby boomers'* are the generation most advisors will readily identify with, since the majority of them are also of this generation. Ironically, advisors' and consultants' own version of baby boomer self-absorption may get in the way of building effective, long-lasting client relationships. This generation will continue to be the primary wealth owners for the next several years, although its concern for its heirs is an integral part of its overall approach to wealth.
- *The 'millennials'* are clamoring for education about and inclusion in the family wealth engine. They are an active and involved version of the silents, wishing to make their marks

117

on wealth decisions and stewardship. Families concentrating on providing such involvement for their millennial members will want advisors and consultants who will also consider such desires and efforts.

Within the last two generational influences are also the influences of women and minorities. Many minorities come from very conservative family traditions that still hold sway over multiple generations. Their international backgrounds and cultures must be considered in serving their wealth optimization needs. The growing impact of women on wealth creation and decisions is another factor that must be addressed within the scope of wealth optimization.

Understanding the importance of family dynamics involves a discovery process. Attitudes toward wealth differ with each successive generation and each generation's attitudes are shaped by its life experiences. These attitudes affect the relationships between family members, their advisors, and the manner in which the wealth may be optimized, which defines the role of the consultant.

[1] Concord Coalition (1998), 'The Truth about Entitlements and the Budget', *Facing Facts Alert,* Vol. IV, No. 8, 10 July, available at www.concordcoalition.org/facing_facts/alert_v4_n8.html
[2] U.S. Department of Health and Human Services (2003), 'US Birth Rates Hit Record Low', press release, 25 June, available at http://pregnancy.about.com/gi/dynamic/offsite.htm?site=http://www.hhs.gov/news/press/2003pres/20030625.html
[3] Howe, Neil, and Strauss, William (1991), *Generations: The History of America's Future, 1584 to 2069,* p. 31, Morrow/Quill; and (2000) *Millennials Rising: The Next Great Generation,* Vintage Books, available at http://www.lifecourse.com/books.html
[4] Howe, Neil, and Strauss, William (1991), *Generations: The History of America's Future, 1584 to 2069,* p. 28, Morrow/Quill.
[5] Author's interview with Sara Hamilton, founder and CEO, Family Office Exchange, September 2003.
[6] 'Silent Generation,' Wikipedia, updated 17 December 2003, available at http://en.wikipedia.org/wiki/Silent_Generation
[7] Howe, Neil, and Strauss, William (1991), *Generations: The History of America's Future, 1584 to 2069,* pp. 29 and 30, Morrow/Quill, available at http://www.lifecourse.com/books.html
[8] Ibid., p. 28.
[9] Author's interview with Maddy Dychtwald, co-founder, AgeWave (www.agewaveimpact.com), January 2003.
[10] Howe, Neil, and Strauss, William (1991), *Generations: The History of America's Future, 1584 to 2069,* p. 31, Morrow/Quill; and (2000) *Millennials Rising: The Next Great Generation,* Vintage Books, available at http://www.lifecourse.com/books.html
[11] Howe, Neil, and Strauss, William (2000), *Millennials Rising: The Next Great Generation,* pp. 14–16, Vintage Books, available at http://www.lifecourse.com/books.html
[12] Author's interview with Andrew Keyt, executive director of the Family Business Center, Loyola University Chicago, October 2003.
[13] Hauser, Barbara R. (2002), *Family Governance: Who, What, and How,* Institutional Investor.
[14] Based on the example on p. 4 of *The Process of Trusting* by Kenneth Kaye and Sara Hamilton, and 'The Big Dilemma for Wealth Creators: Delegating', by Sara Hamilton and Kenneth Kaye, *Trusts and Estates,* May 2003.
[15] Author's interview with Stanley H. Pantowich, partner, TAG Associates, September 2003.
[16] Author's interview with Lee Hausner, Ph.D., partner, DoudHausnerVistar Advisors, September, 2003.
[17] Gettings, John, and Johnson, David (2003), 'Wonder Women: Profiles of Leading Female CEOs and Business Executives', *infoplease,* 16 December, available at http://www.infoplease.com/spot/womenceo1.html
[18] 'Hispanic Wealth Growing Above U.S. Average,' *Business Wire,* 29 May 2003, available at www.hacer.org/current/USOO4.php
[19] Merrill Lynch (2003), 'South Asian Market Fastest Growing in the US', press release, New York, 14 May, available at http://www.ml.com/about/press_release/05142003-1_south_asian_pr.htm

Part III

Competitive advantages of expanding your practice

Introduction to Part III

Following the exploration in Part II of the basic ingredients for wealth optimization, the discussion now moves on to the process of expanding an existing high-level advisory or investment management consulting practice into a business that optimizes the assets of both client and consultant. This process includes:

- knowing how to attract the chosen wealth market tier;
- how to maximize the dynamics of the family to facilitate optimization of all four types of assets;
- knowing how to apply wealth management skills from a wealth optimization perspective;
- the step-by-step process of implementing the expansion; and
- the important role of marketing in building and maintaining optimal relationships with wealthy clients.

The effective expansion of an advisory or consulting practice into a wealth optimization business with an assignable value requires significant investment on the part of the aspiring consultant, but it is an investment that offers exponential rewards to those who make it.

Chapter 9

Education: the differentiating factor when applying wealth optimization skills in the new model

Introduction

Today's high-level advisors and investment management consultants are not fully equipped from a knowledge and educational standpoint to adequately serve the demands of the wealth market-place. This chapter provides an analysis of why education is a critical element, the industry organization educational venues available, the purposes they serve, and how they can be combined to offer the complete educational platform required for those aspiring to adequately serve the family wealth market as wealth optimization consultants.

Why ongoing education is essential

In order to understand why education is such a critical element, the need for a new advisory description must be explained. The terms 'wealth management' and 'wealth management consultant' are losing their significance as their meanings become diluted as a result of interpretations adopted to fit the marketing purposes of the moment. For that reason, a new term is needed to more accurately describe the functions and the type of advisor being sought by the wealthy. That term is 'wealth optimization consultant'. A wealth optimization consultant is a combination of wealth advisor, financial planner, investment management consultant, business consultant, and wealth psychologist.

Educational needs of the wealth optimization consultant include the following, all of which will be discussed in this chapter:

- basic wealth management skills;
- the complexities of wealth management including those involving financial and non-financial assets, family dynamics and wealth psychology, and the dimensions of optimizing the various types of family capital;
- the required new mindset and business focus on the pursuit of long-term, high-level compensation as opposed to monthly, quarterly, or even annual gross fee production; and
- the wealth optimization model.

The easiest way to gain an understanding of the role of the wealth optimization consultant is to look at tax management. All clients with significant financial assets need help managing their tax situations. The larger the assets, the greater the need. However, simply managing tax situations may not be as satisfactory as *optimizing* them by looking at every area that affects the tax liability of that client. These areas include, but are not limited to, the alternative minimum tax (AMT), state income taxes, real estate taxes, gift taxes, and estate taxes. Each type of tax affects the client's overall liability in a different way. By assessing the effects of each type of tax on the client's assets, financial or non-financial, on a year-over-year basis, the client's tax situation can be optimized, allowing the greatest protection of principal from tax erosion and the selection of the best times to pay the taxes owed.

Similarly, optimizing clients' *overall* wealth carries a much greater impact. Optimal investment of the family's four types of assets – human, intellectual, social, and financial – allows the best use of assets, securing the best managers for the assets, and the best performance results of the assets as they relate to each other. Every facet of clients' wealth is optimized for a particular purpose. A well-educated wealth optimization consultant also leads the team of advisors and other consultants in optimizing their services for the overall benefit of the family.

The educational elements necessary to properly equip today's financial advisors and investment management consultants are extensive, but, along with that education, a change in attitude toward the business of managing wealth is necessary. It is no longer adequate to simply manage a client's investments, and advisors who adopt this approach will fall behind consultants who are trained to optimize those investments within the context of the client's overall assets, including human, intellectual, and social assets. Advances in technology will make it easier for any facet of a client's wealth to be managed in a way that also optimizes the other assets. The provision of such depth of service will come to be expected by the wealthy, and the demands of the market-place caused by demographic forces will require consultants to be more and to deliver more.

The vast majority of wealth optimization consultants will spring from the investment management consultant pool since those consultants already have the necessary educational and experiential foundation. Those not yet certified will need the credentials, education, knowledge, and expertise offered by the Certified Investment Management Analyst (CIMA) designation, but they will also need more. To date, there has been minimal conversion from investment management consultant to the wealth optimization consultant needed by the family office industry. However, the opportunity for change and competitive advantage is significant. Investment management consultants across the board are questioning how they need to structure their businesses over the next three to five years. What should they be doing to take advantage of the opportunities available and to be properly positioned, and is what they are being told within the financial services industry going to guide them in that effort?

The answer is, 'only up to a point'. The financial services industry as a whole is not set up to properly equip consultants to remain competitive. A large step back must be taken as well as a much broader perspective; hence, the purpose of this book. The fundamental changes effected by the increasing sophistication of clients, the unsettling effects of the bear market, and the rapid advances in technological capabilities are tending to obscure the market realities. Only by stepping back to see the developments as a whole from the vantage points of both industries can today's investment management consultants transform themselves into the wealth optimization consultants of tomorrow.

Advisors and consultants may be shaking their heads at this point, wondering what more may be required of them after experiencing the ordeal of transitioning to fee-based compensation from transaction-based. And some – in fact, the majority – will decide that the first transition was enough. But a few who realize that the first transition will indeed not be enough will be compelled to take the logical next step, and it is this group who will receive the most compensation over the long term.

Educational resources

The resources available to those who plan to become wealth optimization consultants are increasing, and the Investment Management Consultants Association (IMCA) is a case in point. The organization conducts regular surveys of its membership to make sure its educational provisions are in line with industry demands. According to the 2003 IMCA Major Business Challenges Survey, consultants desire greater education in managing return expectations, implementing tactical risk management, and in building more personalized relationships. Practice management tools, technology tools and how to use them, staying current with industry trends, adopting a profitable business model, marketing proficiency, wealth management skills, and finding qualified partners and building knowledgeable, supportive staffs are all areas of educational interest to consultants. In response to these needs, IMCA is in the process of expanding its certification programs to include programs focusing on practice management, wealth management, qualified retirement plans, endowments and foundations, investment strategy, and alternative investments.[1] The fact that these areas are being recognized as essential additions to prime educational needs indicates the level of interest of investment management consultants in providing more and higher-quality service for their clients. A few short years ago, the list for additional educational needs was non-existent.

According to Richard Joyner, CPA, CFP, CIMA, and president of private wealth management at Tolleson Wealth Management:[2]

> When it comes to IMCA's wealth management program, one of the biggest benefits is its design. Specifically, it is designed to make investment consultants better at what they do by helping them understand the context of the decision-making process within a taxable client environment, because investment decisions are often made in isolation. This program attempts to expand the horizons of those consultants to understand that the decisions they make have a ripple effect. It gives them heightened sensitivity about those issues, whether it's their primary mission to identify and solve those problems. By becoming aware of these things, consultants can bring that awareness to the rest of the advisory team so that they can be part of the solution. That, by itself, is a huge step forward.

The IMCA's program primarily addresses traditional wealth management skills and is a valuable precursor to the educational opportunities provided by the Institute for Private Investors (IPI) and the Family Office Exchange (FOX). Investing in these programs will clearly and easily distinguish wealth optimization consultants from their product-focused competition.

According to FOX, there are four levels of wealth complexity – goals, strategies, structures, and processes. Basically these are the same areas that need to be addressed by investment management consultants, but the components within those levels on the family office side are eye-opening (see Exhibit 9.1). The overlap between steps in the consulting process associated with separately managed accounts (SMAs) are evident from the exhibit. It is also of interest to see the areas where investment management consultants are already stepping out of the traditional consulting model to address the broader needs of their clients. However, investment management consultants today are not equipped to address these areas to the degree required. There may be some who disagree with that statement, but taken in the context of the family office service model its truth becomes clearer. Exhibit 9.2 provides a further breakdown by FOX of the dimensions of wealth management.

Exhibit 9.1

Complexities of wealth management

Level of wealth complexity	Components
Goals	Family assets and liabilities
	Family member involvement
	Family governance
	Family member education
Strategies	Risk assessment
	Lifestyle goals
	Wealth transfer goals
	Investment goals and policy
	Philanthropy goals
Structures	Risk management and insurance
	Cash flow and liquidity management
	Tax planning and compliance
	Trust and partnership structures
	Asset allocation and manager selection
	Gifting and grant-making
Processes	Inventory of collectibles
	Bill-paying and record keeping
	Financial consolidation
	Custody and settlement
	Partnership accounting
	Performance measurement
	Foundation compliance

Source: Hamilton, Sara and Hillerstrom, Hakan (2002), Defining the Family Office, FOX Exchange, February, available at http://www.foxexchange.com/public/fox/news/industry_trends/Defining_The_Family_Office_IBC0202.pdf

Although the area of investment diversification is currently being addressed by top investment management consultants, the results of the services listed under this dimension in Exhibit 9.2 have a direct relationship with the other dimensions. To adequately serve wealthy families, consultants must be able to address the investment diversification dimension more fully and have a working knowledge of and be associated with outside resources designed to address the other dimensions. These investment management consultants seek to know more and to be able to build more personalized relationships with clients; becoming a wealth optimization consultant achieves these goals.

Incorporating family dynamics

The wealth optimization consultant must be educated in areas outside of the normally-thought-of parameters. The influence that family dynamics and the optimization of all areas of family capital have on the overall success of the family (and that of the wealth optimization consultant) cannot be over-emphasized. Regardless of the degree to which the wealth optimization consultant desires to be involved in the dynamics of the family, optimization simply cannot occur without their knowledge and consideration. The complexities of wealth

Exhibit 9.2

Six dimensions of wealth management

Dimension	Components
Family continuity	Clear governance process
	Family member involvement
	100-year goal development
	Leadership training and mentoring
	Stewardship of future generations
Strategic philanthropy	Clear mission and goals
	Strong leadership and governance
	Effective grant-making process
	Measurement of program effectiveness
	Proper policies and procedures
Risk management	Assessment of liabilities and risk
	Assessment of quality financial services
	Thorough due diligence process
	Review of cost of managing wealth
	Development of risk-reducing strategies
Investment diversification	Strategy and policy development
	Risk-adjusted asset allocation
	Manager selection and implementation
	Performance monitoring/analysis
	Strategy review and portfolio rebalancing
Integrated planning	Comprehensive financial audit
	Proactive income tax planning
	Appropriate wealth transfer strategies
	Optimal ownership structures (trusts, partnerships, etc)
	Financial training for owners and trustees
Lifestyle enhancements	Tax compliance
	Insurance coverage
	Trust administration
	Partnership accounting
	Consolidated reporting
	Bill-paying and cash flow management

Source: Hamilton, Sara and Hillerstrom, Hakan (2002), Defining the Family Office, FOX Exchange, February, available at http://www.foxexchange.com/public/fox/news/industry_trends/Defining_The_Family_Office_IBC0202.pdf

strike many emotional chords, and wealth itself is an emotionally charged issue. Of course, family offices traditionally operated around the investment component of the wealth, but, whether the influence of family dynamics has been acknowledged, it has always been present. Today's family offices are addressing every aspect of family wealth. Says DoudHausnerVistar's Lee Hausner:[3] 'There's much greater interest on the part of family offices in the human, intellectual, and social capital now.' There is also much more concern for the way in which family wealth affects the lives of its heirs. Providing access to a wealth psychologist can facilitate the wealth optimization process by creating a solid foundation upon which the consultant can build an optimal relationship between the family dynamics, the assets, and the entire team of advisors.

The role of the wealth psychologist is to discover the attitudes held by family members and make them all work together for the survival of the business, or the successful management of the wealth, or whatever the predominant family goal may be. Family conflict and unexplored attitudes toward the family's wealth can sabotage efforts toward the optimization of that wealth. This can be an outsourced function for the wealth optimization consultant along with other advisory functions that need to be included in the offering mix but which the consultant is either unqualified or has no wish to provide.

Wealth psychologists also play an important role in business succession. According to Hausner:

> Statistics show that only one-third of all family businesses make it to the second generation successfully. So we've lost two-thirds of the wealth already. Of the one-third that gets passed, only one out of eight make it to generation three. So there's a high mortality rate on family businesses and most of the time, it's because the succession process was not managed correctly.

The role of the wealth optimization consultant

Wealthy clients are clamoring for the optimization of all areas of their wealth. To date, this call is being answered by very few in the advisory world. This creates an unprecedented opportunity for those who would become wealth optimization consultants. No other type of advisor can sufficiently address the needs of wealthy clients. Hence, the wealth optimization consultant will have access to more of the assets of wealthy clients (not just financial assets), giving them more sway over, and more profit opportunities associated with, those assets. The critical realization is that the other three areas of wealthy clients' assets are as important, perhaps even more important, than the financial assets themselves. Those who gain the trust of wealthy client families to advise them on all sources of capital in a holistic, completely integrated fashion will ingratiate themselves to these families beyond any preconceived hopes.

The job of the wealth optimization consultant is not to handle everything for the family. Rather, it is to oversee as many areas of the family wealth as may be pertinent to the overall welfare of the family and make sure they are managed optimally to achieve the goals and objectives of the family. In a family office there are multiple goals and objectives, and the wealth optimization consultant must assess and align them so as to achieve the major objectives of the family as a whole.

Families primarily look to the family office to provide guidance in all matters of interest to the family, but family offices can serve many different functions. According to the IPI's Charlotte Beyer, they can be 'a status symbol, a private office catering to a family's special needs or requests, a gatekeeper to keep investment salespeople at bay, or a commercial enterprise open to other families'.[4] But families' experiences with single family offices (SFOs) have not always been good ones. Lack of proper set-up, planning, and management can create disappointment. Contentious heirs can destroy any attempt at smooth, effective management. Uncontrolled costs can create added burdens and make it difficult to retain talent. Mismanagement of expenses by family office executives can compromise family wealth objectives. The wealth optimization consultant can help families avoid these and other disappointing situations by:

- managing the family office as a business;
- defining the purpose of the family office; and
- defining financial goals, family education goals, and charitable goals.[5]

A wealth optimization consultant can guide the family in these processes and help set up the governance structures to keep things running smoothly.

Involvement in the family council

The consultant often can be an effective addition to the family council. The purpose of the council is to educate the family, to discuss the basis for investment decisions, to get feedback from the family on its tolerance for risk, and to gauge attitudes toward the wealth from the different generations involved. The family council can also serve as the 'glue' holding the family together to achieve a common purpose.[6]

The wealth optimization consultant can be a useful guide for the council and the council can be a valuable resource for the consultant. The family council can provide a window to the inner layers of the family so that the consultant can develop a better overall knowledge of family dynamics and how they might affect the wealth optimization program.

For this reason, the family council should include as many family members as possible. Technology enables connectivity and communication between family members and facilitates effective family meetings regardless of the location of family members. Well-planned meetings represent an excellent educational venue for the wealth optimization consultant and can be effectively used to solidify the relationship with the family. At the same time, educating the family is a key component of such relationships.[7] By leading the family meetings, consultants can also establish strong relationships with other family advisors such as CPAs, attorneys, and philanthropy consultants.

In brief, the wealth optimization consultant should report on the financial aspects of the family wealth, discuss the macroeconomic influences on the wealth portfolio, and plan some type of educational presentation either by an outside speaker or the consultant.[8] As a trusted chief advisor for the family, the consultant is then positioned as the team leader of the family and of the other advisors who serve the family's needs, and, as such, can coordinate the efforts of everyone involved in the family's welfare.

Specific education needs

Clearly, the education of advisors to become investment management consultants and of investment management consultants to become wealth optimization consultants demands defined criteria and curricula. The order of education received is also extremely important. The need for ongoing education to support the functions of the consultant and to keep the consultant current on important industry information and trends is a given.

The basic requirement is that provided by IMCA for its CIMA designation. This program provides a foundation in all aspects of the consulting process (as outlined in Chapter 4). IMCA's Wealth Management certification course provides the essential elements of traditional wealth management skills, such as tax planning and compliance, trust structures, gifting, philanthropy goals, wealth transfer goals, risk assessment, and lifestyle goals, but wealth optimization requires these basic elements be expanded as detailed in the following subsections.

Tax planning and compliance

Each type of tax planning, including multi-year planning, estate tax planning, and gifting, must be conducted within the context of family dynamics, ownership structures of family assets, and the family legacy. This comprehensive approach encompasses much more than any single, separated treatment of these planning components. Providing education in these basic areas is critical, but educating consultants in the integrated application of each area is even more critical to wealth optimization.

Trust structures

In order to fully comprehend the complexities of trusts and the need to expand consultant education in this area, we need to look at how control of family wealth is passed through these long-established wealth transfer tools.

Typically, when one thinks of wealth being passed to beneficiaries through trusts, the thought process tends to end there. It is at that point that the trusts end and wealth managers pick up the ball and invest the wealth for the beneficiaries who now own it. But if the inheritance passed through the trust involves ownership of a public company, there can be a lot more involved. It is estimated that as much of one-third of the S&P 500 has significant family ownership.[9] A major change in ownership of a public company can affect the perception of the company's stability. This can be negative if the investing public is not familiar with the new owner and is uncertain how his or her influence will affect the company.

In the past, beneficiaries may have had no knowledge that a trust even existed, much less that they were beneficiaries. Trustees are now required to disclose beneficiary status to the beneficiaries, which will smooth the way for beneficiaries to be more prepared to fulfill their duties responsibly.

Trustee responsibilities can affect holdings in a company. If, for instance, a trust transfers control of the family block of stock to a third party, bids for the company could be attracted and the block of stock sold in the best interests of the beneficiaries. Conversely, a trust or group of trusts controlling a large block of company stock could strengthen a family's position if the voting control is consolidated through the trust. The control provisions for the trust containing the block of company ownership must be carefully planned and should include involvement of the beneficiaries in order for the family, the company, and its shareholders to be well served. A grantor's wishes have much to do with the governance of the trust. If the grantor has not made provisions for changes in circumstances and incorporated some flexibility in the trust document, unintended results could occur that the grantor may never have intended.

All of this goes back to family dynamics, governance, education, and communication. Family leadership is becoming more aware of the need to include provisions in trusts to allow the best decision to be made for the family, not necessarily to follow normally accepted fiduciary rules above all else.[10] The purpose of the trust should be the governing factor, but that purpose must be carefully designed to take account of ramifications for not only the initial beneficiary, but also later beneficiaries such as children or grandchildren.

Trusts can be used in many different ways. They can be established as an incentive to ensure the children achieve a certain goal before being handed their inheritance, or to provide income for a surviving spouse and, after the death of that spouse, an inheritance for the children. Trusts come into play in granting funds or investments to designated charities. Dynasty trusts are becoming more prevalent as a way of ensuring that the family wealth can be more certainly preserved through a series of generations. Also, states are beginning to offer opt-out clauses to attract more trust business for the state.

Of course, the best way for trusts to be well designed and well executed is for families to adopt full disclosure followed by education for involved family members. This process can actually solidify the founding entrepreneur's wishes through greater knowledge and appreciation for the entrepreneur's objectives by the beneficiaries before they actually receive their inheritance. Such a process can only be designed and implemented following careful consideration of family dynamics and by setting up appropriate governance, both inside and outside the trusts.

Philanthropy goals

Training in this area must consist of much more than just the financial aspects, advantages, and implications of gifting. The concern here is the family legacy, which is a deep-seated emotional issue. It is also becoming a training ground for the wealth stewards in successive generations. Gifting and setting up foundations and investments for those foundations are only the first steps in addressing a family's philanthropic objectives, and business succession, estate planning, and wealth transfer all play a part.

Wealth transfer goals

This area is addressed in the trust section above, but the main point to make here is the importance of discovering clients' wealth transfer goals and setting appropriate objectives designed to make those goals a reality. This involves, of course, optimization of all the factors listed in Exhibits 9.1 and 9.2. Proper risk assessment and management as well as life goals factor into wealth transfer and the more emotional issue of leaving a legacy.

Programs

The programs at organizations such as IMCA, the IPI, FOX, and the Association of Investment Management and Research (AIMR) lay a critical foundation for mastering the basic wealth management skills. Each organization requires a certain amount of continuing education credits (including in the area of ethics) to maintain the privilege of using the designations they award. The CIMA is the premier investment management consulting designation, and consultants who achieve this may then add to their training by earning one or more of the additional certification programs mentioned earlier in this chapter.

FOX, as a provider of strategic advice for financial families and of objective information about the wealth management process, is another educational resource. FOX has a strong emphasis on providing education for wealthy families; however, it also provides educational opportunities for advisors and consultants through its regular conference schedule and through special FOX events designed for advisors to wealthy families. The Institute for International Research (IIR) regularly hosts family office conferences with family office industry leaders, covering every facet of family office service and operation, and will soon offer programs providing hands-on training ideal for aspiring wealth optimization consultants.

As yet, the family office industry has no specific designation denoting the expertise of the holder. A discussion is going on, however, about the advantages of having such a designation, as well as the disadvantages. Meanwhile, the CIMA designation, the CFA, and the CFP (Certified Financial Planner) are the most recognized designations and represent high ethical standards as well as a minimum level of expertise.

The CIMA is the prerequisite for any of IMCA's additional certification courses and is the most closely related financial services industry designation to family office level services. Family office professionals comprise approximately 4% of IMCA membership, but that number is expected to grow.[11] While no organization currently has a formal educational program for family office professionals, IPI comes closest. IPI's highest level program is offered by invitation only to consultants whose business focus and educational background qualify them to contribute to as well as benefit from that program.

The educational component is as important (perhaps even more so) than any other wealth optimization component, and, as a result, the wealth optimization consultant's educational program should be organized as follows.

- Earn the CIMA designation to gain the knowledge and expertise to manage financial wealth.
- Become a member of the IPI in order to experience hands-on education involving real family situations and challenges.
- Attend FOX events, either online or at a conference, to learn about family office wealth and also to become known in the family office arena.
- Attend IIR family office conferences in order to learn from top professionals in the family office industry and to develop a professional network.
- Attend Money Management Institute (MMI) conferences to stay abreast of technological developments and financial services industry trends.
- Fulfill the ongoing education required to maintain CIMA and CFA designations.
- Learn by listening to clients and client families. This is an invaluable ongoing education tool.
- Be on the lookout for additional programs sponsored by these and other organizations as they become available.

Conclusions

Financial advisors hear every kind of suggestion from every kind of entity on how to differentiate themselves. The vast majority of those suggestions include the phrase 'add value', but none of them ever mentions education. Education is the only real differentiating factor that can add the value wealth optimization consultants command and their clients demand.

When educating themselves, wealth optimization consultants should consider the edge that ongoing education offers them and the many ways that education can be used in their businesses. One of the most obvious uses for consultant education is in marketing. The investing public today examines the credentials of its advisors much more closely than in times past. They look for experience and expertise, and education can foster each of these components.

Educational opportunities abound. The Financial Planning Association (FPA) provides a broader scope of education from an integrated planning perspective through the Certified Financial Planner (CFP) program, IMCA provides a deeper scope of education from a consulting perspective, and IPI provides the essential skills needed from a wealth optimization perspective. Conferences are regular events for IMCA, AIMR, FOX, IPI, and the IIR. Enterprising entrepreneurs in the financial services industry will realize the value of ongoing education as the way to remain viable as wealth optimization consultants and also to foster best practices.

---

[1] IMCA (2003), *IMCA's Strategic Vision*, the Investment Management Consultants Association, Denver, CO.

[2] Author's interview with Richard Joyner, CPA, CFP, CIMA, president of private wealth management, Tolleson Wealth Management, September 2003.

[3] Author's interview with Lee Hausner, Ph.D., partner, DoudHausnerVistar Advisors, September 2003.

[4] Beyer, Charlotte B. (1999), 'Family Offices in America: Why the Bloom is Off the Rose', *Journal of Private Portfolio Management,* Fall.

[5] Ibid.

[6] Dickstein, Sidney (2003), 'The Family Council: A Useful Adjunct to the Functions of the Wealth Management Professional', *The Journal of Wealth Management,* Spring.

[7] Ibid.

[8] Ibid.

[9] Snyder, Susan D., and Rhodes, Anne-Marie (2003), 'Passing the Baton of Voting Control', *Trusts and Estates,* August.

[10] Ibid.; and personal interview with Susan D. Snyder, partner at Sachnoff and Weaver Ltd, September 2003.

[11] IMCA Membership Demographics Survey, June 2003.

Chapter 10

Attracting the wealthy and their advisors

Introduction

There is a common thread running through the best wealth attraction programs, which can be boiled down to one deceptively simple prescription: focus on the needs of the client. However, this prescription is often misinterpreted in the following ways.

- Focus on what the firm thinks the client needs.
- Focus on what the advisor/consultant thinks the client needs.
- Tell the client what the firm's and/or the advisor/consultant's capabilities, specializations, and philosophies are before even finding out what the client is seeking.
- Tell the client all of these things using the same language and presentation used by every other financial services firm so that the language will be approved by the regulatory bodies and the client will have no way to distinguish one firm or advisor/consultant from another.

Chapter 10 is dedicated to eliminating the confusion and highlighting the most effective ways of attracting the wealthy.

The question of how to effectively attract the wealthy has become a live issue, in part because there are more wealthy people in the world than ever before. The baby boomer generation will soon hold the vast majority of this wealth and are already demanding services designed for the way they want to live their lives and spend their retirement years. Baby boomers have different attitudes toward life and toward their wealth than their 'GI' and 'silent' generation parents. Meanwhile, the millennials' influence on attitudes toward wealth are also beginning to take shape. Only through acquiring knowledge about the attitudes, concerns, characteristics, and life philosophies of these generational forces will wealth optimization consultants be able to maintain control over their positions in the wealth management world.

Chapter 8 provided an overview of demographic influences on family dynamics. This chapter will develop the theme, because only by fully understanding the mindset that great wealth fosters can wealth optimization consultants hope to provide the level of service wealthy families require.

Key characteristics of wealth and the wealthy

The baby boomer generation demand more accountability, knowledge, and expertise from their advisors. They also require advice on a broader scale than their parents did, including help with disability, succession planning, and estate planning. In this sense, certified financial planners (CFPs) may have a slight edge on their financial advisor/consultant counterparts. Financial planners have traditionally approached client wealth from a broader, more comprehensive perspective. Rather than just being interested in a client's investments, financial planners consider insurance needs, estate and tax planning needs, retirement planning needs, and needs brought about by lifestyle changes.

Wealth optimization consultants must offer all of the functions of financial planners but also explore softer issues such as philanthropic interests, the attitudes of each family member toward the family's wealth, how wealth makes their lives different, and what that difference may mean down the road. This chapter will help delineate those attitudes and how they influence the management of the family wealth from generation to generation.

In order to appreciate the influence of the baby boomer generation on today's concept of wealth and how it will shape the lives of those who own it in the future, an examination is necessary of the characteristics that the wealthy seem to have in common. Five words characterize the ultra-wealthy: complexity, control, connections, capital, and charity. An explanation of each follows.[1]

Complexity

The greater the amount of wealth a family owns, the more complex the management and optimization of that wealth. The sheer size of wealth can make it difficult to execute transactions in accounts or adequately diversify financial assets. Some positions may be large enough to influence market prices if trade action is taken. These accounts are hybrids between individual (retail) accounts and institutional accounts. They have the size advantages of institutional accounts and the tax disadvantages of retail accounts – both domestically and globally. Estate tax, state income tax, gift tax, and foreign investment tax swallow sizable chunks of capital unless carefully managed. Foreign taxes and jurisdictions can create layers of international complexity, all in addition to the complexities indigenous to the domicile country.

International ultra-wealthy families may be citizens of more than one country. Their children may attend school in a different country from the one in which they reside. Family dynamics become increasingly complicated when they involve multiple countries and cultures. Social, human, and intellectual capital influenced by those cultures increase the complexity, adding concerns about business succession, divestiture, or other plans.

In addition, larger portions of portfolios are involved in a greater number of non-traditional investments, complicating asset allocation decisions. These investments may take the form of art collections, private equity concerns, commodity accounts, international currencies, investment hedges, personal and business-owned real estate, and so on.

Often, these complexities, combined with the number of voices that must be heard, require families to accommodate rather than optimize.[2] The role of the wealth optimization consultant in all cases is to facilitate optimal accommodation based on the client's specific needs rather than simply optimizing processes and programs. The very term 'wealth optimization consultant' implies optimizing the client's entire family wealth situation. Optimization in this sense may mean instituting less than optimal procedures and structure for the family leader or leaders and more optimization of all assets for other family members involved.

The variety of attitudes within the family regarding wealth, opportunity, family involvement, family business involvement, and many other considerations all serve to add complexity that grows as the family wealth grows. The wealth optimization consultant can play a significant part in the successful functioning and management of that complexity.

Control

Consider the Chapter 6 case study of the patriarch wishing to set up a family office. He had enjoyed total, unquestioned control of all wealth generation, wealth management processes, and the use of the wealth, probably for half a century or longer. The difficulty he encountered in letting go, even to the extent of systematizing the processes that he had been following for all of those years, was only overcome due to his foresight in realizing the consequences of not institutionalizing those processes.

Wealthy people tend to want control, and, in their eyes, wealth gives them the 'right' to be in control through influence and position. In and of itself, control is not to be disdained, but how that control is used for the benefit of the family, society at large, and the management and growth of the wealth can either add to or reduce the complexities cited in the previous subsection. Control, like wealth, is a very emotional issue, involving egos, the outcomes of people's lives, and certain boundaries and restrictions. As mentioned earlier in this book, the list of family members to be included in discussions on family wealth issues can be a source of great consternation and conflict. Siblings who previously showed no interest in the business of the family wealth often develop a 'sudden' interest after finding they are on the outskirts of consideration.

Public markets are also affected. The passing of a controlling interest of a company to heirs is a change in control (see Chapter 9 on trust structures). On another front is the manner in which foundations, trusts, and family limited partnerships are set up: all of these tend to show evidence of the need of the wealthy to be in control.[3]

Connections

The maxim 'It's who you know that counts' has facilitated the business and financial success of entrepreneurs since the days of the first traders. It has shaped societies and governments and offered opportunity where there was none. The wealthy prize their influence, and connections that provide it are of prime importance in the eyes of the wealthy. They are also of prime importance to the wealth optimization consultant. Without connections and influence, ideal clients cannot send ideal referrals and entrepreneurial doors may not be opened.

Capital

The combination of the four types of capital – investment capital, human capital, intellectual capital, and social capital – offers power to the super-wealthy, over their own lives, those of friends and family, and those less fortunate. This power can extend into government and politics; entertainment and medical research, the arts and education. The power of these four types of capital in combination to 'make things happen' lies at the root of the emphasis of the wealthy on wealth preservation,[4] and understanding this is one of the primary keys to attracting the wealthy.

Charity

The growth in philanthropy over recent years is not accidental. The super-wealthy are interested in charity or philanthropy for a variety of reasons. It serves as a way to shelter income

136

from taxes. It can be used as a training ground for heirs. It also preserves the legacy of the wealthy to 'make the world a better place'. It adds purpose to their lives where money often does not.

The needs of the wealthy

The five core characteristics discussed in the previous section comprise a hierarchy of concerns and optimization needs for the wealthy. The underlying complexity at the bottom rung of the hierarchy lays the foundation for attaining the other four levels, much in the same manner as Maslow's hierarchy of human need represents a guide to people's psychological motivations. The complexity of wealth is the largest and most basic component – all advisory needs of the wealthy stem from these complexities. As the wealth increases and the complexities increase, clients desire more control over how those complexities affect their lives and also more control over how the wealth affects the rest of the family.

The complexities of the wealth make control of the effects of taxes, market fluctuations and risk, and the ownership and trust structures involving the wealth of utmost importance. This is the initial level from which the wealthy turn to wealth optimization consultants. Through their advice, the wealthy can control not only the complexities associated with their wealth, but also the way their wealth affects their influence, power, and philanthropic efforts (see Exhibit 10.1).

This gives the wealthy the control they crave, which, in turn, provides connections for developing additional family businesses or opens doors for family members wishing to go

Exhibit 10.1

Hierarchy of wealth characteristics

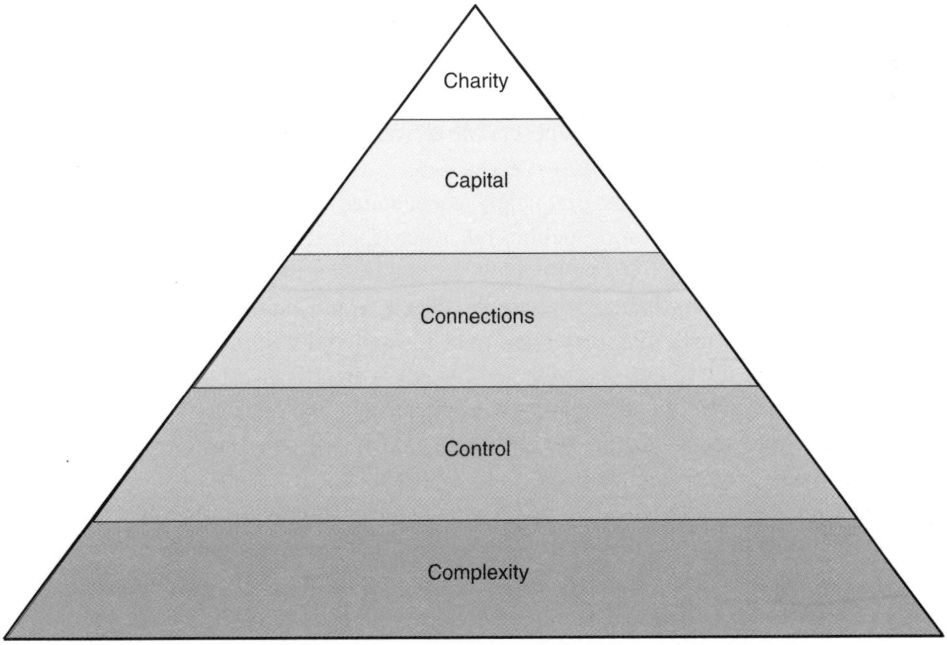

Source: Author's own.

out on their own. Connections influence the opportunities generated for the continued creation of wealth through the entrepreneurial efforts of heirs; they influence access to investment opportunities to preserve and grow the wealth; they influence the power the four forms of capital can wield; and they set up philanthropic opportunities that are not available to the less affluent.

Next to the top is capital, which represents the four forms of capital, namely human, social, intellectual, and financial, outlined in the wealth optimization model. Most importantly, the combination of these assets can give all members of the family serious power by creating more than the sum of the family parts in the operating business, family and business relationships, and in the personal identity of the family.[5] This level is also connected with the desire of the wealthy to show evidence of their wealth by purchasing expensive cars, multiple homes, boats, and other material symbols of success.

The top layer is charity, representing the culmination of what it means to be wealthy and the freedom it provides. Placing structures and advisory supervision of those structures in place to handle the complexity, control the dispersion of the wealth to family members, use the connections to create opportunities and boost influence, and optimize the various forms of capital so the family may concentrate on charitable endeavors illustrates the service requirements for today's family offices. By the time the wealthy are free to concentrate on charitable giving, all the needs preceding this capability have been met sufficiently to proceed to the next phase. Once the complexities are identified, control in the form of preservation becomes the concern; once preservation is in place, connections needed to grow the wealth are sought; then the power to use the wealth and the connections it provides is expressed through the four sources of capital; and, finally, once all the other needs are satisfied, the wealthy are free to give to the causes they favor.

Further characteristics of the wealthy

Most financial advisors do not think of themselves as psychologists, but wealth optimization consultants include wealth psychology as an aid to understanding their clients' needs and in designing their practices to offer the appropriate services. Exhibit 10.2 lists different types of wealth personality.

'Family stewards' (the most frequently encountered type of wealth personality) are common throughout the investing public, but when applied to the ultra-wealthy the type includes factors such as internal control and a general lack of trust. 'Phobics' are the second most common wealth personalities and are the clients who want their advisors to 'just take care of everything for me'. This may seem to be a wonderful trait in a client, but this situation is actually quite difficult to deal with and can create significant relationship management problems. Phobics resent the fact that they are financially and managerially out of control. They are the people who do not like having to take care of their own financial affairs and need financial and other professional advisors to look after them.

'Independents' seek the freedom that having money can provide. They like the security and control over their lives that such freedom gives. This type of personality best personifies the baby boomer generation demographics cited earlier. Although the predominant top two personalities seem to be more generally associated with baby boomer parents and the 'GI' generation, rather than other generational demographics, boomers' rebellious, independent attitudes and outlook will come to predominate as they age and inherit their parents' wealth.

138

Exhibit 10.2

Personality traits of the wealthy

Type	Characteristics
Family stewards	Want to use their wealth to care for their family.
	Want to relieve their family members of financial worries.
	Want to take care of their personal obligations.
Phobics	Hate being involved in financial decisions.
	Not knowledgeable about financial matters.
	Dislike discussing investing.
Independents	See attention to financial issues as a necessary evil.
	Want personal freedom.
	Want to have a safety net if they bail out.
Anonymous	Confidentiality concerning financial matters is key.
	Secretive about their financial dealings.
	Financial success is essential for personal comfort.
Moguls	Financial success is a way of keeping score and winning.
	Wealth brings power.
	Seek personal influence.
VIPs	Financial success is a way to achieve high status.
	Want to be well-known.
	Seek prestige.
Accumulators	Their top goal is asset accumulation.
	Cannot be too rich.
	Their sole objective is to make money.
Gamblers	Treat dealing with financial matters as a hobby.
	Derive pleasure from the machinations of the market.
	They relish the investing process.
Innovators	Perceive investing to be a challenge.
	Want to be on the cutting edge of financial technology.
	Want to be employing state-of-the-art strategies and tactics.

Source: Prince, Russ Alan, and File, Karen Maru (1995), *Cultivating the Affluent: How to Segment and Service the High-Net-Worth Market,* New York, Institutional Investor.

The other personality types in Exhibit 10.2 can be viewed as offshoots of boomer independence and therefore present major considerations for consultants. The 'anonymous' personality (the 'silents') may seem to be a throwback to the GI generation, specifically the 'family stewards', and superficially to contradict typical boomer personality traits, but it actually spans both generations. The patriarch described in the first case study in Chapter 6 is a perfect fit for the anonymous personality. It was extremely difficult for the patriarch to allow the technology consultant access to his private information, but the drive to take care of his family (as family steward) overcame his need to maintain that privacy.

'Moguls' fit the boomer personality in the sense of accumulating more and more assets to provide more and more power, influence, and control. 'VIPs' like the status and prestige their wealth gives them. These are the people who buy expensive 'toys' and possess all the trappings that can give them the prestige to which they feel their wealth entitles them.

'Accumulators' build wealth as a hedge against the future, which cannot be known. The baby boomer generation accumulator may be an entrepreneur who 'started from nothing' or was determined to escape the poverty experienced when growing up. Accumulators are very protective of their wealth since it holds the key to their financial well-being – something about which they exhibit constant concern.

'Gamblers' and 'innovators' represent two other sides to the boomer personality. Gamblers exhibit high self-confidence in their competence to provide for themselves. Thus, they tend to be more aggressive investors and can tolerate more risk than other investors. Innovators are a much milder form of gambler. They are as self-confident, but tend to be more analytical in nature. They want to work with a consultant who will take the time to understand their need to analyze and who will offer them the tools they need to perform their analysis.

Cycles of affluent personalities

In her book *Cycles: How We Will Live, Work, and Buy*,[6] Maddy Dychtwald outlines the changes led by the boomer generation in the way they think about life and seek to control more of their own experiences. Rather than live an age-defined, linear life with traditional expectations for each stage, boomers have created cycles of life that they move in and out of over their lifespan. People begin new careers at age 40, 55, or even 65, while company executives who have sold their businesses or were caught in the layoff downdraft have often gone back to school.

Dychtwald cites examples such as her 80-year-old stepfather who began a company at age 68 and now has a successful second career as a movie promoter. Another example involves a portfolio manager of a large financial services industry firm who left a successful career to go back to school and become a history teacher.[7] Such options were not even thought of, much less available, for previous generations. Technology and the economy have played a part in providing such opportunities for people, but the primary factor has been the way people – principally the baby boomer generation – have begun to view their lives.

Baby boomers have applied this desire to live life differently to their parents by bringing their independent, mogul, VIP, analytical personalities (plus a penchant for taking more gambles in their lives) to managing their wealth. In doing so, they have more control, make the most of their connections and their various forms of capital, and have started a movement among the wealthy toward philanthropy. Bill Gates and Ted Turner are prime examples of this movement, while many others with much less wealth are focusing on how inherited wealth may affect their children and their children's children and are using philanthropy to provide an apprenticeship for the wealth management responsibilities they will have later in life.

Conclusions

Developing a thorough knowledge of the wealthy and their attitudes toward wealth is an essential ingredient for the success of wealth optimization consultants. The ability to optimize a wealthy client's entire portfolio of assets – financial, human, intellectual, and social – in a customized, premium service level capacity has powerful implications for consultants and for their clients. It positions the wealth optimization consultant to attract the wealthy and their advisors by offering them exactly what their personalities and characteristics prompt them to desire. In any industry, the ability to offer such a perfect package for buyers tends to eliminate the competition. It builds a win/win proposition and maintains interest and vitality in relationships so that loyalty can be developed.

By reviewing the history of family wealth and of the financial services industry's consulting model, and by examining family office models, family dynamics, the efficiency and effectiveness of teams, the technology needs of both industries, and the attitudes and characteristics of the wealthy, readers should be formulating ideas about reinventing their practices toward the business of optimizing wealth – any source of wealth – for their clients.

---

[1] Prince, Russ Alan, and Harris, Richard L. (2002), *Advanced Planning With the Ultra Affluent*, p. 17, Institutional Investor Marketing.

[2] Ibid.

[3] Ibid., p. 19.

[4] Ibid., p. 21.

[5] Ibid., p. 21.

[6] Dychtwald, Maddy (2003), *Cycles: How We Will Live, Work, and Buy,* The Free Press, a division of Simon and Schuster.

[7] Author's interview with Maddy Dychtwald, co-founder, (AgeWave (www.agewaveimpact.com) January 2003.

Chapter 11

Expanding advisory practices into wealth optimization businesses: deciding how to compete

Introduction

What will differentiate high-level financial services advisors and investment management consultants as competition in affluent client markets becomes steadily more fierce? The answer lies in the expansion of advisory practices and the transformation of their businesses into service models that optimize the entire portfolio of wealthy clients' assets. This chapter outlines the process required to identify the transition to the most appropriate business models to fit the objectives of aspiring wealth optimization consultants and the affluent market level they choose to serve.

The competitive framework

One of the challenges for family offices and advisors wishing to serve the markets of the wealthy is to be paid sufficiently for the advice they provide. Pat Soldano, CEO of Cymric Family Office Services, cites the frustration caused by financial institutions' business models that have traditionally offered the advice component of their service offerings for free.[1] In a world where that component is becoming much more sought after, efforts to assign it a higher value remain difficult. Sara Hamilton of Family Office Exchange (FOX) agrees:[2]

> The firms that are doing total open architecture are struggling to make enough profit to retain talented professionals against the organizations that are [selling product] and giving the advice away for free. So we're in the midst of a dramatic paradigm shift in terms of what the owner is willing to recognize and to pay for.

Independent advisors such as certified financial planners (CFPs) and registered investment advisors (RIAs) are taking advantage of the opportunities. They are educating themselves in providing the softer services that families need and are moving toward charging for advice. Since they are independent, they have no allegiance to any type of product and can provide the objective advice that wealthy families value. Private banks and financial services firms are attempting to do the same, although private banks with a history of family ownership are closer to realizing this goal.

For the top investment management consultants, the transformation into wealth optimization consultants will be fairly simple. That segment has largely figured out that working with the wealthy requires much more than simply transitioning to fee-based compensation and using separately managed accounts (SMAs) or unified managed accounts (UMAs). Those steps are definitely on the right track, but they stop a long way short of positioning consultants to reap the rewards that providing wealth optimization services can bring.

Wealth optimization will always be a service intensive business. Its profitability has a different character to that with which the financial services industry is familiar. According to Richard Joyner of Tolleson Wealth Management:[3] 'It's a totally different world. The primary difference in the family office business is that the relationships are fewer in number but are much deeper. So you have to adapt to that kind of model.' Joyner suggests consultants who wish to align themselves with family offices get to know family office business models and discover in which areas the services they are accustomed to providing are complementary. By doing so, consultants can determine the right family office service model that would most appropriately house their expertise.

Compensatory concerns

Wealth optimization consultants will do at least as well financially as they did in the financial services industry model, but will need to adjust their compensation expectations. The advice-driven model provides a steadier income spread over a longer time-frame than the product-driven model. The wealth optimization model is unequivocally centered on doing the right thing for the client; if this is prudently accomplished, good compensation will follow.

As indicated earlier, the profit problem now being faced by the financial services industry is caused by the reluctance to completely abandon product-based compensatory methods, whether through transactions, SMA, or UMA accounts. Profits seem set to increase in both industries as technology creates greater efficiencies for operations, but the source of profits for each industry will change. Profits for the large firms will primarily come from the offering of commoditized services to independent advisors and wealth optimization consultants. Fees for advice will increase as clients come to appreciate its value, but customized, fully integrated advice will never become a commodity. Profits will expand for family offices because of the more efficient multi-family office (MFO) model and the changing focus of families seeking to ensure their offices generate profits rather than just break even. So, in a limited way, elements of the two industries are overlapping.

The transformation process

Transforming a practice involves the following steps.

- A thorough re-examination of business goals and personal objectives.
- An examination of the feasibility of the various optimization service models.
- A mindset adjustment in favor of the family office, plus a determination of the level of wealth optimization services the consultant wishes to provide in light of market demands and the desired clientele.
- An adjustment of business and marketing plans.
- Organizing the education and credentials needed to support the new positioning.
- Providing education for clients designed to support optimized service goals.
- Execution of the plan.

Exhibit 11.1

Wealth optimization flow-through

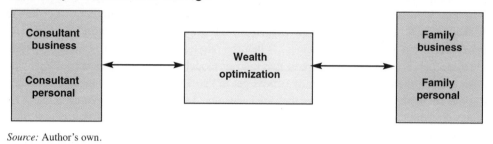

Source: Author's own.

Each of these steps will be examined in the following subsections, and the end result will be a specific, step-by-step plan of action.[4] This transformation process is automatically customized because the answers to questions that must be asked will be different for each consultant.

Business goals and personal objectives

The process required for re-examining business goals should be extended to include a reassessment of personal goals and objectives as well. Contrary to traditional thought, personal lives and business lives most definitely do and should interact. Money is an emotional topic, and family dynamics are based in emotions and opinions. How, then, can the personal aspect realistically and pragmatically be separated from the business? The job of the wealth optimization consultant is to effectively meld sound asset management with the emotional and demographic dynamics of the family.

Bringing personal elements to your business practice does not mean that levels of comfort on either side need to be breached. The key is in finding the right balance for consultant and client, which is the ultimate purpose of re-examining personal and business goals. In carrying out this reassessment, two basic assumptions are made. The first is that the financial advisor or consultant has already created a viable business plan. That should go without saying, but, unfortunately, many practices still operate without a formalized document. The second assumption is that the decision to transform the practice into a business with an assignable value has been made. The wealth optimization process runs in two directions – back through the consultant's business and forward through the client's business (see Exhibit 11.1).

Wealth optimization models

The various wealth optimization models available now or which will soon be available were explored in Chapter 3, while the costs of doing business in today's environment were examined in Chapter 7. By taking a look at the most viable aspects of wealth optimization models and the feasibility of each, consultants will have a useful guide to determining the most workable model for their individual businesses.

The multi-family office model

According to FOX's Sara Hamilton, the multi-family office is set to be the predominant family office model of the future, and it is also one of the easiest ways for consultants to

144

enter the wealth optimization segment.[5] Wealth optimization applies to MFOs in the sense that there is still a gap between the comprehensive functions of the MFO and the most efficient ways of operating and of streamlining even highly customized services. New technology should help close this efficiency gap, but optimizing time-intensive services that are customized for each family will also represent an important development. The idea is not to provide scale in these services, which may be impossible to do, as much as to coordinate and integrate the services in a way that will be more effective for the family as a whole. The result will be optimization of the various forms of capital for both MFOs and the families they serve.

At this stage of development for wealth optimization, there is a dearth of highly qualified consultants available to work for MFOs, so opportunities abound. 'The greatest limitation in our industry today is the small number of talented professionals who have worked across disciplines,' says Hamilton. By this, she is referring to professionals who can effectively integrate the various services families demand. Consultants who educate themselves as recommended in Chapter 9 will be able to take advantage of this shortage.

The MFO does not have to be large in order to provide a wealth optimization consultant with opportunity. An MFO should be judged not on the size of the assets it manages, but on the quality and range of services it provides. Regardless of size, the MFO should be charging a reasonable fee that will cover its service provision and provide at least a small profit for the firm. This balance between services and fees charged and efficiency of operation is difficult to achieve, but it is the deciding factor for investment management consultants who wish to pursue wealth optimization through an MFO.

Consultants wishing to be aligned with an MFO enjoy several advantages. They can 'plug into' a wealth optimization system that is firmly established with a quality clientele to which they can add their own clients. Consultants may make an arrangement with the MFO to grow the business to a certain point, then agree to be bought out by the MFO or leave, take their clients with them, after making a certain amount of money for the office. This allows for an attractive transition by the consultant from early establishment to the capability to stand alone as a fully functioning business. It enables the consultant to have hands-on experience in an established MFO environment without having to participate fully in bearing the costs of running an office. Alternatively, the consultant may become a partner in the MFO and remain with the enterprise throughout his or her career. This enables greater cost-efficiency since the consultant can simply buy into a business that has already been built rather than having to begin one from scratch, and can either join as a specialist or perhaps as a partner, depending on the development stage of the MFO and its needs.

Outsourced resources obtainable through MFOs charge their own individual fees or may have special arrangements with the MFO, depending on the size of the office and the frequency of involvement of the outsourced resource. The fees for these consultants are usually folded into the flat fee charged for overall services. The fee structure at most MFOs is two-tiered. The money manager and consultant fees are paid separately on the investment side and a flat fee is charged for the customized package of other services.

The multi-client family office

This type of MFO is formed specifically for the purpose of providing family office level services to clients. For example, an investment management consultant could decide to become a wealth optimization consultant, taking 60 of her best clients and either go out on her own with a small staff or team up with another type of family advisor or another wealth optimization consultant and set up a multi-client family office (MCFO) with a few basic services, while outsourcing services she does not wish to provide in-house. This arrangement is being explored by the RIA market, which is predicted to experience some of the fastest growth of any advisory segment over the next three to five years. RIAs and independent consultants can either join a type of MFO or simply go out on their own. The MFO is closest to the arrangement investment management consultants have at the big financial institutions where they are currently employed. The primary differences lie in the broad range of services offered and the compensation structures. The MFO is compensated for advice and service. At big financial institutions, the advice portion is currently free; the institutions make their money from the products that are sold.

But that model is changing quickly, which is a theme that has been presented throughout this book. The advice model will win out and clients and those who choose to become wealth optimization consultants will be the ultimate beneficiaries. Consultants who wish to position themselves to thrive in this advice business have no choice about re-evaluating their business models and the way they are paid.

Charlotte B. Beyer cites the primary reason for the disenchantment of families with family office experiences as a lack of attention to the four basic functions a family office should fulfill:[6]

- centralization of record-keeping (bill-paying, cash flow management, tax planning and preparation, and tangible asset accounting);
- centralization of the business management of the family's affairs (sale of businesses or other assets, representation in business affairs, and administration of tangible assets such as real estate, yachts, or airplanes);
- family management (governance, financial and investment education, philanthropy coordination, business succession and wealth transfer planning); and
- investment-related functions (activities involved in the consulting process).

These functions are complex and interrelated, but the business of managing the family assets must be separated from the operating business. They have different objectives and those objectives should be clearly identified.

Going it alone
According to Lydian's Scott Welch:[7]

> There really is a breakeven point of about US$100 million for a family to form its own office. Below that net worth is really the sweet spot for the consulting industry. North of US$100 million, it's very difficult for an external consultant to charge a fee that will allow them to deliver the services that are being demanded at anything resembling a profitable margin. Advisors have to very narrowly define their services if they want to be profitable working with families above US$100 million. But down in the US$10 to US$100 million range you can still do our model and make it work as long as you have an efficient platform to deliver it on.

Firms such as Lydian Wealth Management are examples of businesses that provide platforms for wealth optimization consultants. These platforms offer wealth optimization services and have their own flavor of service provision. Consultants who join these types of firms have the advantage of accessing a built-out platform of services and accessing outsourced resources with whom the firms have built relationships.

This set-up differs from a traditional MFO because it allows the individual consultant more freedom. In one such firm, the consultants work independently but under the firm's name (because they are building a brand). In exchange, the firm provides a buyout of the consultant's business at the end of five years. According to a firm principal: 'Most cream of the crop consultants are in their 50s, so this gives them an exit strategy for the account relationships they're developing, and with the electronic virtual offices, consultants don't have to be based where we are.'

The virtual family office model

The fact that a truly virtual family office (VFO) including front and back office operations and other segments does not exist at this time does not negate the advantages of using what *is* available. The virtual functions that do exist offer consultants a way to have more independence either with a previously established MFO or by establishing their own MCFO. VFO offerings allow consultants to outsource the various platforms needed to provide service and form outsourced relationships with other advisors and consultants. Consulting firms like Family Office Metrics cater to consultants wishing to implement such a set-up and have extensive family office knowledge in addition to providing advice on technology and communications structures.

The independent model is being used by independent RIAs, by CPAs wishing to start their own wealth optimization shops, and by a number of attorneys wishing to move into the wealth optimization business. Whether these efforts succeed depends on the sincerity of service provision and the efficiency of the business model. As noted earlier, relationships with other advisors such as CPAs and attorneys have generally not been successful in the past. But developing the right relationships and teaming up with a CPA or attorney wishing to set up an individual shop can be a winning combination.

VFOs that are founded on the right principles, that have developed quality relationships with other advisors and consultants, and that set up efficient business models will have the ultimate freedom and control to serve their clients and be paid for the advice and service they give. Private banks such as J.P. Morgan and more sophisticated MFOs also offer families private websites as communication and governance tools. In addition, some of the models described in Chapter 3 enable consultants to go out on their own, keep most of their earnings, and build their own wealth optimization organizations.

However, Sara Hamilton cites some problems with the VFO – primarily that it is a difficult model with which to create cohesion for clients:[8]

> It will be much more challenging to deliver consistently from family to family with a virtual structure. It's difficult enough to provide consistency across clients when all the people sit in the same organization. The largest MFO serves 220 client families in its New York office alone, with a team of 65 professionals. You can imagine the diversity across 200 clients. Imagine if you took the same goal and scattered all the advisors and all those relationships across the country.

Hamilton further notes that major players are looking at the family office market for the first time: 'We're going to have dramatic changes in service delivery over the next five years. In the meantime, the client is getting smarter and smarter. The primary change agent is the informed client.'

The adjusted mindset

One of the first mindset adjustments on entry to the family office world must concern service focus. Even for top investment management consultants at larger firms, product still competes with the focus on the client. A wealth optimization consultant must be completely free of any product considerations other than asking the question: 'Out of all the products available, which best suits my client's needs?' This question assumes that complete open architecture exists, which is not the case at this time for any large financial institution. The variety of MFO models discussed earlier have one thing in common: they have no tie to any products. Their business is completely centered on providing advice and services for the client, and they generate profit from providing advice, not from offering products under any contractual relationship.

Investment management consultants need to make a fundamental shift in their thinking, and the easiest way to facilitate the shift is by following the education mandate outlined in Chapter 9. Investment management consultants are educated primarily in the provision of investment management solutions, while the softer services are not yet being emphasized as an essential part of serving wealthy clients. As both industries continue to transform, education in these areas will develop. Top consultants are demanding more and organizations like the Investment Management Consultants Association (IMCA) are rising to meet those demands. However, for now, there are no formalized programs with a focus on educating consultants in comprehensive wealth optimization.

The second mindset adjustment that must be made concerns the manner in which consultants are compensated. In order to successfully make this adjustment, consultants must value the services they provide. Does the value the consultant offers lie in the products recommended or in the advice given? The answer to that question may seem simple; what is not so simple is assigning a value to the advice component. But nothing will change and the transition will not be accomplished until a specific value is assigned to the advice component of a consultant's business.

Once in place, however, the consultant is free to develop a business plan around the advice component. This change in mindset will set off a predictable chain of events. If financial services firms currently give advice away for free, how will the consultant be adequately paid for the advice he or she gives? The answer to this question, along with the increasingly informed client, is driving the changes now occurring.

Another change in mindset that must occur concerns availability to clients, not only from a time standpoint, but also from a nurturing and accommodation perspective. A commitment must be made to give the client service on his or her terms, not on the consultant's. This may mean working with an outside resource such as a family counselor in order to mediate specific situations. If the family office works with more than one member of the family, this can be a complicated process. Not all family members desire their personal information to be shared with other family members, and different outlooks on life or different objectives can cause conflict within the family.[9] Dealing with these types of situations requires patience and a different approach to client care.

Once these three major mindset adjustments have been made – focusing on the advice and service segments of the business, assigning a specific compensatory value to that segment, and introducing a willingness to provide a much broader range of services – consultants are ready to make adjustments to their business plan.

The adjusted business plan

There are preliminary steps that must be taken before actually rewriting the business plan. These involve consultants completing a thorough assessment of the business landscape, reassessing their human capital (team and staff), intellectual capital (expertise and business acumen), and social capital (ideal clients, community involvement, club or other organization memberships), and organizing their practice to become a business entity to which a value can be assigned.

The basic outline for reworking the business plan is as follows.

- State the business objectives.
- Decide how compensation will be structured.
- Delineate the specific services that will be provided within the scope of that compensation. This can be divided into different tiers of service, if desired.
- List the target market (s) that will be attracted to those services (this needs to be much more specific than just 'wealthy individuals and families').
- Design a marketing plan that will attract your target market (s) and build your identity.
- Identify weak points in your service model in light of the new service mandate.
- Filter accepted business structure into your plan. This means a specific outline of procedures to be followed (a policies and procedures manual should be written and a copy given to all staff), including service goals and objectives that are to be consistently met. This is not meant to be an oppressive document, but a guide to the process of integrating the talents of your team and staff.
- Develop accountability structures. These should not be designed as overbearing, morale depleting disciplinary procedures, but rather should serve to keep everyone on track so that the business becomes streamlined in its processes. Make sure to highlight the benefits this type of streamlining has for everyone.
- Develop service awards and other special events that will be used to communicate appreciation to your staff. (Client appreciation events will be included in the marketing plan.)
- Provide a copy of the business plan to everyone who is involved in carrying it out. It is the author's view that all facets of the business plan should be shared with all staff. (This assumes suitable staff have been hired so that confidential information will be protected. If there is any doubt about any staff in this regard – after sufficient time has elapsed to establish a trust relationship – they should be replaced.)
- Review the business plan on a quarterly basis in order to assess adherence, and on an annual basis to evaluate effectiveness.

The business plan should be comprehensive, outlining the reasons for implementing it, the desired results, the specific steps designed to yield the desired results, and how those steps will be implemented and by whom. Such specific planning should be undertaken, realizing that a limited amount of flexibility must be included to accommodate unforeseen complications and the fact that people are, indeed, people. An effective business plan should implement a structure that allows all team members and staff to develop their talent *Novel idea* satisfaction from their efforts. An enjoyable, productive work atmosphere create best identity-builders possible.

Case studies

From a personal standpoint, it is important to identify why the consultant i wealth business in the first place. What rewards does this involvement hold fo personally? How does it affect family life and social life? Dissatisfaction in fa interaction filters into business interactions and relationships, and although the not be visible to the consultant, they will be apparent to the consultant's clients. I when business and personal life are in balance, they actually feed and support eac create a consistent, credible message to the client. Here are two cases in point.

Case study 1: John's high-pressured practice

John had a passion for the investment business. He had carefully designed his practice developing mentoring relationships with some of the top producers in his firm. He had hired an outside business consultant to help him design a business plan and reorganize his team. He had applied what he had learned and was, in the eyes of most people, a huge success. But John was stressed all the time. He had targeted markets that he felt would bring him the most lucrative contacts but he was having a difficult time really 'connecting' with these people. He had studied their likes and dislikes, hobbies, and business profiles, and he was bringing in some accounts. But there was something not quite right.

He was spending a lot of time taking prospective clients to dinner and going to functions he knew would be attended by members of this market. But his staff felt John was never satisfied with their work. They were becoming disenchanted by John's assurance that the push to bring more clients into the business would provide the revenues needed to streamline operations and service. He had also promised to hire more staff at a specific revenue point. But his current staff were frustrated and weary of the extra work that only seemed to keep increasing with no visible evidence of relief.

Meanwhile, at home, John's wife was complaining that all of his attentions were on his business and that he had little time for her and the children. She had tried to be supportive in John's efforts to catapult his business, but his passion for 'making it' with this target market had overshadowed every other aspect of his life. John and his wife were miserable. At the few functions John's wife attended with him, there was a subtle resentment between the two of them. She resented the time he spent away from her and the children. He resented his wife's resentment since he was trying his best to provide a good life for them.

Case study 2: Mark's optimization business

Mark also had a successful practice. He had identified the types of clients who enjoyed the same leisure and business activities he enjoyed, and Mark and his wife had been participating in these activities for a long time. In fact, it was through these activities that they had met 22 years ago. They had built many friendships within the two target markets Mark had identified in his business plan. Their net worths were quite sufficient to provide the type of business opportunities Mark desired, but his primary focus was on finding the types of clients he would enjoy having as personal friends, regardless of whether a close friendship would actually develop. He would leave that to chance.

150

Mark's business definitely had purpose. It was designed to provide a nice and for his family. But it had also been designed to provide that standard of living that would contribute to his own sources of capital – his human, intellectual, and socia~ ital as well as his financial capital. Mark realized that his intellectual capital was the core of his business. He also realized that the human capital represented by his team and staff were a tremendous resource to him, while his and his wife's social capital was of great value in the community. The wisely structured use of all of these types of capital resulted in a visible increase in financial capital, which allowed Mark to further enrich the other three types of capital.

Mark's wife enjoys the social interaction with his clients since she likes being with the same types of people as Mark. She can be herself around them and doesn't feel she has to be 'on' or different when in their presence. Mark's staff also enjoy their work. They are enthusiastic about Mark's goals and appreciate the opportunity to use their skills in a professional capacity. When problems arise, they have a structured process to take care of them. If something unexpected arises, they conduct a team meeting to investigate the proper solution. Everyone has a stake in making the business succeed. Where else would they have the opportunity to do what they enjoy for the kinds of people with whom they enjoy interacting?

Case study review

Realistically, these two case studies have elements that overlap in most consultants' practices. On the other hand, many more elements of one may be present than the other. Given those two qualifying statements, there is value in examining the two studies more closely. The results of these two businesses are quite different. Many of the basic elements are similar, but the manner in which they were implemented yielded two entirely different practices. Most importantly, the results of each practice were only outward symptoms in the case of John's practice or rewarding fruits in the case of Mark's practice of the respective efforts. The real differences in these businesses are deeply embedded within each organization.

John and Mark had hired the same business coach to help them organize their practices and determine workable business plans. Their business plans were both very comprehensive. They had both put business organizational structures in place. But John's focus was strictly on generating revenue. Of course, he felt he had his clients' best interests at heart as well, but the translation of that care was not coming through effectively. John had regular meetings with his team and his staff but they were usually not very productive. His partners and staff were reluctant to express their views. When they had done so in times past, John had either pointed them toward his business plan or had said, 'That's a nice idea but it's not within the scope of what we're trying to do here.' John felt he knew what it took to build a solid business concern. His father had been successful in the business and he had tapped into his father's philosophies as well as the structures and business practices of several successful colleagues. But John was trying to apply those structures and business practices exactly as his colleagues and his father had applied them. He paid no heed to the fact that he did not enjoy doing business that way; it had worked extremely well for everyone else, so it should work as well or better for him, he had thought.

Mark took the ideas and advice he received from colleagues and applied the best of those ideas and advice in ways that best fitted with his team's business plan, his staff's talents and capabilities, and his personal goals. Everything in Mark's business was consistent with those goals. Everything about Mark's business sent the same message to his clients: that Mark and his team were a cut above, that they were truly interested in their clients' welfare and objectives, that they were uncompromising professionals, and that each member of Mark's team really enjoyed their work.

Clients were drawn to Mark's practice as a result. They knew there was something special there. Mark had carefully chosen highly talented individuals with whom to form partnerships and to hire for staff responsibilities. It had taken months of painstaking interviewing and spending time with a number of candidates, but that time had definitely been worth the investment. He had set up effective communication systems within the business, not only to facilitate operations but also to foster the professional yet personalized atmosphere he wished for the entire team. He spent time with each person to explore their personal and professional goals for working with him. He facilitated the disclosure of other talents that they had always wanted to use but had never before found opportunity. He considered their ideas for making the business better. He had given each partner and staff member a personal stake in the success of the business, not only in a monetary sense but also in a personal achievement and satisfaction sense.

Mark had also established very efficient and effective systems for providing high-quality service to his clients. His team was fully integrated in its functions so that if an unexpected need arose it could be fulfilled promptly. Each team member knew what needed to be done and with whom it needed to be accomplished. Granted, things were not perfect. There were times of great stress and even some disorganization, but those times were few and were usually diffused within a reasonable length of time. Everyone worked together to handle the few unexpected crises that occurred, so that each crisis was not only handled well, but handled in a way that would lessen its likelihood of recurring.

The team met regularly, reviewed the week's activities and progress and discussed ideas for improvement or reviewed certain projects that were especially important that week. Mark had aligned his business with each capital asset he possessed. His efforts resulted in a satisfying, balanced business operation that took good care of his clients, offered him and his staff great personal satisfaction, allowed him to enjoy his family and friends, and produced a good living and a solid business.

Consultant education and credentials

This topic is fully discussed in Chapter 9 but its importance merits an additional mention here. Clients are paying much more attention to the educational background, credentials, and expertise of consultants, and they want to see evidence of this training. Although a designation or certification does not automatically qualify the consultant, it is on the list of criteria clients use in selecting advisors.

Continuing education is also expected. Clients want to know their advisors are up-to-date on information and laws that might affect their assets. Just as a doctor needs to stay current in order to improve the overall health of his or her patients, it is imperative for the consultant to maintain the quality of his or her knowledge.

Education for clients

Clients are clamoring for education from their advisors. A wealth optimization consultant is in a prime position to provide that education. Client education is one of the most effective ways of strengthening relationships. Clients who are more knowledgeable understand processes better, appreciate the consultant's services more, and, as a result of being able to see more value, are willing to pay for more advice and services.

An important and often overlooked component of education is that of educating heirs. This education can begin early via informal involvement in the family business, usually on the philanthropic side. But according to a member of the millennial generation who is also involved in educating and advising wealthy families and their heirs, many families contradict themselves. For example, a patriarch may want a son to become involved in philanthropy but the son may wish to support non-profit groups of which the patriarch does not approve. 'He clearly doesn't want his son to be philanthropic,' says this educator. 'He wants his son to be *him*.' The educator says the importance is in emphasizing the process in which the son chose to give to the organization of his choice, not the organization he chose to benefit:

> It's, 'Did he go through all the steps to research all sides; did he go to that organization and ask them why they thought their cause was good or why they think certain things are bad?' It's fine to teach your kids to have an interest in being philanthropic, give them the passion to go find out what these organizations are doing, do the due diligence on them, and let them decide for themselves.

It's not the wealth optimization consultant's responsibility to be the family psychologist, but it is his or her responsibility to guide families to other professionals who can assist in these areas and to consider these factors in the overall optimization of the family's wealth. Client education is discussed further in Chapter 12.

Execution of the plan

The last step is to execute the plan that has been so carefully developed. By the time the consultant has reached this point, he or she should have a clear vision of what is to be accomplished and how to accomplish it. Unless the wealth optimization business is being established for the first time with a completely new team of people, the transformation of an investment management consulting practice into a wealth optimization business will involve a process – it will not happen overnight. However, there are steps that can be taken to facilitate a smooth and relatively quick transition, and these steps are contingent on a clear identification of the benefits to be brought to the business by making the transition.

Given this clarity of purpose, the next step is to make sure you have hired the best team and staff possible, and then to include them in your plans. This, too, is an educational process. It will require educating the team on the wealth optimization process, why it is beneficial, and what it will offer them through the business you wish to form. Ideally, this will be a process that begins with the partners on the team, will become a shared vision, and then will gradually be opened to the staff for their comments, input, and to buy in to the plan.

If the plan includes a team leaving a major firm, of course such a move itself requires significant planning.

- Should the team join an existing MFO? If so, which model will fit the team goals in the best capacity?
- Should the team create its own MFO? If so, what technology should be used? How much in financial resources does the team have to spend on setting up its own platform? Have

the ingredients of the platform been fully identified? Has their integration been well thought out – especially regarding the range of services the team wishes to provide?

- How will compensation and fees be structured? Which services will be provided in-house and which will be outsourced?
- Which clients will go with the team when it leaves? Which clients does the team want to take with it?
- Which coaches and consultants should be hired to help the team make this transition?
- How soon will the projected benefits begin to be realized?
- Which benefits can be expected to be realized first – which benefits need to be realized first?
- How committed is the entire team and staff to making this transition work?

All of this planning may sound burdensome, but in light of the changes in both industries and the devastation of both capital and practices during the 2000–03 bear market, it should give welcome direction to professionals trying to decide which model is for them. The failure to invest in such planning may prove to be even more burdensome as the industry sea change progresses.

Conclusions

Expansion and transformation to the appropriate wealth optimization model requires the following.

- A thorough re-examination of existing business plans, goals, and objectives.
- A change of focus to long-term, higher-level compensation from short-term compensatory gratification.
- A genuine, consistent, deep-seated change in focus in favor of serving the needs of the client, with the realization that compensation will be a natural by-product.
- A willingness on the part of the consultant to educate himself or herself in the components necessary for implementing an optimization level business.
- The realization that educating clients is a prime ingredient to attracting, building, maintaining, and deepening relationships with wealthy individuals and their circles of influence.
- A willingness to implement the processes and steps necessary to create a balanced personal and professional life for the consultant.

The only missing ingredient is the effective marketing to chosen wealthy client markets and building the identity of the wealth optimization consultant within those markets, and this is the subject of Chapter 12.

---

[1] Author's interview with Patricia Soldano, CEO, Cymric Family Office Services, September 2003.
[2] Author's interview with Sara Hamilton, founder and CEO, Family Office Exchange (FOX), September 2003.
[3] Author's interview with Richard Joyner, CPA, CFP, CIMA, president of private wealth management, Tolleson Wealth Management, September 2003.
[4] Author's interview with Scott D. Welch, Managing director, Lydian Wealth Management LLC, October 2003.
[5] Author's interview with Sara Hamilton, founder and CEO, FOX, September 2003.
[6] Beyer, Charlotte B. (1999), 'Family Offices in America: Why the Bloom is Off the Rose', *Journal of*

Wealth Management, Fall 1999, Vol. 2, No. 2, pp. 26–29.

[7] Author's interview with Scott D. Welch, managing director, Lydian Wealth Management LLC, October 2003.

[8] Author's interview with Sara Hamilton, founder and CEO, FOX, September 2003.

[9] McReynolds, Rebecca (2003), 'All in the Family', *Bloomberg Wealth Manager,* November, p. 97.

Chapter 12

Effective marketing and client education

Introduction

What is marketing, and why is it more effective than advertising or sales in attracting the wealthy? The answer to both questions is quite simple. Marketing is the process of relationship building. Therefore, it is a process, not a one-time occurrence like an advertisement. Effective marketing goes hand in hand with wealth optimization.

There are meaningful differences between marketing, advertising, and sales. Viewing marketing as a relationship-building process casts an entirely different light on its purpose, how it is used and implemented, and what it can mean to wealth optimization if designed and implemented effectively. Advertising is not a relationship-building process, and neither are sales. In the wealth optimization world, effective marketing is much more powerful than either advertising or sales. Marketing is an educational, credibility-building, relationship-cementing, efficient way to optimize wealth. Effective marketing focuses on the client, not on the consultant or his or her firm.

This chapter will explain:

- what marketing is designed to do;
- what it is not designed to do;
- the difference between effective marketing for wealth optimization and marketing within the financial services environment;
- how writing adds marketing efficiency by educating clients and by building consultant credibility;
- how to tailor marketing to attract the desired clients; and
- how technology can make marketing more efficient.

What marketing is designed to do

Today, people in general want to be offered the opportunity to buy what they want, not to be convinced that they need a product or service. 'Convincing' is sales; marketing is an invitation. The invitation is the only option the wealthy will seriously consider. Even today's financial industry investment management consultants have the two concepts confused. In their minds, marketing is equated with sales and no distinctions are drawn. Indeed, the entire financial services industry fails to focus on what will truly attract the wealthy, as is evident from its marketing materials. Each firm produces similar marketing material along the following lines: 'Each of our services is highly specialized, demanding in-depth knowledge and expertise. XYZ's professionals are leading experts in their various disciplines and we often provide investment management and financial counsel to multiple generations of the same family and to our institutional clients over many decades. Even today, in our highly mobile society, XYZ employees tend to stay with the company, providing continuity of service and building lasting relationships with our clients.'

So, what is wrong with this? Every firm wants clients to know its professionals have knowledge and in-depth experience, that they are experts in their disciplines, and that those disciplines are varied. In other words, there is a lot of quality to choose from at any firm. So how is a client who reads this great looking, professionally produced piece to know that this particular firm has the right quality in the areas he or she needs? How is the client to choose from the large number of professionals available at this firm the one person who will care for his or her needs satisfactorily? How are clients supposed to have an inkling of the consultant's particular expertise, experience, and philosophy toward client care?

As the investment industry attempts to turn itself around to focus on the client, which in its definition is doing fee-based business instead of selling product (transaction-based business), the mark is definitely and paradoxically being missed in the area of marketing material. Brochures and other written materials still focus on the firm, its expertise, and its specialties – ie, the disconnect comes from the fact that most large firms are still deeply embedded in a product/profit-driven environment.

Granted, some significant changes have been made, and most now offer some form of retail managed money program and some are even venturing into family office level services. But the changes are not homogenous. The material clients read is not written by marketing people with experience in wealth optimization consulting. It is written by large advertising firms hired to help firms in every industry sell everything from laundry detergent to roll-over cell phone minutes. These are the firms that are hired to promote financial services in a world where financial services firms are supposedly trying to attract the wealthy.

The difference between advertising, marketing, and sales

Despite a reluctance to even introduce advertising and sales in a chapter dedicated to marketing effectively to the wealthy and their families, a purpose might be served in showing how these two activities are related in the financial services world. The best way to think of these separate, distinct business-generating activities is as follows.

- Advertising is the process by which a prospective client's attention is gained.
- Marketing draws the client in and is the process by which clients are invited to find out more about consultants and their services.
- Selling is the process by which consultants actually secure the business.

Marketing serves to continually build the relationship, much like the monitoring function of the consulting process serves to continually ensure clients' assets are being well managed. When the consulting process was first introduced to retail advisors, firms still operated primarily on the old product sales mentality. Firms did not really know what consulting was until the late 1980s and did not truly wake up to the benefits of the consulting idea until the mid-1990s. Unfortunately, the marketing process did not develop along with the consulting process.

Like a lot of other buzzwords in the industry, the term 'marketing' has been confused with various other concepts in the business, and, in an effort to dispel this confusion, in the following subsections each segment – advertising, marketing, and sales – will be defined, its uses delineated, and its application shown within today's investment world.

Advertising

Advertising is defined as the activity of attracting public attention to a product or business, as by paid announcements in the print, broadcast, or electronic media. However, in a survey of Investment Management Consultants Association (IMCA) consultants conducted in June 2003, only 6.5% of respondents indicated they obtain new clients as a result of advertising. On the other hand, 75.4% said they get new clients from client referrals. Educational seminars offered by consultants were credited by 21.2% of respondents. So advertising appears to be one of the least effective ways to obtain new clients, at least in the investment management consulting world.

Yet, many consultants (and their firms) spend considerable amounts of money placing advertisements in the newspapers and magazines read by their target markets, conducting direct mail campaigns, and other ineffective but popular ways of advertising. Unfortunately, many of these advertising media are classified as 'marketing', which leads consultants to expect one type of result when their actions are eliciting another. After multiple thousands of dollars have been spent, they realize their efforts did not pay off, but the money is still gone. What they think is an investment in their businesses turns out to be a growing money hole, and they become disenchanted. If the disenchantment arrived after the first experience, it would not be so bad, but advertisers continue to confuse the term with marketing, so consultants continue to put large sums of money into something that will never work as they hope it will.

Although there may be a place for advertising in the financial services world, there is little place for it in the wealth optimization world where families relish their privacy. This is especially in a climate where single family offices (SFOs) are disappearing and less personal multi-family offices (MFOs) are taking their place. There is nothing inherently wrong with advertising, and firms hired to do it do it well. The problem is in distinguishing when advertising is appropriate. Knowing the true purpose of advertising prevents disappointing results that may be gained by applying the wrong approach. It is exactly like managing clients' expectations. They hear all the stories in the market-place and the consultant must continually let them know the types of returns that are realistically possible. So must the consultant be knowledgeable and well educated regarding the appropriate use of advertising, marketing, and sales.

Marketing

Marketing entices clients in to find out what a particular consultant can do to help them, a consultant's personal information, and the qualifications that make the consultant the right fit for their needs. Marketing is the most important aspect of the business-building process. It implements the business plan, attracts ideal clients, and helps build deeper relationships with clients, their children, and their friends.

Why is marketing not sales? The purpose of marketing is not to get the client to sign on the dotted line, but rather to get the client to want to sign on the dotted line. Effective marketing is the most powerful force behind a business. Here are two case studies that show why.

Case study 1

Mitch held an educational client-appreciation event for the top 10% of clients in his target market. The event was well structured, in line with what his target market enjoyed doing, and the educational topic was something he had heard several clients express an interest in. Several of the clients brought friends who were not yet Mitch's clients. After the event, Mitch was able to set several appointments with these new prospects. He gave them some material to look over before they came for their appointments and offered to answer any questions or address any particular concerns they had after reading the material.

As the new prospects came for their first appointments with Mitch, he encouraged them to tell him all about themselves, what their families were like, what they envisioned for their personal future, what they had experienced with other advisors, and what they really wanted from an advisory relationship. He then talked about his own family, situations that he had been in that were similar to what they had experienced, and, when asked, he explained about his group's investment philosophy and how the firm liked to work with clients. At the close of the meeting Mitch asked what else he could do to help them, and they asked if he would mind speaking at their next family meeting.

What contributed to Mitch's success? First, he held a genuinely client-focused event for his best clients. He scheduled activities that he knew they would enjoy and he chose an educational topic that he knew was of interest. He had obviously built solid relationships with these clients because many of them brought friends, who, after liking what they heard, made appointments with Mitch to find out more. His brochure was top notch and his information packet was in sync with his brochure and had specific, client-directed information about how his team catered to clients in his target market. Mitch also had credible, well-written articles that had his name on them.

Mitch used marketing skills in focusing the initial meeting on the client, and not on using it as an opportunity to tout his group's expertise in any area, or to show how successful they had been with other clients. He spent the majority of the time asking the prospects to talk about their lives and their concerns. He paid very close attention to what they said and related their experiences to experiences in his own life. Then he 'invited' them to ask for more, which they did.

Case study 2

John held a seminar for the top 20% of his clients. He also put an advertisement in the local business journal about the seminar, sent reminder cards, and had his staff follow up on the affirmative RSVPs the day before the seminar. He had invited 60 people, and was hopeful a few more would attend as a result of the journal advertisement. The outcome was that 40 responded that they would attend and 20 actually did attend; 18 of the attendees were clients and two were friends who had accompanied clients. No one had come as a result of the advertisement.

After his presentation, John made an appointment with one of the client guests. His other clients patted him on the back and told him what a good job he had done and how much they had enjoyed the presentation. John was disappointed. He had been told that doing seminars was one of the best ways to get new clients. He had spent a lot of time preparing his presentation, and more than a few dollars providing drinks and food. He was not happy with the return on his investment.

What made Mitch's event such a success and John's exactly the opposite? Mitch had done a lot of preliminary work to build solid relationships with his clients. He had hired a

professional marketing consultant who had experience and credentials in the financial industry to help him create a marketing plan that would systematically implement his business
plan, help him focus on his target market, keep him in touch with his client base at regular
intervals, and educate them in the investment process and in the areas Mitch knew matched
their concerns.

Mitch had successfully groomed his client relationships to the point that they loved hear-
ing from him (which they did often through Mitch's well-designed drip system), were excited
about attending the events he held, and wanted to share the experiences with their friends.
They wanted to help Mitch grow his business so they invited friends they knew would be
qualified clients in his target market.

John, on the other hand, had a business plan but no marketing plan. He sent out updates
to his clients on a regular basis. He had spent a lot of money on direct mail campaigns and
sent out a newsletter every quarter that he ordered from a marketing firm and could brand
with his firm's logo and his own team's name and information. John's efforts were uncoordi-
nated, unfocused, and had no consistent theme. They also came across as impersonal.

Sales

Sales are the last thing on the minds of wealth optimization consultants. With a well-designed
marketing plan that properly implements a business plan based on the needs of the client,
sales become a natural conclusion. No convincing needs to be done; the signatures on the
dotted line just happen. By the time a consultant begins telling prospects about his or her
value proposition, the consultant is in the sales process. If the marketing has been done correctly, prospects will ask the consultant for that information without any need for the topic to
be introduced. The right level and methods of marketing will set up the sale from such a solid
foundation that a concerted effort would have to be made to keep the sale from happening. It
sounds like a lot to expect, but that is precisely how powerful effective marketing can be.

The source of marketing success

Marketing success is based on deciding which markets to address, correctly analyzing those
markets and becoming intimately familiar with their needs, and designing a business around
serving those needs. The marketing plan is the instrument designated to carry out the business plan. As such, the most important part of the business plan is the marketing plan. A business plan can be created, but in the absence of a well-designed marketing plan the business
plan may be implemented in an ad hoc fashion. Activities are not coordinated, and clients
may get one message from one part of the team and another message from another part, creating confusion. The most important aspect of marketing is consistency. The message being
communicated must consistently be represented by every activity, every event, and every
action by members of the wealth optimization consultant's team or staff. This consistency can
only be achieved as the result of careful planning.

Although more consultants are creating marketing plans with their business plans – a
show of hands at a recent IMCA conference indicated about half are doing so – the quality
of those plans is questionable. Most marketing coaches associated with the financial services
industry are still of the sales and advertising mindset, which seeps through almost every business coaching program available throughout the industry. Financial services firms are large

corporations, and large corporations hire big advertising firms to design their marketing materials. This is evident from the similar content of marketing materials not only of major industry firms, but also of the individual advisors who create brochures or other marketing material to identify their team businesses within the firm structure. The problem is not so much the consultants but rather the marketing message to which they are exposed. Business coaches attempting to be marketing experts have booths at major industry conferences. These conferences also invite advertising companies to speak to consultants about marketing – something totally foreign to them, especially from a consulting perspective.

The following is an example of brochure material generated by consultants responding to the marketing message sent by the financial services industry. The example shows the huge difference to the message simply by changing the focus from the firm or the consultant team to the client.[1] Keep in mind that this brochure was designed with no particular target market in mind.

Example brochure copy

Original copy (partial)

Integrity – integrity is at the heart of all our relationships. We put our client's interests first by:

- maintaining complete confidentiality;
- avoiding conflicts of interest;
- offering full disclosure and objectivity;
- always doing the right thing; and
- adhering to the Uniform Fiduciary Standards of Care.

Service – our clients deserve courtesy, respect, and prompt response. We will exceed our clients' expectations by:

- handling all questions promptly (return phone calls and e-mails promptly);
- being accessible 24/7;
- providing accurate monitoring of investments; and
- anticipating the needs of our clients.

Revised copy (using only the copy above as a guide)

Integrity. Service. Value. Quality. Rather than give you our view of those criteria, we prefer you offer us yours. No one knows the demands of your financial life as well as you. The XYZ Group centers its uncompromising focus on offering standards of service that surpass your expectations.

You expect:

- complete confidentiality;
- objective, high-quality advice; and
- uncompromising integrity.

In addition, The XYZ Group gives you:

- prompt response to your concerns and questions;
- 24/7 access;
- accurate monitoring of your portfolio; and
- your needs anticipated without your having to ask.

Analyzing the messages

Although the first set of copy had a good message, the question is which would more effectively draw the client to pursue more information, and why? The first set of copy stated basically the same things that every firm throughout the financial services industry states, and there is little, if any, differentiation of this investment management consulting team from any other.

The second set of copy conveyed the same message, but in a much more effective manner. Its focus was entirely on the client. It 'talked' to the client as if it were viewing the team of consultants through the clients' eyes, and it clearly distinguished this team from any other team.

The marketing plan

The marketing plan should follow a similar outline to the business plan, with one key difference – the business plan focuses on the consultant's or consulting team's practice, while the marketing plan focuses strictly on the clients it desires to attract. This point cannot be over-emphasized because it is a complete 'about face' from the modus operandi of the financial services industry.

The wealth optimization consultant's marketing plan should incorporate the business objectives, identify appropriate target markets and specific, client-focused ways to approach them. It should delineate the specific services that will be provided, how clients will benefit from those services, how the services are to be delivered, and the measuring systems designed to gauge the effectiveness of the marketing plan and feedback from clients.

One of the first steps in any transformation of a business is to survey – preferably by phone or in person – existing clients regarding the services provided, the manner in which they are delivered, and clients' overall satisfaction with their experience. No matter how well consultants think they know their clientele, such a survey will always include revealing results. Most of these results are likely to be positive, but learning about the less positive ones may be even more beneficial. This survey would ideally be conducted before the marketing plan is drafted so that the results can be incorporated into the planning stage of the marketing process.

It is important that the marketing plan incorporates only activities that the consultants and their staffs enjoy. This may sound like a reverse in focus, but the reality is that consultants should only be trying to attract people they enjoy being around and who enjoy similar activities. Like John in the Chapter 11 case study, trying to force a team or staff into a particular mold never works. Of course, there is a direct link here to choosing the appropriate target markets in the first place.

Target markets should be aligned closely with the consulting team's natural markets. In other words, the markets already served by the consulting team should be evaluated from several standpoints. The 'A', 'B', and 'C' client categories espoused by so many financial industry business consultants are applicable here only from the perspective of identifying 'A' level clients if that process has not be previously accomplished. 'A' level clients should then be evaluated for attributes in common among the client group as well as with the consultants. It is rare for 'A'clients not to have several common attributes with the consultants and with each other, and assessing these will make planning marketing activities much easier and more fun. Business should be fun. It should not seem like 'business'.

Marketing materials

The marketing materials generally required for wealth optimization businesses include the following.

- *A personal brochure* designed to attract readers to find out more about what the wealth optimization consultant can do for them.
- *A well-written biography* of the wealth optimization consultant's (or team's) experience and credentials. This helps indicate to clients the possible fit between them and the consultant or consulting team.
- *Powerful, interesting, inviting presentations.* Now that clients are interested, they want to know what a wealth optimization consultant might have to say that would make them want to set up a personal meeting.
- *Trade magazine articles.* These further establish a consultant's expertise. Some marketing firms recommend that only applicable quotes from articles be sent to clients and prospective clients, but a full article with a wealth management consultant's by-line at the top builds more credibility than isolated quotes.
- *Research and educational materials.* These do two things; they maintain and improve the consultant's standing as an expert, and they help the consultant transform his or her clients into exceptional, ideal clients.
- *Books.* These represent an excellent and powerful way to accomplish a range of marketing goals in one fell swoop and to make the most of other marketing activities.

The brochure

Of course, it is important for clients to see the consultant's credentials, hear the right message, and feel confident in the consultant's expertise, but inviting clients to seek that information is the correct focus of a brochure, not getting that information 'out' to them. The message of the brochure must match the message sent by the entire team in any situation, and it should be a message that high net worth investors are eager to hear. The best place to begin is by looking at the market environment for the consultant's particular expertise and the goals laid out in the business plan. Here's an example of how the development of an effective brochure works.

Brochure case study

John is a well-educated, well-credentialed wealth optimization consultant. He views his clients' wealth as not only including their financial assets, but their human, intellectual, and social capital as well. John has developed a business plan outlining the steps needed to accomplish the growth objectives he has set for his business for next year. He has also developed a pragmatic marketing plan for implementing those steps in a way that is realistic and efficient for himself and his staff.

John has identified his primary target market as successful executives of software firms.

163

Software executives have specific common experiences, needs, and problems. John has a particular fascination with software and how it is developed and he has followed software companies for most of his career. These executives certainly experienced the bear market but they experienced it in a very different way than the general investing public. John is aware that they are looking for a consultant who knows the ups and downs of the software industry, is familiar with the competitive forces of their industry, and who can help them protect and optimize the use of all of their assets during tough environments.

John needed help physically connecting the message he wanted to send to these executives with the message he knew they wanted to hear. With professional assistance, John was able to develop a professional looking brochure that addressed the concerns of software executives and showed how his expertise could meet their needs. It was brief, to the point, and inviting. It 'grabbed' its readers and invited them to find out more about John. John uses the brochure as outlined in his marketing plan. He gets regular phone calls from software executives wanting to find out more about the services he provides.

Obviously, John's brochure was not some magical client attraction tool, but it did generate enough interest from software executives for them to want to know more about John and his services. It prompted them to take action from what they read, and it opened the door for John to begin the process of earning their trust and their business.

Biographies, presentations, and articles

The proper place for biographies and relevant articles is in the information packet or at a presentation, not in the brochure. The biographies of team and staff, presentations used in client meetings, family meetings, or in educational settings, and articles and research that is published with the consultant as author – for all of these, the message must match the primary message being communicated by the wealth optimization business, regardless of the topic under discussion. This consistency builds a true identity – what general marketing professionals and business coaches call 'branding'. The message the wealth optimization consultant wishes to convey must be in sync with his or her identity and the reason for being in the wealth optimization business. This will create an identity for the consultant that is unmistakable and which will automatically enter the minds of client families as well as prospective client families anytime the consultant's name arises.

Sophisticated presentations may be impressive, but too many technology gimmicks will lessen the quality of the presentation. It should be clean, well-designed, and well-executed. The presenter must know the topic well enough to necessitate minimal use of cards or other prompts. It is easy for presentations to spend too much time on one area, be too busy visually, or look 'thrown together'. The presentation must look professional, must convey the overall message, but must also be directly related to the topic discussed with no efforts to promote the team other than from the team's identification on the first slide and its contact information on the last one.

Books

Books are perhaps the most efficient and effective business-building tools available. A well-written book that conveys the wealth optimization consultant's message and expertise and is truly helpful to the target audience creates greater visibility, authenticity, and status in its eyes.

A book can bring all other marketing activities and messages together in a comprehensive and integrated fashion. It promotes consistency, and it adds excitement to the business.

If marketed correctly, a book will 'touch' clients outside of the wealth optimization consultant's circle of influence, serving as a much broader invitation for qualified clients to make contact. However, like everything else in the marketing plan, a book must be carefully constructed and must be in keeping with the consistent message of the business.

Efficiencies through writing and technology

A survey conducted by the Institute for Private Investors (IPI) in 1999 found that eight out of 10 private investors considered themselves computer literate; nine out of 10 used e-mail; favorite websites were Bloomberg and Yahoo; and almost half had online links to at least one of their money managers and their custodians.[2]

At the time of writing, it can safely be assumed that all private investors and wealthy families are comfortable with technology. These investors also want consultants to educate them rather than 'talk at them', and they expect to be more involved in the overall optimization of their wealth.[3] These desires and expectations provide the perfect backdrop for the wealth optimization consultant to employ writing and technology in educating clients. This chapter has defined marketing as a relationship builder, a consistent communicator of a wealth optimization consultant's message and identity, and as the implementation of the business plan. Another role marketing plays is that of educator. With all of the changes wealth optimization consultants must accommodate during the reinvention of their businesses, marketing through writing can be one of the most effective tools at their disposal. In line with a well-designed marketing plan, writing can educate clients on the new way of doing business, outline the benefits they will receive, and the enhanced relationship they will experience. Even with fewer client relationships to manage, the depth of these relationships requires consistent contact. Writing – especially when combined with technology – is a powerful communication and contact enhancer. It 'touches' clients more regularly than a consultant can. It leaves no client without attention, and it provides the education clients seek.

A consultant's website can be a powerful marketing tool. The author would venture to say that the primary point of having a website is to provide consistent marketing through education and 'contact' with clients. By consistently posting personal messages from the consultant, or by providing an avenue through which clients can send e-mails directly through the site, clients feel in closer contact with the consultant even when it is impossible to talk directly. E-mail is not a substitute for a phone call, but it is a mode of communication as commonly used as the telephone.

Posting educational material on topics of interest is another way to build relationships, add credibility, and foster trust between client and consultant. Trust and high-quality relationships must continually be earned and nurtured. Using writing and technology to facilitate this process increases the impact of a marketing plan exponentially.

Conclusions

The financial services industry commonly confuses marketing with sales. Sales is the process of convincing a buyer he or she needs the services and products of the seller; marketing is the process of attracting the buyer by discovering the buyer's needs and providing a complete and satisfactory solution to those needs. The successful wealth optimization consultant will be able to communicate the marketing message effectively and pragmatically, building a competitive identity that attracts his or her chosen market.

Education of clients should be focused toward all generations who will be affected by the family wealth. This education can be accomplished by marketing, writing, and using technology. Educational material posted on the consultant's (or the family's) website or distributed by some other means automatically supports phone or face-to-face communication. It helps the client and the consultant get to know each other and establishes a comfort level that can be carried to any other interaction between the two.

---

[1] This example is taken from the brochure created for a graymatter STRATEGIES LLC client in 2003.
[2] Beyer, Charlotte B. (1999), 'A Profile of the High Net Worth Investor', presentation at the NYSSA's *Issues Facing the High Net Worth Investor Conference*, 15 September.
[3] Ibid.

Chapter 13

The new family office: the optimization of family office services

Introduction

The state of the financial services and family office industries today is one of disruption and uncertainty, causing confusion for investors and for those who would advise them. However, during times of substantive change, opportunities abound for those who seek them. But how many of today's advisors and consultants will respond to those opportunities? In the same way that financial industry firms are 'stuck' in their cash cow mindset, so financial industry advisors are stuck in business-hampering mindsets of their own. They tend to adhere to methods that 'have always worked', seeing no need to change what has fostered their past success. But the world is different now. Older advisors getting close to retirement may indeed not need to change, but the vast majority of the advisory population must choose how they will compete going forward. If they do not consciously do so, the choice will be made for them.

Some of the most serious obstacles in the way of advisors' and consultants' success today comprise practitioner shortcomings, including:

- not knowing today's investor market-place;
- not knowing or properly defining target markets;
- improperly assessing team talent and the best ways to use it;
- thinking that being a good salesperson or a good consultant automatically makes you a marketing expert; and
- not being willing to let go of preconceived ideas and ways of doing business.

Readers may take issue with the above list, but if they are honest with themselves many of these points will hit home. Those who are well positioned to capitalize on the opportunities presented by the sea change now occurring in the market-place will most certainly increase their wealth exponentially. But that capitalization must begin with a willingness on the part of the advisor or consultant to eliminate preconceived notions and explore uncharted waters.

More than ever, wealthy families are demanding highly customized relationships with credentialed advisors. They are also seeking ways to obtain more productivity and efficiency out of their family offices. Rising costs make it almost impossible to keep top-level talent, so families are seeking viable alternatives that will still provide the range and depth of services they demand. Client families are becoming more willing to pay for quality advice, and astute advisors and consultants will offer it. Even the most sophisticated advisors and consultants in the financial services industry today are missing the mark on the quality of their advice. They must offer advice that considers every aspect of their clients' wealth and every type of capital, including financial, human, social, and intellectual capital. They must have more investment education and sophistication, and access to more options for customized investing than ever before.

The advisory perspective

Today's advisors and consultants have an opportunity to reinvent themselves and their businesses in ways that will offer them more control over their business and personal lives by targeting the types of clients they enjoy working with and establishing more balance between business and personal life. Whether financial services industry firms will rise to the challenge of successfully changing their product-based culture and providing these consultants with the tools they need remains to be seen.

The author believes that the roles of industry firms and top consultants are metamorphosing, perhaps in ways that may offer several levels of support for advisors. It would be ideal for wealth optimization consultants to be able, at some point, to operate objective businesses at major firms since they have the funds to support such businesses. Firms are making great strides to solve the technology problems hindering the industry, but the educational component so acutely needed by aspiring wealth optimization consultants is the weakest area on both industry sides. Wealthy families require much more from the same services that have always been provided by their family offices. They want greater integration of investments whether traditional or non-traditional, more education, and a deeper understanding of their needs by advisors. They want optimal management of their assets, optimal attention, and optimal comfort with their advisors.

Financial services industry firms will have to make the conscious decision to address these desires or change their focus to a less demanding market segment. The process is still occurring in a trial-and-error fashion, with most firms simply scrambling to realize margins wherever they can. As financial market conditions improve, firms may have more leeway in 'appropriating' funds, which will greatly affect their choice of market. It will take courage to offer a wealth optimization-friendly atmosphere, but the firms who do so can become more profitable than ever. In the interim, astute advisors and consultants are answering the call, whether through multi-family office (MFO) or multi-client family office (MCFO) involvement via the creation of independent businesses, or within the confines of the large firms.

A new business model

A new concept in wealth management is set out in this book – wealth optimization consulting. The concept of optimizing a family's entire portfolio of assets allows consultants the freedom to serve clients in the way they want and with the independence they want, regardless of their physical business status. It also allows wealthy families access to a highly educated, highly qualified, and objective advisory and consulting resource. By looking at the exhibits in Chapter 6 and the consulting process discussions in Chapter 4 comparing family office functions and needs to those most often provided by financial services industry firms, the gap in the overall service offerings are all too apparent. Only by providing in-depth consulting that encompasses all aspects of family assets, attitudes and dynamics, asset allocations to both financial and non-financial investments, cash management, ownership structures, and a host of other considerations can consultants hope to remain competitive over the next three to five years.

The transformation to the new business model will not be easy, but many consultants are already well on the way. The consultants who succeed in making the transformation will set themselves and their businesses in a leadership position in the industry and will become attractive to the very markets they previously sought through other means. A clear view of the process required has been outlined in this book. By stepping back and looking at the history and development of the family office and financial services industries, the dynamics of the family, the realities of the industry sea change, and the opportunities for serious consultants who have their clients' welfare uppermost in their minds, the wealth optimization consultants of tomorrow can obtain the vision necessary to secure their futures. From a financial services industry perspective, the family wealth market is elusive, yet has a powerful hold on the industry. To owners of those assets, their search for the advisory relationship they have long sought is coming to an end. For wealth optimization consultants, attaining the business ideals they have long sought but have previously had no support for realizing is finally on the horizon.

Optimization is the key

The family office is the business model of choice, but in forms other than the traditional single family office (SFO). The family wealth market – also called the private investor market by the Institute for Private Investors (IPI) – is a market whose demands for higher-quality service at a fair price are filtering into the realm of the less affluent. The definition of higher-quality service may vary from investor to investor, but each desires his or her particular needs to be met, and the new family office model – the wealth optimization consulting model – addresses these concerns.

Again, the opportunities are not limited to the top advisors and consultants. In addition, those who find a niche market to address with a high specialty focus can become quite prosperous. Here are a few examples of how niche development within the context of wealth optimization can occur.[1]

- *Example 1*. A wealth optimization consultant earns a performance fee from her work in negotiating favorable prenuptial agreement terms for her wealthy male clients. After the divorce petition is filed, she is again consulted regarding the effective structuring of the assets so that the opposing parties (the wives) secure as few of the assets as possible.
- *Example 2*. A group of cousins started an offshore family office for Latin American families. Services provided included tax optimization, asset protection, and charitable estate planning. The role of the cousins has been to research and perform in-depth due diligence on asset management firms tailored to fit the needs of their clients. They currently advise on over US$3.7 billion in Latin American family assets.
- *Example 3*. A cash flow broker arranges the purchase of income streams. These income streams could come from any number of sources – annuities, workmen's compensation, privately held mortgage notes, lottery winnings, etc. This particular broker is a financial advisory firm that works in 16 states that allow lottery winnings to be assigned. The broker generates millions of dollars in fee income and often is given the opportunity to invest part of the lump sum payments.

These examples are from fairly young companies who have used their resources in innovative ways to create more wealth for all the parties involved. Most of these firms are boutiques and are virtually ignored by large financial institutions. The most important observation about these firms is that they offer invaluable insights into best practices for wealth optimization consultants. Each has found its own unique way to serve the wealthy, and each captures significant wealth in compensation as a result.

The focus of the wealth optimization consultant

Although many MFOs downplay the profitability side of their operating equations, there is obviously great potential for doing well by serving wealthy families. And no one can fault the wealth optimization consultant who identifies a particular need of the wealthy that is currently underserved. It is entrepreneurial spirit that fostered the business examples cited in the previous section, and it is entrepreneurial spirit that will forge the success of wealth optimization consulting.

Wealth optimization is a seriously underestimated need. The opportunities can only be seen by stepping back and looking at both industries – the family office/private investor and financial services industries – from a broader, clearer perspective. Taking a view from above the fray of industry dynamics and the sea change that has wrought so much disappointment and confusion in both camps can offer consultants a path to the optimization of their own wealth as well as that of their clients.

But that path can only be successfully traveled by serving the needs of the client. Touting services provided in the hopes that they will fit a few clients' needs is a poor and frustrating way to position oneself. By using a little intellect and adopting a broader view, a much more productive and satisfying result can be obtained. As well as providing advantages, wealth in the family wealth/private investor segment can cause problems, and these are complicated by a number of factors previously outside consultants' radar screens. However, wealth optimization can alleviate many of those problems through an understanding of family dynamics, the psychology of wealth, and the importance of optimizing all four forms of family capital, plus knowing how to integrate that optimization among ownership structures, asset classes, and influential factors.

As in all worthwhile endeavors, maintaining the correct focus benefits all parties involved. This does not mean the profitability of the business is ignored, but that aligning the goals of the wealth optimization consultant with those of his or her clients results in the optimization of all types of capital on both sides of the equation.

An unprecedented position

The spillover of the open architecture culture of the family office into the financial services industry has raised awareness among top consultants in the investment management consulting industry of the opportunities that are available. For the first time, investment management consultants can provide an unbiased service for wealthy families. This ability for the consultant to be genuinely objective, bound by no firm's association or contracted agreement with a product vendor, breaks down barriers that made investment consultant membership on the family council undesirable. It also opens the door for the investment management consultant to assume the role of wealth optimization consultant or, as Family Office Metrics' Jon Carroll describes it, the role of chief advisor for the family.[2]

But this is just the beginning. There are many underserved areas in this market that wealth optimization consultants can address in order to realize their personal and business objectives. As investment management consultants research those areas, they will be able to expand their concepts of client service to accommodate the best mix for their business focus. As Frank L. Campanale has stated, control of the business is moving into the hands of the consultant.[3] Financial services firms have been afraid of that development, but they have not been able to stop it. As the control shift develops, financial industry firms will find ways to realign their business focuses to serve wealth optimization consultants. Campanale has been one of the most influential forces in the financial services industry in fostering the 'client-first' focus. His work at Salomon Smith Barney was groundbreaking and will serve as a solid foundation for continued efforts to create awareness in large financial institutions regarding not only the approaches that should be taken with the markets they wish to serve, but also in providing the critical educational component for consultants wishing to elevate their levels of service.

Because each firm is at a different stage of implementing the consultative approach, the outcome of this development may be in the form of hybrid service levels concentrated within a certain net worth range. For instance, the large industry firms of today may be attractive alternatives for the underserved less affluent investors with net worths between US$1 million and US$5 million. The next level is the US$5 million to US$10 million market, which is currently ignored by both industries. Wealth optimization at this level can certainly be accomplished, especially as technology advances and creates greater efficiencies that lower the inhibitions placed on these investors by the relatively small size of their funds. Clients with US$10 million and above are welcomed by many MFOs. When realizing that some of the members of the largest legacy families with multiple hundreds of family members have as little as US$10 million as their share of the family wealth, the US$10 million investor outside of a large family becomes much more attractive.

At whatever level wealth optimization occurs, the author is convinced that optimization consulting is the only viable model for today's investment management consultants. In Example 1 earlier in this chapter the prenuptial consultant optimized her wealthy male clients' divorce outcomes; in Example 2 the cousins optimized the assets of Latin American families through targeted services particularly relevant to them; and in Example 3 the cash flow broker optimized its clients' winnings by facilitating the purchase of their income streams and investing a large part of the proceeds.

Never before in either industry has the investment component served either the client or the consultant as well as in the optimization model. The independence of the individual consultant will allow him or her to take advantage of the family wealth market in a way that will be impossible for large financial institutions because of their size and the limited number of wealthy available. However, opportunities arise when money is in motion and the onset of the most expansive wealth transfer in history has already occurred. New wealth is being created by the surge in entrepreneurial activity over the past few years, and perhaps the wisest and most prudent generation ever is entering adulthood and seeking to make its mark on its inheritance.

Models of the future

Models of the family office and the financial services firm of tomorrow cannot be accurately predicted. This book has attempted to highlight the most viable of the models available

171

today, but the proof will not materialize for perhaps another five years. According to FOX's Sara Hamilton:[4]

> There are only a handful of firms operating with successful business models that are profitable enough to sustain and attract enough talent for them to stay in business at a high level. Until we raise the price we charge to the owner, [that will continue to be the case.]

The ability to raise the fees for advice will increase as investors become more knowledgeable about the value of advice. The primary way for them to obtain that knowledge is through education from the consultants providing the advice. As management fees and separately managed accounts (SMA)/unified managed account (UMA) wrap fees reduce, consultants are seeking a way to be compensated for the services they provide and the advice they give. Wealth optimization provides that educational venue, supported by purposeful and appropriate business and marketing plans designed to build relationships by invitation only.

Through whatever model that invitation is extended, wealthy families or private investors will respond. Wealth optimization answers their key questions about who to trust, who should oversee their interests, and how to educate their progeny to live successful and productive lives. What better role could a wealth optimization consultant have? The future of the financial services and family office industry advisories lies in their own hands. Unprecedented options for building the ideal business model exist today and will increase exponentially over the next three to five years as the monumental sea change affecting both industries begins to settle out. Through wealth optimization consulting, astute, forward-thinking industry participants will emerge from the current confusion as the industry leaders of tomorrow.

---

[1] Examples are based on information contained in, 'Under the Radar Screen', by Russ Alan Prince, *Institutional Investor,* 2003.

[2] Author's interview with Jon Carroll, MBA, CPA, co-founder and managing director, Family Office Metrics, LLC, September 2003.

[3] Author's interview with Frank L. Campanale, former president and CEO, Salomon Smith Barney Consulting Group, September 2003.

[4] Author's interview with Sara Hamilton, founder and CEO, the Family Office Exchange (FOX), September 2003.

Appendix

Outsource resources for wealth optimization businesses

This appendix details resources that may be outsourced or subscribed to in order to round out consultants' wealth optimization service offerings.

Philanthropy

- Giving Capital, www.givingcapital.com
- DoudHausnerVistar, www.dhvadvisors.com
- National Center for Family Philanthropy, www.ncfp.org

Educational organizations

The following organizations provide community and support for a variety of financial professionals.

- Investment Management Consultants Association (IMCA), www.imca.org: Licensors of the Certified Investment Management Analyst (CIMA) designation and a key educational resource and ethical standard bearer for investment management consultants and their clients.
- Financial Planning Interactive, www.financial-planning.com: A free, all-you-need-to-know service which provides educational and up-to-date information for financial planners and wealth optimization consultants. The website for *Financial Planning* magazine.
- Association of Investment Management and Research (AIMR), www.aimr.org: Licensors of the Chartered Financial Analyst (CFA) designation and a global leader in educating and examining investment managers and analysts and sustaining high standards of professional conduct. AIMR's membership is global in scope and its activities are worldwide.
- Institute for Private Investors (IPI), www.memberlink.net: Innovative educational and networking resource for families with substantial assets and their advisors. Educational resource for advisors to the affluent.
- Family Office Exchange (FOX), www.familyoffice.com: Providers of intellectual capital for the wealth management community. Network of advisors to families of wealth.
- The Money Management Institute (MMI), www.moneyinstitute.com: The organization for staying current on financial services industry marketing and technological development. The organization is an influential forum for change and competitive development within the managed accounts industry.
- The Institute for International Research – USA (IIR), www.iir-usa.com: This organization hosts a series of family office conferences designed to provide education in all areas of

family office wealth management.

- Alternative Investment Management Association (AIMA), www.aima.org: The alternative investment industry's global trade association. AIMA is a purely educational organization and is a conduit between a highly complex industry and all those wishing to understand, regulate, and invest within it, and aims to increase understanding, encourage best industry practice, and work with the regulatory authorities to enhance the existing regulatory environments.

Web-based client service platforms

The following companies provide customized and integrated web-based platforms for wealth optimization consultants.

- Finaplex, www.finaplex.com: Comprehensive family office/financial planning/wealth optimization platform enabling multi-currency, customizable tax optimization across all accounts and asset classes, user-defined performance reporting including dollar and non-dollar assets, employee and restricted stock, customized hedge structuring, strategies, and scenario analysis among many other integrated elements.
- SS&C Technologies, Inc, www.ssctech.com: Provider of financial software, consulting, and premium application outsourcing services for seven vertical markets – commercial lending, financial institutions, hedge funds and family offices, institutional asset managers, insurance entities and pension funds, municipal finance, and real estate property managers. Technology platform specifically designed for family office and complex wealth optimization demands.
- eMoneyAdvisors, www.emoneyadvisors.com: Comprehensive financial planning platform with support for advisors converting from transactional to fee-based compensation.
- Lydian Wealth Management, www.lydianwealth.com: Provides 'Integrated Wealth Management (IWM) Solution' to a select group of advisors, banks, and wealth managers. As Lydian's partners, these individuals and institutions access core investment-consulting platforms and value-added wealth management services, and integrate them with their own operations.
- ADVISORport, www.advisorport.com: Third party separate account services platform designed by CIMAs for CIMAs. Recently purchased by PFPC Worldwide, Inc, which provides technology and managed account services to enterprise sponsors, RIAs, and money managers.

Performance measurement and attribution

- PPCA, Inc, www.ppca-inc.com: Creators of StokTrib and Portfolio Opportunity Distributions (PODs), PPCA is an investment consulting firm specializing in innovative analytical tools for investors.

Connectivity

- The Family Wealth Alliance, www.fwalliance.com: An organization dedicated to creating the right 'fit' between wealthy families and advisors.
- FOX: In addition to its educational services, FOX has an extensive roster of qualified advi-

sors for wealthy families to access.

- IPI: IPI's membership consists of families and their advisory professionals. It is purely an educational and network hub for its members.

Virtual connectivity

- Private Family Networks, www.pfn-usa.com: Web-based networking service that provides virtual family office software and consulting services for high net worth individuals, families, and for the advisors that service their wealth management needs.
- Family Office Network, www.familyofficenetwork.com: A service that facilitates the creation of a web-based relationship among independent attorneys, accountants, investment managers, and other advisors that enables them to work together for the benefit of their mutual clients.
- Fugent, www.fugent.com: Virtual meetings can efficiently and cost effectively facilitate communications with clients and other advisors. Fugent's offerings are specifically tailored to support wealth optimization consultants' educational, presentation, conferencing, and marketing needs.

Technology service providers for financial institutions

The following firms have the potential to provide family office level services.

- Integrated Decision Systems, www.idsnet.com: Leading global portfolio management solutions company providing automated financial portfolio management, accounting, performance measurement, online compliance and trading systems. A single database of automated decision support and straight-through processing.
- CheckFree Investment Services, CheckFree APL, www.checkfreeinvsvcs.com: CheckFree Investment Services provides outsourced trading, portfolio management, accounting, reporting services, and data to broker/dealers and money managers in separately managed accounts. CheckFree APL serves as a separately managed accounts platform, providing remote processing services to sponsor firms, money managers, and financial advisors for the automation of investment management, trading, portfolio performance, and investor reporting.

Industry trade magazines

- *Family Business Magazine*, www.familybusinessmagazine.com: Provides insights into the needs of family entrepreneurs.
- *Financial Planning* magazine, www.financial-planning.com
- *Registered Rep* magazine, www.rr.com: In addition to its traditional offerings, RR now follows family office trends in the financial services industry.
- *Senior Consultant*, www.srconsultant.com: A resource for developments in areas of interest to high-level investment consultants.

Institutional Investor journals

- *Journal of Wealth Management*

- *Journal of Portfolio Management*
- *Journal of Private Equity*
- *Journal of Alternative Investments*
- *Journal of Risk Finance*
- *Journal of Derivatives*
- *Journal of Fixed Income*

Other journals

- *CFA Journal (AIMR)*
- *Journal of Investment Consulting (IMCA)*